Contents

THE EIGHTEENTH-CENTURY NOVEL
AND THE SECULARIZATION OF ETHICS

To Stephen

The Eighteenth-Century Novel and the Secularization of Ethics

CAROL STEWART

ASHGATE

Published by
Ashgate Publishing Limited
Wey Court East
Union Road
Farnham
Surrey, GU9 7PT
England

Ashgate Publishing Company
Suite 420
101 Cherry Street
Burlington
VT 05401-4405
USA

www.ashgate.com

British Library Cataloguing in Publication Data
Stewart, Carol.
The eighteenth century novel and the secularization of ethics.
   1. English fiction – 18th century – History and criticism. 2. Ethics in literature.
   3. Women in literature. 4. Women – Great Britain – Social conditions – 18th century.
   5. Books and reading – Great Britain – History – 18th century. 6. Religion and ethics.
   I. Title
   823.5'09353–dc22

Library of Congress Cataloging-in-Publication Data
Stewart, Carol (Carol Ann)
   The eighteenth-century novel and the secularization of ethics / by Carol Stewart.
      p. cm.
   Includes index.
   ISBN 978-0-7546-6348-5 (hardback: alk. paper)—ISBN 978-1-4094-0371-5 (ebook)
   1. English fiction—18th century—History and criticism. 2. Ethics in literature.
3. Christian ethics in literature. 4. Religion and literature—England—History—18th century. 5. Latitudinarianism (Church of England)—History—18th century. I. Title.

PR858.E67S74 2010
823'.509353—dc22

                                                                                    2009052680
ISBN 9780754663485 (hbk)
ISBN 9781409403715 (ebk)

Mixed Sources
Product group from well-managed forests and other controlled sources
www.fsc.org Cert no. SA-COC-1565
© 1996 Forest Stewardship Council

Printed and bound in Great Britain by
MPG Books Group, UK

Acknowledgements

This book began life as a doctoral thesis supervised by Ian Campbell Ross at Trinity College, Dublin. His consistent support for this project, from its earliest days until publication, has been invaluable. He brought rigour, scholarship and remarkable patience to his reading and re-reading of my writing, and continues to go well beyond the call of duty as a supervisor. I want to take this opportunity to record my thanks. All mistakes contained herein are, of course, my own.

Parts of Chapters 1 and 5 previously appeared as 'Pamela and the Anglican Crisis of the 1730s', in the *Journal for Eighteenth-Century Studies*, 32.1 (March 2009), and 'The Anglicanism of Tristram Shandy: Latitudinarianism at the Limits', in the *British Journal for Eighteenth-Century Studies*, 28.2 (Autumn 2005).

My thanks also go to Stephen Stewart, whose encouragement and faith in me have been unwavering over very many years. This book is dedicated to him.

Introduction

Writing to a friend in April 1749, Captain Lewis Thomas recommended Henry Fielding's recently published *Tom Jones* as a work of great moral efficacy, which was likely to do more good than any number of clerical homilies: 'If my design had been to propagate virtue by appearing publickly in its defence, I should rather have been ye Author of Tom Jones than of five Folio Volumes of sermons'.[1] This view was not universal. Samuel Johnson was famously shocked to hear Hannah More quote from 'so vicious a book'. In 1750 Thomas Sherlock, Bishop of London, issued a pastoral letter on the occasion of the earthquake tremors experienced in London, warning of divine retribution for the publication of 'Histories and Romances of the vilest Prostitutes'.[2] The bishop could have been referring to John Cleland's *Memoirs of a Woman of Pleasure* (1748–1749), more usually known as *Fanny Hill*, but 'Eubulus', writing in *Old England*, a journal happy to publish attacks on Fielding and his friend and patron George Lyttleton, took the opportunity to interpret Sherlock as meaning the hero of Fielding's novel 'who is a Male-Prostitute'.[3] Still, if the moral credentials of *Tom Jones* (1749) were disputed – as had been other novels before it, not least Samuel Richardson's *Pamela, or, Virtue Rewarded* (1740) – the idea that particular novels, if not the novel as a genre, could promote morality in a way that sermons failed to do was beginning to take hold in the mid-eighteenth century. Alexander Pope believed that *Pamela* would do more good than a sermon and the novel was recommended from the pulpit of St. Saviour's Church in Southwark. Lady Mary Wortley Montagu considered that Lady Vane's scandalous memoirs, which form a significant part of Tobias Smollett's novel *Peregrine Pickle* (1751), might, if 'rightly consider'd', be 'more instructive to young Women than any Sermon I know'.[4] The idea that the clergy were not the most effective communicators of moral teaching was certainly commonplace. The Postscript to the third edition of Richardson's *Clarissa* (1751) makes a forceful statement:

> [The Author] has lived to see Scepticism and Infidelity openly avowed and even endeavoured to be propagated from the *Press*: The great doctrines of the Gospel brought into question: Those of self-denial and mortification blotted out of the catalogue of christian virtues: and a taste even to wantonness for

---

[1]   Ronald Paulson and Thomas Lockwood (eds), *Henry Fielding: The Critical Heritage* (London: Routledge and Kegan Paul, 1969), 162.

[2]   *Henry Fielding: The Critical Heritage*, 235.

[3]   Ibid.

[4]   Lionel Kelly (ed.), *Tobias Smollett. The Critical Heritage* (London: Routledge and Kegan Paul, 1987), 88.

out-door pleasure and luxury, to the general exclusion of domestic as well as public virtue, industriously promoted among all ranks and degrees of people.

In this general depravity, when even the Pulpit has lost great part of its weight and the Clergy are considered as a body of *interested* men, the Author thought he should be able to answer it to his own heart, be the success what it would, if he threw in his mite towards introducing a Reformation so much wanted: and he imagined, that if in an age given up to diversion and entertainment, he could *steal in*, as may be said and investigate the great doctrines of Christianity under the fashionable guise of an amusement; he should be most likely to serve his purpose.[5]

Interestingly, the Postscript might not have been written by Richardson himself: in *Samuel Richardson's Published Commentary on* Clarissa *1747–1765* (1998), Thomas Keymer suggests that it might have been partially written by William Warburton or Edward Young, both clerics and friends of Richardson's.[6] If so, one might read into it a certain vexation about the decline in influence of clergy and pulpit. In *The Citizen of the World* (1762), Oliver Goldsmith, writing in his persona of Lien Chi Altangi, a Chinese visitor to England, proposed that the writer, however impoverished, was of more use in a refined society than the preacher:

In a polished society, that man, though in rags, who has the power of enforcing virtue from the press, is of more real use than forty stupid brachmans, or bonzes, or guebres, though they preached never so often, never so loud, or never so long.[7]

A contributor to the *Monthly Magazine* of 1797 listed Robert Bage and Thomas Holcroft among the authors who 'have probably diffused more liberal and more just ideas, than could, in the same space of time, have been inculcated upon the public by a thousand sermons, or by as many dry political disquisitions'.[8]

This study is an account of how it was that the novel (or extended prose fiction), a kind of writing regarded with suspicion at the beginning of the eighteenth century, began to supplant sermons and other religious works as a possible source of moral instruction for the reading public: the legitimization of fiction may be regarded as an episode in the history of secularization.[9] My approach has something in

---

[5]   Thomas Keymer (ed.), *Samuel Richardson's Published Commentary on* Clarissa *1747–65*, 3v. (London: Pickering and Chatto, 1998), Vol. I, 255.

[6]   *Samuel Richardson's Published Commentary on* Clarissa *1747–65*, 3v., Introduction by Jocelyn Harris, ed., with head notes by Thomas Keymer (London: Pickering and Chatto, 1998), Vol. I, 46–7, 51–2.

[7]   Oliver Goldsmith, *The Citizen of the World*, in *Collected Works of Oliver Goldsmith*, ed. Arthur Friedman, 5v. (Oxford: Clarendon Press, 1966), Vol. II, 238.

[8]   Cited by Pamela Perkins, Introduction to *Hermsprong, or Man as He Is Not* (1796) by Robert Bage (Peterborough, Ontario: Broadview, 2002), 23.

[9]   There is a debate about the meaning of the term *secularization* and whether such a process has in fact taken place. I have followed the more restricted definition as employed by B.R. Wilson in *Religion in Secular Society* (London: C.A. Watts, 1966) and Steve Bruce in *Religion and Modernization. Sociologists and Historians Debate the Secularization*

common with that of William B. Warner in *Licensing Entertainment: The Elevation of Novel Reading in Britain, 1684–1750* (1998). The question Warner asks is not 'how did a literary genre, called the novel, come into being?' – the question asked by such studies as Ian Watt's seminal *The Rise of the Novel* (1957), Michael McKeon's *Origins of the English Novel* (1987) or Margaret Doody's *The True Story of the Novel* (1996) – but rather, how did the kind of entertainment that the novel represented become *respectable* reading? Warner traces the development of the novel as a genre through mutations of amatory fiction, from Aphra Behn through Mary Delarivière Manley, Eliza Haywood, Daniel Defoe's *Roxana* (1724), Richardson's *Pamela* and, finally, *Joseph Andrews* (1742). Despite Warner's distancing of his study from *The Rise of the Novel*, the conclusions he reaches about Richardson and Fielding are not dissimilar to Watt's. *Pamela*, it seems, fostered a kind of uncritical, 'absorptive' reading, which Fielding corrected by creating, through his rhetorical strategies, a more self-reliant, critical reader. As with Ian Watt, Richardson's fiction is distinguished by its ability to persuade the reader of the reality of what it represents, whereas Fielding supplies moral assessment. Warner, like Michael McKeon, concludes his study without considering *Clarissa* and *Tom Jones*, two novels that played a major part in legitimizing the genre.

I am concerned, then, with the novel's claims to social respectability. Appropriately, then, I begin my discussion of novels with the publication of *Pamela*. One searches in vain for serious votes of confidence in prose fiction in England before 1740. I approach the question of the novel's rise from the moral end of the spectrum, rather than (as Watt did) the issue of realism. I argue that the novel began to be taken seriously by authors and readers when it was used as a means of motivating readers to whatever was seen as moral behaviour. (It should be said from the outset that those ideas of moral behaviour were strongly inflected by a politics of gender.) The impetus for such a development came from a perception of the clergy as inadequate or ineffective moral teachers. The immediate context for Richardson's intervention into a religious and ethical debate, which intervention took the shape of *Pamela* (1740), may be found in the Anglican crisis of the 1730s. With *Shamela* (1742), Fielding began a dialogue with Richardson's fiction that in turn produced *Joseph Andrews* (1742), *Clarissa* (1747–1748) and *Tom Jones* (1749). All of Richardson's and Fielding's novels argue an Anglican and Whig position. Once prose fiction began to acquire a degree of legitimacy, however, it was taken up as a medium for proselytizing quite different points of view: by the Scottish Tory Tobias Smollett, in works of fiction from *Roderick Random* (1748) to *The Expedition of Humphry Clinker* (1771); and more radically by women writers such as Sarah Fielding, Charlotte Lennox and Frances Sheridan.

Thesis (Oxford: Clarendon, 1992): that is, a decline in the social significance of religion. Recent commentators speak, usefully, of the transference of religious ideas to other spheres, or a mutation. See Grace Davie, *Religion in Modern Europe: A Memory Mutates* (Oxford: Oxford University Press, 2000) and Vincent P. Pecora, *Secularization and Cultural Criticism: Religion, Nation and Modernity* (Chicago: University of Chicago Press, 2006).

In *The Life and Opinions of Tristram Shandy, Gentleman* (1759–1767), the Rev. Laurence Sterne used fiction to put forward an idiosyncratic and very liberal interpretation of the eighteenth-century Anglican ethos. Thereafter novels began to multiply and diversify, achieving relative moral, intellectual and social legitimacy by the end of the century. As well as dealing with the important transitions of the 1740s, this study is also an account of the uses to which the genre was put as novels, and novel-writing became more respectable: as a new arena for moral and political controversy; as a means of supporting the prevailing order or protesting against it; and as a means of gaining fame, influence and – not least – money, by those who frequently had little other opportunity to gain one or all of these.

The broader context for the legitimization of the novel as a genre is the secularization of ethics in England in the seventeenth and eighteenth centuries, especially in the post-Restoration period. By 'secularization of ethics' I mean the separation of ethics – ethics both in the broader sense of moral philosophy and in the narrower sense of rules for moral behaviour – from religion. Religion itself was 'secularized', that is, it became less a system of belief or a body of doctrine and was increasingly defined as morality. With the decreased social significance of institutionalized religion in the period, moral instruction could more easily pass to the laity. The conception of 'politeness', as it replaced religion as a cohering force in society, is also of major importance. We need to begin with the separation of ethics from religion. From a political point of view, the separation of ethics from religion in England in the eighteenth century can ultimately be traced back to the confused nature of the English religious settlement.[10] After Henry VIII broke with Rome in 1533 and made himself head of the church, the established religion of England was essentially dependent on the religion, or disposition, of the monarch.

Elizabeth I enforced the Protestant religion by law: the Act of Uniformity required attendance at church on Sundays and holy days and the Oath of Supremacy reinforced the split with Rome. The law forbade the saying or hearing of mass. The English church was catholic but it was not Roman, though neither was it sufficiently organized on Calvinist lines as far as Puritans were concerned. By the end of the sixteenth century, the doctrine of the English church as laid out in the Thirty-nine Articles favoured the Calvinists by virtue of its assertion of predestinarianism, but the Elizabethan Prayer Book implicitly contradicted it.[11] By 1633 Calvinist archbishops had been replaced by anti-predestinarian Arminians and Calvinist teaching was subject to censorship. The Arminians, following the teaching of the Dutch Protestant Jakob Harmensen (otherwise Jacobus Arminius), placed greater

---

[10]   The religious and philosophical positions involved in the long debate about the relationship between morality and religion are discussed fully by Isabel Rivers in *Reason, Grace and Sentiment: A Study of the Language of Religion and Ethics in England, 1660–1780*, Vol. I, *Whichcote to Wesley* (Cambridge: Cambridge University Press, 1991); and Vol. II, *Shaftesbury to Hume* (Cambridge: Cambridge University Press, 2000).

[11]   For an account of the established Church before the Restoration, I am indebted to Nicholas Tyacke, *Anti-Calvinists: The Rise of English Arminianism c.1590–1640* (Oxford: Clarendon Press, 1987).

emphasis on the sacraments and therefore on the authority of the clergy and less on preaching and sermons. Under Archbishop Laud, the more liberal theological doctrine was joined to the Elizabethan commitment to discipline. During the Civil War of 1642–1649, the reformers held sway and the Westminster Confession of Faith, a full and coherent statement of Calvinist theology and the Larger and Shorter Catechisms were brought before Parliament (though never ratified) as the creed of the national Church.

The role of William Laud as Archbishop of Canterbury from 1633–1645 resulted in the strict enforcement of a mixed doctrine, a situation that was reproduced after the restoration of the monarchy in 1660. The Act of Uniformity of 1662 required from clergy subscription to the Book of Common Prayer, the Thirty-Nine Articles, renunciation of the Solemn League and Covenant (the terms of which had rejected episcopacy) and ordination by a bishop. The dominant clerical teaching in the post-Restoration period was hybrid, emphasising the importance, as aids to salvation, of grace and works, though favouring the latter. This may be seen as a way of combating the twin threats of popery and dissent. Bishop Jeremy Taylor's doctrine of 'Holy Living' and seventeenth-century teaching concerning the Gospel generally, was partially driven by the fear of antinomianism, that is, the supposed freedom of the 'elect' to disregard the moral law.[12] An emphasis on the free nature of grace and forgiveness could be seen as a threat to social order. John Tillotson, Archbishop of Canterbury from 1691–1694, articulates the concern from an Anglican standpoint:

> If our Saviour *came not to dissolve* and *loosen* the obligation of *moral* duties, but to *confirm* and *establish* it and to *enforce* and *bind* the practice of these duties *more strongly* upon us, then they do widely and wilfully mistake the design of Christianity, who teach that *it dischargeth men from the obligation of the moral law*, which is the fundamental and avow'd principle of the *Antinomian* doctrine.[13]

However, it was also a central part of the Anglican tradition to assert the value of works against the superstitious observances of popery. Tillotson attacks the doctrine of supererogation, which allowed for 'excess' merit on the part of some individuals to be attributed to those who were deficient in it, as tending to enervate the Christian religion, so that it loses its power over the 'hearts and lives' of men.[14] The greatest heresy is a wicked life. The Church of Rome has 'a thousand solemn devices' as a substitute for moral reform.[15]

Religion became increasingly redefined as morality and morality as the essence of Christianity might be emphasized as a way of eliminating religious discord.

---

[12] C.F. Allison, *The Rise of Moralism: The Proclamation of the Gospel from Hooker to Baxter* (London: SPCK, 1966), 185.

[13] John Tillotson, *Works*, 3v., ed. R. Barker (London: 1728), Vol. II, 317.

[14] Tillotson, *Works*, Vol. III, Sermon XXXI.

[15] Tillotson, *Works*, Vol. II, 296.

The Latitudinarians, who came to dominate the Anglican Church, argued for a Protestantism uncomplicated and undivided, by 'matters indifferent'. Benjamin Whichcote (1609–1683), one of the Cambridge Platonists, asserted roundly that 'The *State* of Religion lies in a good Mind and a good Life; all else is *about* Religion: and Men must not put the *Instrumental part* of Religion, for the *State* of Religion' – a statement that would presumably have the effect of rendering institutionalized religion entirely redundant.[16] Aiming at those Protestants who would not conform to the national church, Whichcote contended that ceremonies and observances not specified exactly in the Scriptures are not crucial to salvation, for this would impose too great a burden on the individual memory – to which, again, the answer might be that there was no need to impose them. In matters which are crucial, conscience can be relied on to guide us: 'If the Thing be good in itself; I am admonished daily how to act, by *the Rectitude of my Temper*'.[17] This is not to say that Whichcote discounts Christ's atonement for sin and the necessity of grace: but in his account of the obligations placed on us by Christianity, such matters are explicitly secondary.

Tillotson, who was chief among the second generation of Latitudinarians, does not discount the importance of grace either, but he sees it as an aid to reform rather than as an end in itself: 'a sufficient Aid and Strength to enable us to conquer the rebellious motions of Sin'.[18] For Whichcote, the moral life itself sanctifies men: 'every piece of It doth sanctifie by its presence'.[19] Melding together an older vocabulary with the same thought the Cambridge Platonist Ralph Cudworth (1617–1688) finds that safe conclusions may be drawn 'concerning our state and condition' from our conformity to the 10 commandments. He discriminates between the '*dead Law of outward Work*' and the '*Law of the Spirit of Life …* written within upon the *Fleshly Tables of our heart*', a statement which might be seen as conferring a spurious spirituality on the moral life.[20] For John Smith (1618–1652), who shared the values of Whichcote and Cudworth, the attributes of the religious man are '*Liberty and Amplitude, the most free and generous spirit*' and the divine virtues are love, joy, peace, longsuffering, kindness and goodness.[21] However, as has often been remarked, the concern with a moral life could make the lines between sermons and the conduct-books of the period rather thin. Tillotson's sermons on the education of children would be a case in point. For their High Church and Puritan opponents alike, the Latitudinarians were 'mere moral men'.

The Latitudinarian sermons also appealed to self-interest. It could be said that they diminished the radicalism of the philosopher Thomas Hobbes, author of *Leviathan* (1651), not so much by refutation as by appropriating the Hobbesian

---

[16]   *The Cambridge Platonists* (1969), ed. C.A. Patrides (Cambridge: Cambridge University Press, 1980), 334.

[17]   Ibid., 67.

[18]   Tillotson, *Works*, Vol. III, 257.

[19]   *Cambridge Platonists*, 69.

[20]   Ibid., 123–4.

[21]   Ibid., 158.

vocabulary.[22] J.G.A. Pocock has referred to a 'condition of thought about 1700 in which a bourgeois ideology, a civic morality for market man, was ardently desired but apparently not to be found'.[23] Perhaps the Latitudinarians provided just such a morality. There are many appeals to pleasure and utility to be found in the sermons Anglican divines such as Jeremy Taylor (1613–1667), Isaac Barrow (1630–1677), Thomas Sherlock (1677–1761), Edward Stillingfleet (1635–1699) and, above all, John Tillotson (1630–1694). Taylor's sermon on 'Apples of Sodom: Or, The Fruits of Sin' shows the disadvantages of sin: 'it is a great truth, that *there are but very few sins that pretend to pleasure* … most kinds of sins are *real* and *prime troubles* to the very body'.[24] Stillingfleet answers the proposition that religion is inconsistent with the civil interests of men.[25] In Tillotson's sermon 'The Advantages of Religion to Particular Persons', we find that religion is compatible with and indeed promotes, health and longevity, the ownership and management of estates, a good reputation and the welfare of relatives.[26] Tillotson's rationale is this:

> To recommend Religion to men from the great and manifold advantages which it brings both to *publick Society* and to *particular Persons* … to *vindicate the practice of it* from the suspicion of those *grievous troubles and difficulties* which many imagine it to be attended withal.[27]

Bishop Sherlock justifies usury by arguing that Scripture prohibits it only in relation to poor people. Charging interest on money lent 'is not properly Usury, but Traffic and Commerce'.[28]

In general, Latitudinarian clerics wanted to absorb and de-radicalize those elements that militated against their own authority. Such was their approach, in general terms, to the nonconformists. Such was their approach, also, to the Whig Revolution of 1688.[29] When the dynastic issue split the Church following the abdication of James II, those who prospered and went on to become the dominant voice in the Church of England, were the pragmatists.[30] Allegiance might be given to William and Mary as *de facto* rulers, without prejudice to James II's divine

---

[22]   Rivers, *Reason*, Vol. I, 85.

[23]   J.G.A. Pocock, *The Machiavellian Moment, Florentine Political Thought and the Atlantic Republican Tradition* (Princeton: Princeton University Press, 1975), 431–2.

[24]   *The English Sermon*, 2v., ed. C.H. Sisson (Cheadle: Carcanet, 1976), Vol. II, 26.

[25]   Ibid., Vol. II, 153.

[26]   Ibid., Vol. II, 196–200.

[27]   Tillotson, *Works*, Vol. III, viii.

[28]   *The English Sermon*, Vol. II, 213.

[29]   See J.P. Kenyon, *Revolution Principles, The Politics of Party 1689–1720* (Cambridge: Cambridge University Press, 1977), Ch. 3.

[30]   The characterisation of the Latitudinarians as the dominant party is agreed by Norman Sykes, *Church and State in England in the XVIIIth Century* (1934) (Hamden: Archon, 1962), 257–87; G.R. Cragg, *From Puritanism to the Age of Reason. A Study of Changes in Religious Thought within the Church of England 1660 to 1700* (Cambridge: Cambridge University Press, 1966), 86; and Isabel Rivers, *Reason*, I, 26.

right. William Stephens, adopting the persona of a Deist, put the point rather more caustically: 'The *Shiboleth* of the Church now is King *William's de facto Title*'.[31] Barrow and Tillotson absorb the Hobbesian vocabulary so as to undermine the persuasiveness of Hobbesian ethics or, to put it another way, the Latitudinarian sermons present a Christianized version of Hobbes. In so doing the Latitudinarian sermons helped to forge one of the most powerful ideas in eighteenth-century ethical thought: the notion that self-interest is compatible with virtue. This thinking carried the *imprimatur* of the Anglican Church.

The counter to such thinking lay in the reforming, or as it subsequently became, the nonconforming tradition. For Calvinists, the Latitudinarians placed a dangerous, not to say unscriptural, emphasis on Man's free will and reason. In the Westminster Confession of 1647, an important statement of Calvinist principles, the individual is corrupted by original sin and therefore 'utterly indisposed, disabled and made opposite to all Good and wholly inclined to all Evil'.[32] Adam's sin of disobedience broke the first covenant of God with Man, which was a covenant of works and mankind is now wholly dependent on the second covenant, the covenant of grace. The majority are damned but a select few, the elect, are predestined for salvation. This is not because of any merit on their part:

> Those whom God effectually calleth, he also freely justifieth: Not by infusing Righteousness into them, but by pardoning their Sins … Not for anything wrought in them, or done by them, but for Christ's Sake alone.[33]

The individual is completely passive and devoid of agency in this account. She or he cannot earn their salvation. Indeed, 'Works done by unregenerate Men … are therefore sinful and cannot please God'.[34] The 'darknesse' in Thomas Goodwin's *A Child of Light Walking in Darknesse*' (1636) is 'that darknesse which accompanies the want of the sense of God's favour'. As we find in John Bunyan's *Grace Abounding to the Chief of Sinners* (1666) or later, *The Pilgrim's Progress* (1678), the inner struggle is with pride, ignorance, temptation, despair and doubtfulness of one's election by God. Agency comes only with the Spirit and then good works are the fruit of election, not its cause. Adherents of this theology were themselves conscious of the danger of antinomianism. In the Confession and the Catechisms '[a]ny interpretation of the doctrine of grace that slights human action or frees the regenerate from the obligations of the moral law is also fundamentally wrong'.[35] The question of the precise weight which could be accorded to human agency in the process of justification was one on which Congregationalists, Baptists and Presbyterians differed.

---

[31]   William Stephens, *An Account of the Growth of Deism in England* (1696), The Augustan Reprint Society, 261 (Los Angeles: William Andrews Clark Memorial Library, 1990), 12.

[32]   *The Confession of Faith*, (Glasgow: 1749), 50.

[33]   Ibid., 71.

[34]   Ibid., 90–91.

[35]   Rivers, *Reason, Grace and Sentiment*, Vol. I, 15.

The redefinition of Christianity as morality was expressed in Latitudinarian sermons. It could also take the form of John Locke's *The Reasonableness of Christianity* (1695). Christianity offers a uniquely authoritative and practical scheme of morality, and the only 'law of faith' is that we should believe in God and in Christ as the Messiah. Or it could take the form of Matthew Tindal's *Christianity as Old as the Creation* (1730): the gospel is simply a republication of the law of nature. The logical and more far-reaching outcome of Tindal's thought may be found in his earlier and misleadingly titled *The Rights of the Christian Church Asserted* (1706):

> a Rational Religion will not make Men depend much on the Authority of the Priests; because themselves can judg of that by its' own Evidence.[36]

The moralism and rational piety of the English eighteenth century followed from the marginalisation of popery and enthusiasm by the Restoration Anglican church. The peculiarity of the English situation was that the sceptical, scientific, modernising tendencies we associate with the Enlightenment were, given the nature of the Anglican Church at this time, essential to the preservation of the Establishment.[37] Anglicanism absorbed those potentially destructive elements. A rationalistic and moralistic faith could also, though, become the programme of freethinkers and militate against the power of the Church. Reason and science undermined revelation, and in the post-Revolution state, it was more often expected that men should be bound by laws to which they had agreed. Locke rejected the Calvinist doctrine of reprobation on the grounds that it was an unfair law. Morality could therefore be used as a weapon against the Christian apologists. After the lapsing of the Licensing Act in 1695, it was possible to air such views. The writings of Charles Blount (1654–1693), John Toland (1670–1722), Matthew Tindal (1657–1733), and Anthony Collins (1676–1729) all belong to this period. Collins maintained that an antecedent knowledge of the natural law was necessary to understand the nature of the moral duties prescribed by Scripture, though in the letter that precedes the work he also concedes that self-evident truths are so far from being self-evident that they are not acknowledged by everyone.[38] A literal and historical reading of the Bible, to which the Latitudinarians also largely subscribed, could be used against revelation. From the standpoint of natural morality, the French Protestant scholar Pierre Bayle (1647–1706) criticized the cruelty and political chicanery of David.[39] Collins could

---

[36] Matthew Tindal, *The Rights of the Christian Church Asserted, Against the Romish and all other Priests who claim an Independent Power over it* (London, 1706), 191.

[37] See Knud Haakonssen, 'Enlightened Dissent: an introduction', in *Enlightenment and Religion, Rational Dissent in Eighteenth-century Britain*, ed. Knud Haakonssen (Cambridge: Cambridge University Press, 1996), 3.

[38] Anthony Collins, *A Discourse of Free-Thinking (1713)* bound with *An Answer to Mr. Clark's Third Defence of his Letter to Mr. Dodwell (1708)*, in *Atheism in Britain*, with an introduction by David Berman (Bristol: Thoemmes Press, 1996), Vol. I, 3.

[39] Pierre Bayle, *Historical and Critical Dictionary*. Selections, trans. Richard H. Popkin (Indianapolis: Bobbs-Merrill, 1965), 45–62.

enlist Socrates, Plato, Cicero, Epicurus, Plutarch, Seneca and many more, as both freethinkers and examples of virtuous heathens.[40] Joseph Addison (1672–1719), though no freethinker, was more inclined to recommend a particular virtue 'by the Precepts or Examples of the ancient Heathens'.[41] The ideal of the moral life could be used by Whigs against the High Church party. Whig writers John Trenchard (1668–1723) and Thomas Gordon (?–1750) find that the High Church priest stresses matters of little importance 'to the Neglect of Morality and that Holiness of Life, which is the End and Design of all Religion'.[42] What is required is, rather, 'a Religion of Reason, free from the blind mazes ... of Popish Priests and beneficial to Society at first View'.[43] Natural morality could be used as a weapon against the clergy and against revelation, but, as may be suggested by the comment above, freethinkers and deists subscribed no less than Anglicans to the principle of social utility. Low Church Anglicans such as Samuel Clarke (1675–1729), an advocate of natural religion and moralism, thought that their version of religion could be validated by its utility: Trenchard and Gordon would say the same for theirs.

In the seventeenth century, the clergy, whether Anglican or nonconforming, could adjudicate over what was or was not sinful by means of the literature and practice of casuistry. The Church of England also had at its disposal the ecclesiastical courts, which could adjudicate over misconduct by the clergy, offences against conformity, tithes, wills, matters of sexual morality, drunkenness, usury (though this was the subject of changing legislation), ribaldry, disruption of church services, attendance at church generally and more specifically, neglect of baptism, communion and catechism.[44] I will return to the question of the courts and their decline, in a moment.

As a phenomenon of the late sixteenth and the seventeenth centuries, casuistry was intimately linked with the crises of conscience and authority that distinguish the period.[45] For Roman Catholics living under the Protestant Queen Elizabeth,

---

[40]   Collins, *Discourse*, 121–50.

[41]   Donald F. Bond (ed.), 2v., *The Spectator* (Oxford: Clarendon Press, 1965), Vol. II, 334.

[42]   J. Trenchard and Thomas Gordon, *The Independent Whig*, XLV, Wednesday, 23 November 1720.

[43]   Trenchard and Gordon, *The Independent Whig*, LIV, Wednesday, 18 January 1721.

[44]   On legislation regarding usury, see Martin Ingram, 'Reformation of Manners in Early Modern England', *The Experience of Authority in Early Modern England*, ed. Paul Griffiths, Adam Fox and Steve Hindle (Houndmills: Macmillan 1996), 70–71.

[45]   See Keith Thomas, 'Cases of Conscience in Seventeenth Century England', *Public Duty and Private Conscience in Seventeenth Century England*, ed. John Morrill, Paul Slack and Daniel Woolf (Oxford: Clarendon Press, 1993), 29–56; Camille Wells Slights, *The Casuistical Tradition in Shakespeare, Donne, Herbert and Milton* (Princeton: Princeton University Press, 1981), 4; Margaret Sampson, 'Laxity and Liberty in Seventeenth-Century English Political Thought', *Conscience and Casuistry in Early Modern Europe*, ed. Edmund Leites (Cambridge: Cambridge University Press, 1988), 72–118; and John S. Wilks, *The Idea of Conscience in Renaissance Tragedy* (London: Routledge, 1990), 1–43. An episode in the practice of casuistry has been described by Michael Hunter, 'Casuistry in Action: Robert Boyle's Confessional Interviews with Gilbert Burnet and Edward Stillingfleet, 1691', *Journal Of Ecclesiastical History*, 44 (1993), 80–98.

casuistry was a way of dealing with the problem of compliance with a religious settlement which they believed damned their souls.[46] In practical terms this could mean tortuous considerations about verbal ambiguities in the penal laws, such as how one construed such questions as 'do you go to church?', or what mental reservations were allowed when answering. In the early seventeenth century, Puritans who disagreed with the liturgy or sacraments of the Established Church were not subject to any penalties. The problem for Puritan clergy was how far they could, in conscience, comply with a half-reformed Church. Protestant casuistry could take as its starting point the need to attack Roman casuistry, as is the case with William Perkins (1558–1602) and Jeremy Taylor. The laws of the land were not initially a particular issue. Since Martin Luther's break with Rome in 1521, the scriptural justification for obedience to the civil power had been Romans 13:i: 'The powers that be are ordained of God'. However, in due course, Romans 13:i came to be used in support of the Royalist and Laudian cause.[47]

Protestant casuistry was always concerned with moral behaviour. Though written for the clergy, it was assumed that the readership for casuistry could include that part of the laity who were masters and employers.[48] The rationale for developing a distinctively Protestant casuistry may have been primarily the proneness to despair at the heart of Calvinism.[49] Early in William Perkins's *Cases of Conscience* (1613) we find the question of '*How a man beeing in distresses of minde, may be comforted and releeved?*'[50] In casuistical writing, it was assumed that Christian ethics should regulate all human activity and casuistry could negotiate the potential conflicts between the obligations of religious faith and the exigencies of daily life.[51] It may also be the case that Protestant casuistry of the later seventeenth-century period was concerned with regulating the unruly conscience that would be a law unto itself. Possibly addressing the danger of antinomianism Richard Baxter (1615–1691), who was himself a nonconforming minister ejected from his living after 1660, warns that 'There is a dangerous Errour grown too common in the world, that a man is bound to do every thing which his Conscience telleth him is the will of God'.[52]

The two major works of English casuistry in the post-Restoration period are from the Anglican side, Jeremy Taylor's *Ductor Dubitantium* (1660) and,

---

[46]   Elliot Rose, *Cases of Conscience. Alternatives open to Recusants and Puritans under Elizabeth I and James I* (London: Cambridge University Press, 1975), 7.

[47]   See Sampson, 109–14.

[48]   Thomas, 40.

[49]   Sampson, 99. See also John Stachniewski, *The Persecutory Imagination. English Puritanism and the Literature of Despair* (Oxford: Clarendon Press, 1991).

[50]   William Perkins, *Cases of Conscience*, in *The Workes of That Famous and Worthy Minister of Christ, in the University of Cambridge, Mr. William Perkins* (London: 1613), Vol. II, Booke I, Ch. VII, 22.

[51]   See Slights, 3.

[52]   Richard Baxter, *A Christian Directory: or, a Summ of Practical Theologie and Cases of Conscience* (London: 1673), Tome I, 134.

from the nonconformists, Richard Baxter's *A Christian Directory* (1673). The differences between these two works in terms of style and emphasis point up the different emphases in doctrine. Jeremy Taylor is more literary, theoretical, allusive and humanist and prefers 'lawful' and 'unlawful', to 'sinful' and 'innocent'. The *Christian Directory*, on the other hand, is plainer, 'lower' in terms of literary style and informed by a consciousness of the possibility of sin at every point, despite its concessions to the realities of commercial life. The *Christian Directory* also points up the importance of writing and reading from the point of view of nonconformity. As Isabel Rivers observes:

> After the ejection of the nonconformist ministers in 1662, reading became a necessary substitute for preaching for those congregations who could not attend secret prayer meetings and would not attend their parish churches.[53]

Baxter himself put the point succinctly: '*Preachers* may be silenced or banished, when *Books* may be at hand'.[54] Taylor, on the other hand, writes from the Latitudinarian position, and the Latin title itself suggests the kind of educated readership he envisaged.

However, both works are concerned to regulate or guide the perplexed conscience, by taking due cognisance of the circumstances which may alter cases. Both subscribe to the concept of a rule for the conscience, however voluminous the qualifications and exceptions. As Keith Thomas has remarked, 'So long as the idea prevailed that a single right answer existed for every moral dilemma, then the notion of moral expertise made sense'.[55] The individual must always follow his own conscience: on that *principle* the Protestant casuists were clear. The conscience is the voice of God in Man and not to follow it is a sin. However, to follow an erroneous conscience is also a sin. The remedy for the erring conscience is, Baxter says, to change one's judgement – presumably with Baxter's *Directory* as a guide. On the vexed question of obedience to a political order with which one did not necessarily agree, Jeremy Taylor concedes that the condition of a man who has to choose between disobeying his superior (a sin) or obeying against his conscience (a sin) or obeying his erroneous conscience (another sin) is 'indeed perplexed'.[56] The only way for this man to avoid sin, apparently, is to correct his error and then obey authority.

The *Christian Directory* is both comprehensive and minutely detailed. Baxter considers private duties, family duties, church duties and duties to our rulers and neighbours. It would be impossible to convey in brief the sheer volume and density of the arguments and the method of query, prescription and qualification militates

---

[53]　Isabel Rivers, 'Dissenting and Methodist books of practical divinity', *Books and their Readers in Eighteenth-Century England*, ed. Isabel Rivers (Leicester University Press, 1982), 134.

[54]　Baxter, Tome I, 60.

[55]　Thomas, 53.

[56]　Jeremy Taylor, *Ductor Dubitantium*, 3rd ed. (London: 1676), 86.

against definitive statements or judgements. We might take as an example of the play between authority and qualification Baxter's response to the much-discussed issue of parental control over children's choice of a spouse. The question is, Is it sinful to disobey a parental prohibition on marriage? Baxter answers:

> *Children* are not (ordinarily) called of God to marry, when their Parents do absolutely and *peremptorily* forbid it. For though Parents *Commands* cannot make it a duty, when we are sure it would hinder the interest of God our ultimate end; yet Parents Prohibitions may make it a sin … Because, 1. Affirmatives bind not *semper & ad semper* as Negatives or prohibitions do. 2. Because the sin of disobedience to Parents will cross the tendency of it unto good and do more *against* our ultimate end, than all the advantages of marriage can do for it.[57]

Baxter's method is often to set a Scriptural absolute, either directly or by implication, against the exigencies of ordinary life. Implicitly addressing difficulties with the fifth commandment, Richard Baxter answers the question of whether self-defence is lawful. He concludes that it is.[58] And in answer to the question '*Is it lawful to take away anothers Life, in the defending of my Purse or Estate*', he replies: 'If the Law of the Land allow you to take away a Mans Life in the defending of your Purse, it removeth the scruple' – meaning the scruple of conscience.[59] To the question, '*May I ask in the Market more, than my Goods are truly worth?*' he answers: 'Ordinarily it is better to ask no more at all than a just gain'.[60] We find, too, against the Scriptural ban on usury, that 'there is some Usury which is not unlawful'.[61]

The *Christian Directory* offers stern strictures about the sinfulness of broken, disingenuous or hypocritical oaths, but one is still left with the impression that there was considerable room for manoeuvre. Baxter offers as a 'rule' the following:

> There are so great a number of Sins and Duties that are such by accidents and circumstantial alterations, and some of these are greater and some less, that it is a matter of exceeding great difficulty in morality to discern when they are indeed sins and duties and when not, which must be by discerning the preponderancy of accidents; and therefore it must be exceedingly difficult to discern when a Vow shall weigh down any of these accidents and when not.[62]

His advice is that one should then turn to a wise and faithful counsellor of great ability. Taylor offers the Latitudinarian solution to the issue of oaths. In a passage which seems to refer to the restoration of the Anglican Church, Taylor answers the query as to whether it can be 'lawful' for a man to subscribe to a religious settlement he does not believe to be true. In other words, should he swear a false oath for the

---

[57] Baxter, Tome II, 477.
[58] Baxter, Tome IV, 65.
[59] Ibid., 66.
[60] Ibid., 120.
[61] Ibid., 126.
[62] Baxter, Tome III, 712.

sake of the public peace? At first Taylor replies that this is hypocrisy and that it should be punished, but then qualifies the position. The Church should rather avoid requiring subscription to articles which are not strictly necessary, and the 'temporal regards' of the supreme power must take precedence. As a last resort:

> let the articles be made with as great latitude of sense as they can; and so that
> subscriptions be made to the form of words, let the subscribers understand them
> in what sense they please which the truth of God will suffer, and the words can
> be capable of. This is the last remedy, but it is the worst.[63]

Whereas it may be a principle of casuistry that human law is placed in the context of a hierarchy of laws in which divine law is superior, the Protestant casuists obviously made concessions to, or integrated, other principles which come nearer to natural law: that is, the eternal law as known by every rational creature without the aid of revelation. Taylor resolved the potential opposition between divine law and human positive law (and skated over the allegiance question) by identifying one with the other:

> The whole measure and rule of conscience is, The Law of God, or Gods will,
> signified to us by nature, or revelation, and by the several manners and times and
> parts of its communication it hath obtained several names. The law of Nature.
> The consent of Nations. Right Reason. The Decalogue. The Sermon of Christ.
> The Canons of the Apostles. The laws Ecclesiastical and Civil of Princes and
> Governors. Fame, or the publick reputation of things, expressed by Proverbs and
> other instances and measures of publick honesty.[64]

In the end, both *Ductor Dubitantium* and the *Christian Directory*, written from different tendencies within seventeenth-century Protestantism, attest to a modifying of doctrine to accommodate temporal realities.

In an atmosphere of scientific rationalism, and with religion a cause of national dissension, the literature and practice of casuistry duly mutated into other forms. Keith Thomas suggested that Hobbes's thinking about morals and politics in *Leviathan* (1651) should be seen as part of the literature of casuistry:

> *Leviathan* abounds in solutions to traditional casuistical dilemmas: do covenants
> made under force oblige? must one keep faith with heretics? are poor men
> justified in stealing in order to keep alive? is revenge lawful? what excuses
> for crimes are allowable? may a soldier flee from the field of battle? what can
> Christians do to escape persecution?[65]

As he also notes, the immediate object of *Leviathan* was to address the dilemma of conscience facing Royalists in 1651, but it ended by offering a *de facto* theory of kingship that pleased nobody. If Hobbes addressed traditional casuistical dilemmas, he brought the new scientific understanding to bear on them, and

---

[63]   Taylor, 692.
[64]   Taylor, 6.
[65]   Thomas, 45.

offended accordingly. Clerical casuists, as we have seen, integrated natural law and temporal realities into their schemes: Hobbes made the nature of man, and man's needs, the starting point for his. The political order was not, after all, sustained by oaths. Man, like the Galilean universe, was to be understood as matter in motion, a bundle of appetites and aversions. Natural law was a series of 'theoremes' reached by calculating, self-interested Man. Only in *Leviathan* Part III does Hobbes deploy the arguments from Scripture to justify his rational theory of absolute sovereignty. In all of this, Hobbes's project, like that of the Latitudinarians, is to quell dissension and ensure peace:

> And though in matter of Doctrine, nothing ought to be regarded but the Truth; yet this is not repugnant to regulating of the same by Peace. For Doctrine repugnant to Peace, can no more be True, than Peace and Concord can be against the Law of Nature.[66]

The extent to which Hobbes may be said to be a Christian writer remains arguable to this day, and may be seen as proof in itself of his equivocal stance.[67] In fact, Hobbes could not allow into his scheme – even supposing that he believed in them – any supernatural obligations such as could take precedence and disrupt civil order. The guarantor of peace is the Leviathan, the *mortal* god. The section on natural law is a series of fudges whereby Hobbes sidesteps the question of natural law's divine provenance. As D.D. Raphael has rightly said, 'Hobbes wants to keep authority in morals while discarding it for belief'.[68]

Hobbes represents the starting point for the ethical naturalism of the eighteenth century: the conception that ethical conclusions and accounts of obligation can be established on the basis of facts about human beings and their world. The empirical understanding of human nature was subsequently replicated, with variations, in the ethical and political thinking of John Locke (1632–1704), Anthony Ashley Cooper, Earl of Shaftesbury (1671–1713), Francis Hutcheson (1694–1746) and David Hume (1711–1776). Some kind of supernaturalism could be incorporated back into this system by way of the Platonism that passed from the Cambridge Platonists to Shaftesbury, or by the divine voluntarism retained by Locke in *The Reasonableness of Christianity*, or by Hutcheson's divinely implanted 'moral sense' in *An Inquiry Concerning the Original of our Ideas of Virtue or Moral Good* (1725). On the whole, though, transcendence is notable by its absence, and the recurring problem is to establish a theory of obligation on merely natural grounds. For the ethical naturalists, the grounds of obligation have to be man's desire for happiness. Pleasure and pain are the motivating forces in human nature.

---

[66]   Thomas Hobbes, *Leviathan* (Harmondsworth: Penguin, 1985), 233.

[67]   See, for example, Howard Warrender, *The Political Theory of Hobbes: His Theory of Obligation* (Oxford: Clarendon Press, 1957); A.P. Martinich, *The Two Gods of Leviathan: Thomas Hobbes on Religion and Politics* (Cambridge: Cambridge University Press, 1992).

[68]   D.D. Raphael, *Hobbes: Morals and Politics* (London: Allen and Unwin, 1977), 17.

The political writings of Robert Filmer (1588–1653) and John Locke were also generated by the vexed question of legitimate authority, and they too may be seen as part of the literature of casuistry. In *Patriarcha, or the Natural Power of Kings asserted*, published posthumously in 1680 but possibly written in the 1630s, Filmer argued that God gave Adam absolute sovereignty over Eve, over the world, and over Eve's offspring, and that kings derived their authority by hereditary succession from Adam. The authority of a king over his subjects was the same as the natural paternal authority of a father over his children. Filmer's position is not without its difficulties and ambiguities, and is perhaps better seen as an attempt to refute the idea that men were at liberty to choose what form of government they pleased. This conception can be traced back to the Levellers and the period of the Civil War.[69] Filmer's absolutism provided the point of departure for Locke's perhaps equally incoherent argument for authority by virtue of an original contract, and a separation of the family and the state. The power of a magistrate over a subject, Locke argued, was not to be equated with that of a father over his children, a master over his servant, a husband over his wife, and a lord over his slave.[70] These were all distinct and different relationships. What this meant, though, was that patriarchy might remain in place in the family while its tenability had been denied in terms of the state. Having demolished Filmer's argument in his *First Treatise of Government*, which was probably written in 1680–1681, though it was not published until 1689, Locke, in the *Second Treatise* (1689), constructed an alternative system based on a notional 'state of nature'. Locke's justification of male superiority is couched in terms of 'natural' gender difference: 'it ... being necessary, that the last Determination, i.e. the Rule, should be placed somewhere, it naturally falls to the Man's share, as the abler and stronger'.[71] Locke's argument, in turn, prompted a reply by the polemicist Mary Astell (1666–1731): 'If absolute sovereignty be not necessary in a State, how comes it to be so in a Family? Or if in a Family why not in a State; since no reason can be alleged for the one that will not hold more strongly for the other'.[72] Arguments about authority in the state, in the family, and in marriage, were inextricably entangled.

At the end of the seventeenth century, periodical literature took up the casuistical challenge, to be followed in the eighteenth century by the prose fiction that, in part, emerged from it. John Dunton's *Athenian Mercury* (1692), originally entitled *The Athenian Gazette: or, Casuisticall Mercury, resolving all the most nice and curious questions proposed by the ingenious of either sex*, addressed some typical casuistical topics such as matrimony, divorce, the obligatory force of vows, and contracts, but

---

[69]   See Rachel Weil, *Political Passions. Gender, the family and political argument in England 1680–1714* (Manchester: Manchester University Press, 1999), 32–6.

[70]   John Locke, *Two Treatises of Government*, ed. Peter Laslett, 2nd edition (Cambridge: Cambridge University Press, 1967), 286.

[71]   Locke, *Two Treatises*, 339. For a feminist critique of Locke, see Carole Pateman, *The Sexual Contract* (Cambridge: Polity, 1988).

[72]   Mary Astell, 'Reflections upon Marriage', *Astell: Political Writings*, ed. Patricia Springborg (Cambridge: Cambridge University Press, 1996), 17.

it departed from normal practice by presenting the queries in the first person and allowing for much more circumstantial detail. It also allowed rather more scope to the judgements of the reader, and it was not written by the clergy. It combined, or attempted to combine, the goals of instruction and entertainment in a commercial form. Typically, a popular periodical cost one penny for a folio half-sheet, issued twice weekly. The content of the *Athenian Mercury*, and other periodicals, was pitched to a readership outside the educated minority; and audience participation, which included participation by women, was invited by the printing of what were presented as readers' letters. Whether these were genuine or not remains a moot point.[73] A major portion of each essay in Daniel Defoe's *Review* (1704–1713) was concerned with politics or trade, but in the second issue Daniel Defoe began a briefer feature called '*Mercure Scandale: or, Advice from the Scandalous Club*', in which he undertook to answer readers' queries on such matters as duelling, drinking, newswriters, magistrates, love or marriage, thus continuing the approach of the *Athenian Mercury*. As Kathryn Shevelow puts it:

> In the hands of such middle-class entrepreneurs as John Dunton and Daniel Defoe, the popular periodical became an agent in that larger struggle to assert another set of Puritan inspired, but increasingly secularized, moral and economic values against those perceived as traditional, aristocratic, and morally suspect.[74]

The *Tatler* and *Spectator* continued the practice of answering readers' queries, and Addison was described by John Gay as 'the best Casuist of any Man in England'.[75] In *Defoe and Casuistry* (1971), G.A. Starr argued that the concern of casuistry with cases, and crises, of conscience strongly informed Defoe's own conduct manuals, such as *The Family Instructor* (1715–1718), *Religious Courtship* (1722) and *A New Family Instructor* (1727), as well as his fiction.[76] Richardson's 'familiar letters', which in turn formed the basis for *Pamela*, drew on the casuistical tradition, and Thomas Keymer has discussed the casuistical inheritance in Richardson's *Clarissa*.[77]

Although the powers of the ecclesiastical courts were wide ranging, the period of maximum severity against immorality should in theory have occurred during the Interregnum, when they were in abeyance.[78] The Commonwealth would have punished incest and adultery by death, without benefit of clergy, but the Act remained virtually a dead letter: 'Godly rule and reformation proved to be an image in which

---

[73]   Kathryn Shevelow, *Women and Print Culture. The Construction of Femininity in the Early Periodical* (London: Routledge, 1989), 26.

[74]   Shevelow, 29.

[75]   Cited by Donald F. Bond (ed.), *The Tatler*, 3v. (Oxford: Clarendon Press, 1987), I, xi.

[76]   G.A. Starr, *Defoe and Casuistry* (Princeton: Princeton University Press, 1971).

[77]   Thomas Keymer, *Richardson's* Clarissa *and the Eighteenth-Century Reader* (Cambridge: Cambridge University Press, 1992), 85–137.

[78]   See Ingram, 'Reformation', 66.

the world stubbornly refused to be remade'.[79] The power of the ecclesiastical
courts, sweeping as they may seem to modern eyes, fell short of the Puritan ideal.
Offences were 'sins' for which the guilty party must do penance, the most enduring
of these being the practice of having an adulterer stand in a white sheet before
the congregation. For the offence of double adultery, a Quaker in the diocese of
St. Asaph in 1683 was punished by so standing without a hat, holding a white
staff, and reading a schedule of penance on three successive Sundays.[80] Seventy
years later, the Rev. Laurence Sterne oversaw the same punishment in the case
of Jane Harbottle, who had given birth to an illegitimate child.[81] Heresy might be
punished by 'excommunication, deprivation, degradation, and other ecclesiastical
censures, not extending to death'.[82] Excommunicates could not plead at law nor act
as executors, and in theory, at least, they lost the right to Christian burial. In the
late seventeenth century, excommunication was increasingly used against more
minor offences like nonpayment of tithes or nonattendance at church, despite the
declared intention of the Church of England under Archbishop Sancroft to give
greater solemnity to the penalty. The excommunicate was supposedly to be cut
off from all social contact with his or her community.[83] In a case of last resort, the
sheriff could seize and imprison an excommunicate under a writ of *excommunicato
capiendo*, and the offender could potentially remain in prison for life.

It is notoriously difficult to assess the effectiveness of the courts and therefore
even more difficult to make definitive statements about their later decline. The
actual evidence for the decline of ecclesiastical courts is suggestive but not
conclusive. The regional picture seems to have been highly variable, with public
penance still taking place in some areas until the middle of the nineteenth century.[84]
In other parts of the country, the consistory courts were clearly in decline.[85] The
decline of the Church courts may be attributed to James II's Declaration of
Indulgence (1687), which removed all penalties for recusancy and nonconformity,
and to the Toleration Act of 1689, which allowed Dissenters to worship outside

---

[79]   Derek Hirst, 'The Failure of Godly Rule in England', *Past and Present* 132 (1991),
33–66.

[80]   Spurr, *Restoration*, 214.

[81]   See Ian Campbell Ross, *Laurence Sterne: A Life* (Oxford: Oxford University Press,
2001), 150–51.

[82]   Cited by Norman Sykes, *From Sheldon to Secker, Aspects of Church History 1660–
1768* (Cambridge: University Press, 1959), 60.

[83]   Spurr, *Restoration*, 214–15.

[84]   John Walsh and Stephen Taylor, 'Introduction: The Church and Anglicanism in the
"Long" Eighteenth Century', *The Church of England c.1689–c 1833. From Toleration to
Tractarianism*, ed. John Walsh, Colin Haydon and Stephen Taylor (Cambridge: Cambridge
University Press, 1993), 6.

[85]   John Addy, *Sin and Society in the Seventeenth Century* (London: Routledge,
1989), 212.

of the Anglican Church.[86] The effectiveness of the courts in enforcing religious conformity may have been compromised by the existence of religious divisions from the Reformation onwards, and most particularly after the Restoration.[87] Appeal was open, in any case, to the secular courts, which could stop proceedings in the spiritual courts by means of a 'prohibition'. The laity were perhaps more ready to submit questions of property to the perceived impartiality of the secular courts.[88] Norman Sykes has also argued that the ecclesiastical courts became progressively less effective in the post-Restoration period, in part because of lay resistance to, and dislike of them.[89]

The absence of the Court of High Commission also vitiated the power of the Church. It alone had the power to fine and imprison, and it was also capable of enforcing censorship. Confusion about the power of Convocation to punish heresy in the absence of the Court of High Commission ended in the censure, rather than the trial, of Anglican cleric and Lucasian Professor of Mathematics William Whiston.[90] The gradual decline of the provincial synods, which might meet to consider changes in the liturgy, canon law and the ecclesiastical courts, was also a factor. The Long Parliament of 1641 asserted the need for both parliamentary and royal assent to canons passed by Convocation. Sitting Convocations were suspended in 1664 after Archbishop Sheldon's decision to include taxation of the clergy to be included in money bills before Parliament. This apparently pragmatic decision had far-reaching consequences. The Convocation, which met in 1689 to consider the revision of canon law and the ecclesiastical courts, never got beyond the election of an anti-revisionist prolocutor. It too was subsequently prorogued. As Norman Sykes observes, the Church thus failed in the project of self-reform both after the Restoration, and after the Revolution.[91]

In the period c.1690–1740, the cause of moral reform was in some measure taken up by the Societies for the Reformation of Manners. The dates of their activities are suggestive, and throughout their history the Societies were most closely identified with the Whigs.[92] Henry Rock argues that the Societies movement reflected the contemporary Anglican crisis of authority: '[The movement] was an attempt to supplement, and even to supplant, the coercive traditions and agencies which had

---

[86] G.V. Bennet, 'Conflict in the Church', *Britain after the Glorious Revolution 1689–1714*, ed. Geoffrey Holmes (London: Macmillan, 1969), 159–62. See also I.M. Green, *The Re-Establishment of the Church of England 1660–1663* (Oxford: Oxford University Press, 1978), 141.

[87] Martin Ingram, *The Church Courts, Sex and Marriage in England, 1570–1660* (Cambridge: Cambridge University Press, 1987), 373.

[88] Christopher Hill, *Society and Puritanism in Pre-Revolutionary England* (London: Secker and Warburg, 1964), 293–4.

[89] Sykes, *Sheldon*, 22; *Church*, 40.

[90] Hill, 345.

[91] Sykes, *Sheldon*, 63.

[92] Tina Isaacs, 'The Anglican Hierarchy and the Reformation of Manners 1688–1738', *Journal of Ecclesiastical History*, 33 (1982), 399.

characterized the Established Church, including some brands of Puritanism, ever since the Reformation'.[93] However, the Societies may also need to be seen in terms of the long perspective. The Reformation inaugurated a battle over reformation of manners that remained a persistent feature of English social life.[94] The Societies were not, therefore, a new and unusual development. They were rather a new mutation of an old programme. The Societies may be seen as part of a long Puritan tradition that evolved to address different enemies and take on different causes.[95] They responded to Restoration libertinism and to the flood of sceptical writings that followed the expiry of the Licensing Act in 1695. The Societies' conception of the moral life is recognisably Puritan: activity rather than passive piety, self-denial, avoiding immoral company. As is appropriate for a society, they invoke man's nature as a communal being as an argument for moral behaviour. Enthusiasm for a reformation of manners may stem from the immediate aftermath of the Glorious Revolution.[96] The cause of moral reform could be identified with the security of the post-Revolution constitution.[97] Every libertine was therefore a friend to popery and a traitor. Virtuous men were the true patriots.[98] A sermon preached by Archbishop Tillotson in 1688 gave thanks for the deliverance of England by William III, and at the same time asked for moral reform. As God has delivered us, and punished us less than we deserve, 'Should we again break his Commandments?'[99] Immorality tempted Providence: 'Righteousness exalteth a nation' was a favourite text. The Church in a sense needed a moral revolution to vindicate the political revolution.[100] Added to the constitutional anxieties was a reaction to the social problems brought about by war and urban growth.[101] The Societies were a distinctively urban development.

One version of the development of the reform movement is that the Societies for the Reformation of Manners were exercised first by popery and then by Court corruption: they subsequently became associated with the Country opposition, and

---

[93]   Henry Rock, 'Religious Societies and the Origins of Methodism', *Journal of Ecclesiastical History*, 38 (1987), 589.

[94]   Ingram, 'Reformation', 51 *et passim*.

[95]   David Hayton, 'Moral Reform and Country Politics in the Late Seventeenth Century House of Commons', *Past and Present* 128 (1990), 52; T.C. Curtis and W.A. Speck, 'The Societies for the Reformation of Manners. A Case Study in the Theory and Practice of Moral Reform', *Literature and History* 3 (1976), 59.

[96]   Dudley W.R. Bahlman, *The Moral Revolution of 1688* (New Haven: Yale University Press, 1957), 14.

[97]   Bahlman, 7.

[98]   Ibid., 9.

[99]   Tillotson, *Works*, Vol. II, Sermon XXXII.

[100]   John Spurr, 'The Church, the societies and the moral revolution of 1688', *The Church of England c.1689–c.1833. From Toleration to Tractarianism*, eds John Walsh, Colin Haydon and Stephen Taylor (Cambridge: Cambridge University Press, 1993), 130.

[101]   Hayton, 51.

then with the Low Church, and therefore the Whigs.[102] The difficulty for the Anglican Church was that the Societies, while not irreligious, were an extra-ecclesiastical agency. Accounts of the history of the Societies agree about the ambivalence of the clerical response to them. Liberal Churchmen cautiously endorsed their activities, while High Churchmen emphatically opposed them, though the dates given by historians to periods of support and distrust may vary. The High Church cleric Henry Sacheverell (1674–1724) began his career with a pamphlet partly devoted to an attack on the Societies for the Reformation of Manners, seeing clearly that they subverted the primacy of the Church by depending on the magistrates to enforce the laws against immorality. The Church of England essentially faced the same problem with the Societies that it did with the Dissenters, that is, whether to absorb or exclude them. The Societies for the Reformation of Manners were initially Anglican but broke away from the Church by including Dissenters. The Church rejoined the movement in 1699 under the direction of Thomas Tenison, and 53 Anglican ministers preached to the Societies between 1696 and 1739.[103] The real division of the reform movement into High and Low Church factions may be dated to the growth of the evangelical societies, who directed their reforming efforts to sending out missionaries, establishing schools and workhouses, and providing Bibles and prayer books.[104] Charity schools themselves became embroiled in politics in the early eighteenth century, first attracting Dissenting support, which was subsequently alienated by High Churchmen, and then being suspected, in turn, of Jacobitism.[105] In due course, the Societies for the Reformation of Manners prospered and then became bogged down in factionalism and party politics.

In the period after the expiry of the Licensing Act in 1695, the cause of reform was taken up by lay figures in the periodical press, most notably Richard Steele and Joseph Addison's *Tatler* (1709–1711) and *Spectator* (1711–1712; 1714). The *Tatler* first appeared in April 1709 in the form of a miscellany, combining news from the war with France, comment on books and plays, advice on manners, letters and sketches of characters, some real, and some imaginary. In the earlier papers, satire on amateur interpretation of the news featured frequently, but Richard Steele (1672–1729), in his persona of Isaac Bickerstaff, also closed the first *Tatler* with a warning to London society to mend its manners, as he would from time to time print bills of mortality in which the 'deceased' (that is, those who were 'good for nothing') would be listed. Reflecting on the achievements of the first year of the *Tatler*, Bickerstaff tells readers that he took upon himself 'the Title and Dignity of *Censor* of *Great Britain*'.[106] However, if the paper had reformist ambitions which are recognisably Puritan, its ideas of reform were

---

[102] W.A. Speck, *Stability and Strife: England, 1714–60* (London: Edward Arnold, 1977), 5–6; Hayton, 56.

[103] Isaacs, 396–9.

[104] Hayton, 55.

[105] M.G. Jones, *The Charity School Movement. A Study of Eighteenth Century Puritanism in Action* (Cambridge: Cambridge University Press, 1938), 111–13.

[106] Donald F. Bond (ed.), *The Tatler*, 3v. (Oxford: Clarendon Press, 1987), Vol. II, 402.

less rigorous and more adapted to metropolitan middle-class life than those of the crusading Societies. The most frequently canvassed topic in the *Tatler* is London itself. Bickerstaff is a frequent theatre-goer and in *Tatler* 3 we read that he 'cannot be of the same Opinion with my Friends and Fellow-Labourers, the *Reformers of Manners*, in their Severity towards Plays' (*Tatler* I, 31). In *Tatler* 14, similarly: 'tho' I am a Reformer, I scorn to be an Inquisitor' (*Tatler* I, 118). Bickerstaff is a man about town, a frequenter of coffee- and chocolate-houses, and a wit, even if, as one of his admiring correspondents pointed out, his 'wholesom Project' was to make wit useful (*Tatler* I, 446). His case, in *Tatler* 61, for an agreed standard for female behaviour also suggests a man who enjoyed courting women's company:

> We have no such Thing as a Standard for good Breeding. I was the other Day at my Lady *Wealthy*'s and ask'd one of her Daughters, How she did? She answer'd, She never convers'd with Men. The same Day I visited at Lady *Plantwell*'s, and ask'd her Daughter the same Question. She answers, What's that to you, you old Thief. And gives me a Slap on the Shoulders. (*Tatler* I, 424)

The title *Tatler* was itself invented in honour of 'the Fair Sex', and Steele was obviously conscious from the very beginning that many of his readers would be women.[107] An occasional contributor to the paper was Isaac Bickerstaff's half sister, Jenny Distaff.

The paper campaigned against swearing, gaming, duelling, sexual license, matrimonial strife, vanity (especially female vanity), female scolds, extravagance, affectation and freethinking, as well as offering guidance on such matters as marriage, raillery and unseasonable visits. The ideal state was one of matrimonial felicity, with men and women in distinct gendered roles:

> The Woman's Province is to be careful in her Oeconomy, and chast in her Affection: The Man's, to be active in the Improvement of his Fortune, and ready to undertake whatever is consistent with his Reputation for that End. (*Tatler* I, 368)

Female dress, speech and habits of mind were all worthy of detailed attention, however condescending the tone. Male misdemeanours could sometimes be less severely treated. In *Tatler* 60, Isaac Bickerstaff tells the story of Tom Wildair, a dissolute law student, who is cured of his whoring, drinking and gaming by a rather surprising gift from his father of £4,000. Nevertheless, the ideal masculine character was to be one of self-restraint. In his earlier pamphlet, *The Christian Hero* (1701), Steele proposed that the military gentleman should perform his role with temperance and moderation, in accordance with the new ethic of politeness:

---

[107] Kathryn Shevelow distinguishes between the earlier periodicals, which reflected the ferment of debate at the turn of the century, and occasionally endorsed a radical feminism, with the more prescriptive productions of Addison and Steele.

'to Assault without Fear, Pursue without Cruelty, and Stab without Hatred'.[108] Likewise, in *Tatler* 176, he reflects with admiration on:

> those heroick Spirits, which in the Conduct of their Lives seem to live so much above the Condition of our Make, as not only under the Agonies of Pain to forbear any intemperate Word or Gesture, but also in their general and ordinary Behaviour to resist the Impulses of their very Blood and Constitution. (*Tatler* II, 459)

He himself had behaved so badly while suffering from toothache as to have broken two pipes and a pair of spectacles.[109]

While the *Tatler* aimed at reform, its methods were those of persuasion and suggestion – what Steele described as 'all gentle Methods imaginable' – rather than admonition and exhortation (*Tatler* II, 111). It would entertain as well as instruct, and do so by means of example as well as precept. The paper abounds in anecdote, story and character sketch as well as brief drama, and 'vision'. The tone was light, ironic and conversational and Steele cultivated a dialogue, either real or implied, with correspondents and readers. The project was continued and extended in the rather graver *Spectator*, which began appearing daily on 1 March 1711, just two months after the last *Tatler* was published in January of the same year. Where Isaac Bickerstaff had been a frequenter of ladies' assemblies and coffee houses, Mr. Spectator was styled a taciturn man, a looker-on, who was constantly in public places, though seldom recognized (*Spectator* 1). He was an independent gentleman, having been born to an hereditary estate passed down through the family since the time of William the Conqueror. Where Bickerstaff wrote from a variety of locations, which indicated the content of each essay – poetry and drama from Will's coffee house, news from St. James's coffee house, and so on – *Spectator* 2 promised variety by introducing a club of the author's 'ordinary companions'. These were the old-fashioned Tory squire, the young man about town ostensibly studying the law, the merchant of 'indefatigable industry', the modest but courageous captain, the gallant, and last of all, the philosophical clergyman. Mr. Spectator is unsure whether the cleric should be spoken of as one of the company, 'for he visits us but seldom'.[110] In the end, the club and its members played rather less of a part in the subsequent *Spectator* volumes than this introduction might have led the reader to expect. The paper had a unified viewpoint in its *persona*, and the single essay which occupied the whole paper gave the *Spectator* a more purposeful demeanour than the motley *Tatler*. On the other hand, a diverse correspondence from readers, much

---

[108]   Richard Steele, *The Christian Hero*, ed. Rae Blanchard (London: Oxford University Press, 1932), 10.

[109]   On self-restraint, see Edmund Leites, 'Good Humor at Home, Good Humor Abroad: The Intimacies of Marriage and the Civilities of Social Life in the Ethic of Richard Steele', *Educating the Audience: Addison, Steele, and Eighteenth Century Culture*, eds. Edward A. and Lillian D. Bloom, and Edmund Leites (University of California Los Angeles: William Andrews Clark Memorial Library, 1984), 51–89.

[110]   Donald F. Bond (ed.), *The Spectator*, 5v. (Oxford: Clarendon Press, 1965), Vol. I, 13.

of which Donald F. Bond adjudges to be genuine, took up a greater proportion of space in the *Spectator* than in the *Tatler*.[111]

The papers Joseph Addison (1672–1719) contributed to the *Spectator* trod over the same ground as the Latitudinarian sermons, and on more than one occasion lengthy passages from Tillotson's sermons were included. It rehearsed as well the campaigns of more obviously Puritanical writers, such as Jeremy Collier. In place of religious zeal, the *Spectator* promoted low-key moral virtues: cheerfulness, compassion, modesty, indifference to praise or censure, self-control and self-criticism.[112] *Spectator* 93 promoted the social, charitable virtues, such as advising the ignorant, comforting the afflicted and relieving the needy. Women's diversions, duties, appearance, faults and foibles were a major concern of the *Spectator*, as they had been of the *Tatler*, with the argument for separate spheres continued:

> Men and Women ought to busie themselves in their proper Spheres, and on such Matters only as are suitable to their respective Sex. (*Spectator* I, 241)

The missionary purpose of the *Spectator* had to be disguised, though, for fear of alienating the very readers moral instruction was aimed at:

> I must confess, were I left to my self, I should rather aim at Instructing than Diverting; but if we will be useful to the World, we must take it as we find it. Authors of professed Severity discourage the looser part of Mankind from having anything to do with their Writings ... The very title of a Moral Treatise has something in it Austere and Shocking to the Careless and Inconsiderate. (*Spectator* II, 205)

Readers must be entertained and amused. Morality would be enlivened with wit, and in this way, unthinking readers would be 'insnared into Sentiments of Wisdom and Virtue'. On the other hand, wit would be tempered with morality. There would be nothing ill-natured, offensive, or obscene.

In some respects, the moral programme of the periodicals – enlivening morality with wit, and tempering wit with morality – can be seen as an attempt to bypass party, and fuse together Puritan and Cavalier idioms. A correspondent to *Spectator* 461 remarked that thanks to the paper's reforming mission, it was now possible to be a fine gentleman without being 'a Keeper nor an Infidel'. In Steele's Preface to the collected *Tatler*s he asserted that the paper was above party, citing his favourable characterization of two High Church Tories, George Smalridge (1662–1719) and Francis Atterbury (1663–1732), as proof of his impartiality. In *Spectator* 125 Addison characterized the rage of party as being likely to produce bloodshed and civil war: 'It fills a Nation with Spleen and Rancour, and extinguishes all the Seeds of Good-Nature, Compassion and Humanity' (*Spectator* I, 510). Party rage was particularly inappropriate for women:

---

[111]   Donald F. Bond, 'Introduction', *The Spectator*, I, xxxix.

[112]   For a comprehensive list of the *Spectator*'s moral topics, see Peter Smithers, *The Life of Joseph Addison* (Oxford: Clarendon Press, 1954), 218.

> Women were formed to temper mankind, and sooth them into Tenderness and Compassion, not to set an Edge upon their Minds, and blow up in them those Passions which are too apt to rise of their own Accord. (*Spectator* I, 242)

The *Spectator* did cross party lines insofar as it attracted a wide readership, and the list of subscribers to the collected octavo edition of 1712–1713 included Tory and Whig peers.[113] Nevertheless, both the *Tatler* and the *Spectator* were Whig journals written, for the most part, when the Tories were in power. Even the swipes at party rage and party amongst women were themselves shots in a party war against Queen Anne's backing for the Tories under Robert Harley, as new peers were created to give the Tories a majority in the Lords.[114] The emphasis on morality, and the secular means by which it is to be inculcated, come from a Whig – which is to say Low Church, and possibly anti-clerical – perspective, as contemporaries were well aware. The Tory *Examiner* ridiculed the moral and literary pretensions of a 'weekly Retailer of loose Papers', and the anonymous author of 'A Spy upon the Spectator' objected to the marginalisation of the Church in the *Spectator* as much as in the Constitution itself.[115] The concern of the *Tatler* and *Spectator* to reform manners or encourage politeness by near-covert non-authoritarian means indicates a perceived need to construct a society cohering on the basis of shared social codes rather than religion. The concept of politeness as a socially desirable goal, encouraged by the *Tatler* and *Spectator*, was Whig ideology. Lawrence Klein has argued that Shaftesbury formulated this concept of culture to 'characterize and legitimate the post-1688 world'.[116] Politeness, as Shaftesbury conceived of it, was owing to liberty; politeness could then be used as weapon against political opponents. Royal courts, the Church and religious zeal were apparently not congenial to true politeness.

When Addison addressed the issue of games of chance in *Spectator* 191, he ridiculed them as being against reason rather than against the laws of God. In his praise for a country Sunday, the Church is very definitely subordinate to a goal of politeness:

> I am always very well pleased with a Country *Sunday*; and think, if keeping holy the Seventh day were only a human Institution, it would be the best method that could have been thought of for the polishing and civilising of Mankind. (*Spectator* I, 459–60)

---

[113]   Donald F. Bond, Introduction, *The Spectator*, I, lxxxvi–lxxxviii.

[114]   Angus Ross (ed.), *Selections from* The Tatler *and* The Spectator (London: Penguin, 1982), 50.

[115]   Edward A. Bloom and Lillian D. Bloom (eds.), *Addison and Steele. The Critical Heritage* (London: Routledge and Kegan Paul, 1980), 232.

[116]   Lawrence Klein, 'The Political Significance of "Politeness" in Early Eighteenth Century England', *Politics, Politeness and Patriotism*, eds Gordon J. Schochet, Patricia E. Tatspaugh and Carol Brobeck (Washington, DC: The Folger Shakespeare Library, 1993), Vol. 84.

Addison's remark may be seen as an exemplification of one way of conceiving of the relationship between the established Church and society.[117] It was possible to regard man's sociability as being of divine institution, while the forms of worship were merely conventional. As Addison sees it, morality might conceivably be endangered by adherence to religion, but this danger can be obviated by subscription to religion as formulated by the post-Revolution Anglican Church:

> the greatest Friend of Morality, or Natural Religion, cannot possibly apprehend any Danger from embracing Christianity, as it is preserved pure and uncorrupt in the Doctrines of our National Church. (*Spectator* IV, 120)

In this sentence, Christianity understood as synonymous with Anglicanism seems to be merely an additional cohering force in society, and social utility, as we have seen above, is really Addison's highest criterion. Moreover, 'the greatest part of Morality ... is of a fixt eternal Nature, and will endure when faith shall fail, and be lost in Conviction'. Fortunately, faith is not of prime importance: 'a person may be qualified to do greater Good to Mankind, and become more beneficial to the world, by Morality without Faith, than by Faith without Morality' (*Spectator* IV, 118). The near-irrelevance of the Church, from the point of view of the Whig conception of moral reform, might be judged by the fact that when Addison, in *Tatler* 267, wanted an exemplar of piety and true religion, he ignored 'very shining Examples from among the Clergy' which might have been cited, and chose Sir Francis Bacon instead.

Steele praised Jonathan Swift's 'Project for the Advancement of Religion and the Reformation of Manners' (1709), but there were really only superficial similarities between his conception of reform and Swift's.[118] By recommending religion as a criterion for political advancement in the 'Project', Swift was implicitly supporting the authority of the Established Church, and the imposition of Test Acts. Addison and Steele only represent one side of the argument: their careers are contemporaneous with those of High Churchmen like Francis Atterbury and Henry Sacheverell. Atterbury's campaign for the rights of Convocation, and its Lower House in particular, enjoyed some partial triumphs. Nevertheless, Whig politics became dominant. John Loftis argues that after the success of Nicholas Rowe's political play *Tamerlane* in 1701, dramatization of principles used to justify the Revolution became a commonplace of tragedy.[119] By 1713, Whigs and Tories vied with each other to applaud references to liberty in Addison's *Cato*. There were no tragedies celebrating passive obedience and divine right. 'Politeness' became the norm. Bishop George Berkeley's *Alciphron*, published in 1732, was partly concerned to refute the Shaftesburian account of virtue and taste, but *Alciphron* was cast as a series of polite dialogues in the style made popular by Shaftesbury,

---

[117] Haakonssen, 6–7.

[118] Bertrand Goldgar, *The Curse of Party. Swift's Relations with Addison and Steele* (Lincoln: University of Nebraska Press, 1961), 46.

[119] John Loftis, *The Politics of Drama in Augustan England* (Oxford: Clarendon Press, 1963), 23.

Addison and Steele.[120] William Law's *Serious Call to a Devout and Holy Life* (1729) made a case for a more heartfelt version of religion, but by the same method of character sketch and narrative that we find in the *Spectator*, and with the same assumptions about its middle-class audience. One chapter describes the 'wise and religious use of our estates'.

By 1714, the succession of George I assured the supremacy of the Whigs. Bishop Benjamin Hoadly provoked a furious controversy by defending the rights of the secular power to penalize the non-jurors who would not take the oaths of allegiance to William and Mary. He also argued that the Church of England had, in effect, no divine right: it was, rather, analogous to a voluntary society. It followed, then, that the clergy possessed no unique privilege to interpret the Scriptures or regulate individual consciences. At this point, the radical anticlericalism of those Protestants who would have a priesthood of all believers (an anti-clericalism which, as J.G.A. Pocock has argued, fed into Deism) meets, almost by accident, the factionalism of eighteenth century politics.[121] Convocation was prorogued in 1717 to silence opposition to Hoadly and did not sit again until 1741. When it did meet it attempted to address, once again, the old problems of enforcing moral discipline, delay in the courts and the courts' prerogatives, but the suspicion of a libel upon the Constitution forced an adjournment.

Anticlerical feeling seems to have been particularly strong in the 1730s, when a series of bills proposed restrictions on Church prerogatives. Suits for tithes were to be restricted and church rates were to be decided by Parliament, the latter in effect a sweeping attack on the jurisdiction of ecclesiastical courts.[122] The Mortmain Act of 1736 sought to limit the accumulation of Church wealth by preventing death-bed donations. The Quakers' Tithe Bill would have transferred jurisdiction from the ecclesiastical courts to the local magistrate. Moreover, in the case of *Middleton v. Croft* in 1736, the Lord Chief Justice delivered a judgement that came to be seen as the definitive assertion of the supremacy of statute over canon law.[123] Bishop Edmund Gibson (otherwise known as Walpole's Pope) constructed a lengthy and detailed response but acknowledged that in the present climate the cause of Church authority, as he saw it, was weak.[124] The question of the relationship between Church and State was resolved for the time being by William Warburton's *The Alliance between Church and State*, published in 1736. The future Bishop of Gloucester justified the current arrangement on Lockeian principles, construing the Church as giving up its 'natural right' of independence in order to enjoy the protection of the State, which then protected the Church by the imposition of Test Acts.

---

[120] Klein, 97.

[121] J.G.A. Pocock, 'Post-Puritan England and the Problem of the Enlightenment', *Culture and Politics from Puritanism to the Enlightenment*, ed. Peter Zagorin (Berkeley: University of California Press, 1980), 93 *et passim*.

[122] Sykes, *Sheldon*, 202–3.

[123] Paul Langford, *A Polite and Commercial People. England 1727–1783* (Oxford: Clarendon Press, 1989), 41–3.

[124] Sykes, *Sheldon*, 203.

By the 1730s, then, the Anglican Church was not well placed to address the challenge to its authority that arose from within the Established Church itself in the form of the Evangelical Revival. The revival was a diverse movement, but in theological terms it was a reaction against the largely ethical preaching characteristic of the post-Restoration Church, and it marked a wish to return to the doctrines of justification and regeneration as laid out in the Thirty-Nine Articles.[125] Through the irregular practices of itinerant and lay preaching, meetings in the open air, private chapels and meetinghouses, societies and conferences – not to mention the notorious 'love-feasts' – adherents of the Revival moved outside the organisational structures of the Church of England. This, by itself, was liable to arouse alarm. An extract from the *Weekly Miscellany*, reprinted in the *Gentleman's Magazine* of 1739, objected to the Methodist stance of remaining within the Church of England whilst seeming to preach against it, and outside of its walls. Religious difference might be permissible but only so long as it was regulated by the Toleration Act:

> Provided they maintain no Doctrines destructive of Religion in general, or of Civil Government, different as their Sentiments can possibly be from those of the Church of *England*, wild and enthusiastical as they are in themselves, yet in the Name of God, in the Name of Justice, as *Christians*, as *Englishmen*, as *Men*, let them enjoy the Benefit of the *Toleration*, but let them entitle themselves to it by a proper Licence from the *Civil* Power. That they should have the Liberty of worshipping God in their own Way (tho' *they* have endeavoured to interrupt us in our Worship) this is the Voice of God, of Reason, and of our Laws; but that every Man should be at Liberty, when, and where, and how he pleases, without first subscribing to some Articles of Faith, and without any warrant from Publick Authority, to preach up whatever Doctrines he shall think proper, abusing the Establish'd Clergy … this is a Procedure destructive of all Order and Religion, and dangerous to the Peace and Safety of the State.[126]

The Methodist might have replied that he (or she) was returning to precisely those Articles of Faith which the Church, at this date, had chosen to discount.

Abuse of the Anglican clergy there certainly was. In his controversial *Journal*, entitled 'A Short Account of God's Dealings with the Reverend Mr. George Whitefield' (1738), George Whitefield (1714–1770), who preached in the open air to the colliers at Kingswood near Bristol, in February 1739, and who by the late 1730s had begun preaching to large congregations in Gloucester, Bath, Bristol and London, responded to a letter from William Warburton, now Bishop of Gloucester, advising him to confine his preaching to the congregation to which he had been appointed. Whitefield replied:

> I hope your lordship will inspect the lives of your other clergy, and censure them for being *over-remiss*, as much as you censure me for being *over-righteous*.

---

[125]   Isabel Rivers, *Reason*, I, 205–6.
[126]   *Gentleman's Magazine*, 9 (1739), 241.

It is their falling from their Articles, and not preaching the truth as it is in Jesus, that has excited the present zeal of those, whom they, in derision, call the *Methodist preachers*.[127]

And again in 1739:

I heartily wish all the Lord's servants were prophets; I wish the Church of England was the joy of the whole earth; but I cannot see her sink into papistical ignorance, and refined Deism, and not open my mouth against those who, by their sensual, lukewarm lives, and unscriptural superficial doctrines, thus cause her to err. (*Journals* 312)

The late 1730s and early 1740s were accordingly a time of acute concern about the rise of Methodism. The Rev. Richard Green's 1902 bibliography of anti-Methodist publications has just one entry for 1732 – an anonymous letter in *Fogg's Weekly Journal* – followed by four entries for 1738, then 87 for the year 1739, 23 for the year 1740, 22 for 1741, 14 for 1742, 9 for 1743, and then an increase again in the period of the '45 Rebellion.[128] Methodism was charged with enthusiasm, schism, cryptopapism, antinomianism, and a tendency, above all, to promote disorder.[129] An anonymous pamphlet of 1744 usually attributed to Bishop Gibson suggests, in effect, that an excess of faith may distract people from their duties:

Whether Notions in Religion may not be heighten'd to such *Extremes*, as to lead *some* into a Disregard of Religion itself, through Despair of attaining such exalted *Heights*? and Whether *others*, who have imbib'd those Notions, may not be led by them into a Disregard and Disesteem of the *common* Duties and Offices of Life; to such a Degree at least, as is inconsistent with that Attention to them, and that Diligence in them, which Providence has made necessary to the well-being of private Families and publick Societies, and which Christianity does not only require in all Stations and in all Conditions, but declares at the same Time (*Col.* III:22. *Ephes.* vol. 6.) that the Performance even of the lowest Offices in Life, *as unto God*, (whose Providence has plac'd People in their several Stations) is truly a *Serving of Christ*, and will not fail of its Reward in the next World?[130]

The biblical references make the anxiety about the question of obedience more explicit. Colossians 3:xxii, reads: 'Servants, obey in all things your masters according to the flesh; not with eyeservice, as menpleasers; but in singleness of heart, fearing God'. The text from Ephesians is 'Let no man deceive you with vain

---

[127] George Whitefield, *George Whitefield's Journals* (Edinburgh: Banner of Truth Trust, 1960), 300.

[128] Richard Green, *Anti-Methodist publications issued during the eighteenth century …* (London: C.H. Kelly, 1902).

[129] See Albert M. Lyles, *Methodism Mocked. The Satiric Reaction to Methodism in the Eighteenth Century* (London: Epworth Press, 1960).

[130] Anon., 'Observations upon the Conduct and Behaviour of A Certain Sect, Usually Distinguished by the Name of Methodists' (n.p., n.d.), 9.

words: for because of these things cometh the wrath of God upon the children of disobedience'. From the Anglican point of view, Whitefield and Wesley posed a threat to the Church of England's emphasis on works and duty. Whitefield ill-advisedly attacked both Tillotson's sermons and that essential Anglican work, *The Whole Duty of Man* (1657), in his letters.[131]

While the bishops might issue reproofs to the Methodists, they were unable to take effective action to stop them. Gordon Rupp has spoken of the 'disciplinary paralysis' of the Church of England between 1662 and 1850.[132] The cessation of Convocation, to which reference has already been made, was a major absence. A writer in the *Gentleman's Magazine* in 1741 referred to the 'universal Feebleness and Debility' of the Church and called for a revival of the synod to control the activities of Methodists. By the time Samuel Richardson came to offer his version of the Latitudinarian ethic in *Pamela* (1740), then, or indeed Fielding his version of natural religion in *Tom Jones* (1749), the authority of the Anglican Church had been fatally undermined in the long term by the Toleration Act of 1689, and in the shorter term by the dominance of Whig politics and politicians. The Toleration Act was a limited measure, merely granting Dissenters exemption from the penalties of statutes that remained in force, but it effectively legitimized schism, and abolished the offence of recusancy. Church authority was undermined again by the Whig supremacy after 1714. Bishop Gibson ensured that only Walpole supporters sat on the bishops' benches in the House of Lords. Clerical authority was also potentially undermined by the scramble for places in an oversubscribed profession, with the 'clerical subalterns', as Addison described them, often being doomed to uncertain tenure and inadequate stipends. Pluralism, meaning the holding of more than one living, was widespread, as was nonresidence, both practices scarcely contributing to an idea of spiritual commitment.

Recent scholarship has attempted to rehabilitate the reputation of the Hanoverian Church, taking up Norman Sykes's case for a more balanced and historically sensitive view.[133] However, a sense that the Church of England was incapable of effecting moral reform, and a belief that the clergy were self-serving, lax, and even venal, was common enough at the time, and was not unique to Methodists. In *Pamela*, the heroine herself reflects that 'it was impossible I should have edify'd under any Doctrine preached by Mr. *Peters:* So I apply'd myself to my private Devotions'.[134] Fielding's Parson Trulliber in *Joseph Andrews* (1742) offers a damning portrait of a country parson. Isabel Rivers has written of the dissatisfaction with Anglican literature in the 1730s and 1740s that prompted the

---

[131] Gordon Rupp, *Religion in England 1688–1791* (Oxford: Clarendon, 1986), 378.

[132] Gordon Rupp, Introductory Essay, *A History of the Methodist Church in Great Britain*, eds. Rupert Davies and Gordon Rupp (London: Epworth Press, 1965), Vol. I, xix.

[133] See the introduction to *The Church of England c.1689–c.1833. From Toleration to Tractarianism*, eds John Walsh, Colin Haydon and Stephen Taylor (Cambridge: Cambridge University Press, 1993).

[134] Samuel Richardson, *Pamela; or, Virtue Rewarded*, eds Thomas Keymer and Alice Wakeley (Oxford: Oxford University Press, 2001), 140.

writing of alternative works of practical divinity by Dissenters and Methodists. These works had to be 'experimental, affectionate, and evangelical':

> By 'experimental' they meant that it must be based on the personal religious experience of the writer, or appeal to that of the reader, or narrate that of others; by 'affectionate' that it must be directed at the reader's heart and excite his passions; by 'evangelical' that it must teach the gospel doctrine of salvation by faith.[135]

If we substitute for the gospel doctrine of salvation the idea of virtue as compatible with earthly happiness, then this account might well serve as a description of *Pamela*. Contemporaries noticed the parallels. Richardson wrote to George Cheyne that 'the principal complaints against me by many, and not Libertines neither, are, that I am too grave, too much of a Methodist, and make Pamela too pious'.[136] Where the Methodists addressed themselves to the shifting and rapidly growing population to which the Anglican parochial system was unable to adjust itself, Richardson used the democratic appeal of fiction, and its proven ability to engage the reader's passions to make his case for moral reform.

In 1739 the Methodists' emphasis on a renunciation of worldly pursuits and pleasures was attacked from the pulpit and in print in the form of four sermons by Joseph Trapp (1679–1747), collectively entitled 'The Nature, folly, sin, and danger of being righteous over-much; with a particular view to the doctrines and practices of certain modern enthusiasts.' Here Trapp rehearsed the eighteenth-century Anglican view that virtue and self-interest were compatible. 'Do not', writes Trapp, 'out of an immoderate, and mistaken Sanctity utterly reject all enjoyment of worldly Pleasures, Honours, Riches, etc ... must we allow ourselves no pleasure in worldly Things?'[137] Against Whitefield, Trapp argued that a Christian might be rich, he might bequeath estates, practise a trade or profession, or go to law to defend his property. The sermons were extracted in the *Gentleman's Magazine* for June 1739. A vigorous riposte followed from the Methodist side in the form of pamphlets and sermons, among them Jonathan Warne's 'Trapp try'd, and cast; and allowed to the 10th of May next to recant' (1739); 'Dr. Trapp vindicated from the imputation of being a Christian' (1739) by 'Lover of Truth'; 'A proper Reply to the Anti-overrighteous Dr. Trapp's Sermons against Mr. Whitefield' (1739); 'The Folly and Danger of being not righteous enough' (1739), a sermon by Whitefield; and 'The folly and danger of parting with Christ for the pleasures and profits of life' (1740), also by Whitefield. Vindications of Whitefield also appeared in the *Gentleman's Magazine* for June and August of 1739.

---

[135] Rivers, 'Dissenting', 128.

[136] John Carroll (ed.), *Selected Letters of Samuel Richardson* (Oxford. Clarendon, 1964), 47.

[137] Joseph Trapp, *The Nature, Folly, Sin and Danger of being Righteous over-much; with a particular view to the Doctrines and Practices of Certain Modern Enthusiasts*, 3rd edition (London: 1739), 4.

Here then, was a vigorous controversy in 1739 revolving around the old split between Calvinism and Latitudinarianism, calling up the old fears of antinomianism and disorder. Richardson intervened from the Latitudinarian side with a work that dramatized the benefits of adhering to virtue, conspicuously subtitling his novel 'Virtue Rewarded'. *Pamela*'s relationship with the Whitefield/Trapp controversy was more than tangential.[138] The point at issue between them was central to Richardson's novel. While Richardson wrote to support the Anglican ethos, he deployed the methods of nonconformity: print, immediacy, a demotic vocabulary. *Pamela* also enacted the secular creed of politeness, in which virtuous femininity would tame an otherwise rough and lawless masculinity. The work of reform is not effected by the Anglican clergy, in the shape of Parson Williams, Mr. Peters, or the Dean, but by the example of Pamela herself, and by her writings. Henry Fielding would reply in 1742 with *Shamela*, a work that homed in on *Pamela*'s quite deliberate appeal to worldliness and self-interest, attributed Richardson's intention to his heroine, and found her 'virtue', in every sense of the word, entirely bogus. Thus began a dialogue between the novels of Richardson and Fielding that played out in a new arena the debate about the motivation to virtuous behaviour which had long divided Calvinists and Arminians. The issues were not debated or dramatized by adherents of opposing tendencies within Protestantism, but between two writers who were both moderate and rational Anglicans. Questions of morality and virtue were not contested in the old style of pamphlet and sermon, but in the new style of fiction written for a middle-class market. I want now to turn to these works.

---

[138]   The view that *Pamela* is 'tangentially implicated' in the Trapp/Whitefield controversy by way of Fielding's reference to the dispute in *Shamela* is briefly stated by Thomas Keymer and Peter Sabor in *Pamela in the Marketplace. Literary Controversy and Print Culture in Eighteenth Century Britain and Ireland* (Cambridge: Cambridge University Press, 2005). Fielding had his Parson Williams preach on the text 'Be not righteous overmuch'.

Chapter 1
Secularizing Ethics:
From *Pamela* to *Tom Jones*

Samuel Richardson's successful and controversial novel *Pamela; or, Virtue Rewarded* can be read as an enactment of Latitudinarian thinking. In her successive roles as daughter, servant and wife, Pamela is an exemplar of duty as advocated in *The Whole Duty of Man* (1658). From Chapter X of *The Whole Duty*, readers might learn the duty of obedience to kings, clergy and parents. In Chapter XI, wives could learn how they must obey their husbands, following Col. 3:18: 'Wives submit yourselves to your husbands, as is fit in the Lord'. The duty required of servants by *The Whole Duty* is 'Obedience to all lawful commands'. The reader's attention is directed to this dimension of Pamela's character from the beginning of the novel. In the first letter, Pamela expresses her sense of duty towards her parents in almost the exact words of *The Whole Duty*:

> I am sure it is my Duty, and it shall be my Care to love and cherish you both; for
> you have lov'd me and cherish'd me, when I could do nothing for myself. (*P* 12)

She signs herself 'Your most dutiful Daughter', 'Your ever dutiful Daughter', and at one point apologizes for failing, on every occasion, to subscribe herself as she ought: 'I am sure you will always believe it is not for want of Duty' (*P* 44). Before, as she hopes, leaving the service of her master, Mr. B. – an undutiful act – she vows to 'do all the Duties of my Place first, if I may' (*P* 39). So she must put the linen in order before she leaves or embroider Mr. B's waistcoat. In the verses composed on her departure, she coaches her fellow servants in their duties:

> One thing or two I've more to say;
> God's holy Will, be sure obey;
> And for our Master always pray;
> …
> Your Parents and Relations love:
> Let them your Duty ever prove;
> And you'll be blessed from above. (*P* 90–91)

As a servant, Pamela values order. Mrs. Jervis is praised by Pamela for making her master's interests her own and for keeping 'good Rule and Order'. In the second volume, Pamela is an exemplar of wifely duty: servant readily translates to wife. Mr. B. becomes, at every turn, 'my master'. It is too great an honour to accompany him in his chariot, and she cannot deserve his goodness to her: 'if I can, by the most chearful Duty, and resigned Obedience, have the Pleasure to be agreeable to you, I shall think myself but too happy' (*P* 262–3).

Somewhat inconsistently, however, *Pamela* is also an enactment of the Latitudinarian idea that virtue was compatible with commercial life, with self-interest, and with pleasure, as reiterated in the sermons of Tillotson, Barrow and others. As Richardson construed it, a servant girl would naturally desire money, clothes and social elevation, and the plot allows Pamela to gratify all of what her creator conceives of her wishes. Pamela turns down the 'wicked articles' in which B. offers her all but one of these in exchange for sex, but in the end she gains exactly what was on offer, as well as the higher prize of social elevation, by remaining chaste. Evidently Richardson thought that servants, or even women in general, needed the incentive of tangible rewards to induce them to accept subordination.

Pamela departs from Anglican teaching in any of its forms, though, in its conception of the agent of moral reform. The novel offers the reader a picture of one character in need of reform – the young and rakish Squire B. – and another, his servant Pamela, who manages to effect a change in B.'s manners. In Volume I, we see how B. wants sex outside marriage, is often angry and behaves roughly. By the second volume, he is more moderate in temper, addresses Pamela affectionately and is willing to marry her. *Anger* is a recurring word in the first volume: in the second volume, *kindness*, *chearfulness* and *forgiveness* are the terms that reappear. The work of reform is effected by the example of Pamela herself and by her writings. By means of these writings, she is able to convert B. from one style of behaviour and speech to another.

Pamela's reforming powers also extend to the wider society outside the marriage. When she appears in church at the end of the novel, her presence assembles the gentry in the congregation. Squire Martin, a bachelor who seldom attends church, tells B. that if he and Pamela come every Sunday, he will never absent himself. The Dean says that her behaviour as a bride would not only be 'very edifying to his congregation', but also 'encouraging to himself' (*P* 489). By the end of the novel, B.'s sister, Lady Davers, is asking whether she may see Pamela's journal, in the hope of moral improvement:

> the Sight of your Papers, I dare say … will disarm my Pride, banish my Resentment on Lady *Betty*'s account, and justify my Brother's Conduct; and, at the same time, redound to your own everlasting Honour, as well as to the Credit of our Sex. (*P* 456)

Pamela's moral character also has the power to maintain the Whig idea of legitimate government. In terms of political allegory, her role is pivotal: the example of Pamela transforms B. from the Stuart-like tyrant of the first volume to the benevolent constitutional monarch of the second.[1]

---

[1]   For a political reading of *Pamela*, see Jocelyn Harris, *Samuel Richardson* (Cambridge: Cambridge University Press, 1987), 17–37.

From Richardson's point of view, in fact, Pamela has remarkable powers, *power* being a word that recurs notably in the narrative. She has power over B.'s mood. A dilemma for Pamela is that her letters, which will eventually effect B.'s reform, also enrage him. Yet. in terms of the code of politeness, anger should be discouraged and restrained, particularly by women.[2] As Mrs. Jervis tells Pamela:

> you have made our Master from the sweetest-temper'd Gentleman in the World, one of the most peevish. But you have it in your Power to make him as sweet-temper'd as ever. (*P* 48)

From the beginning, B. seems fearful of Pamela's power over his reputation – hence his extraordinary watchfulness over her powers of communication and expression. He speaks of 'the Liberty she has taken with my Character, out of the House and in the House' (*P* 58), and her 'licentious tongue' (*P* 210). She has talked, he says, 'a little too freely'. By virtue of her looks, Pamela has the power to attract B., and, seemingly, compel him to behaviour over which he has no control. Mrs. Jewkes tells Pamela that 'you have so great Power over my Master, that you may soon be mistress of us all' (*P* 110), and, later, 'you may do anything with him' (*P* 137). If she has the power to attract him, she also has the power to make him a cuckold. B. asks for assurances, over and over again, that she has no hidden regard for Parson Williams (*P* 216–17). So important is this issue that she must swear it, at one point, in the presence of God. B. is always ready to interpret Pamela's action as meaning that she prefers another man.

Pamela, then, advances the claims of duty and obedience for women at the same time that it endows the beautiful and virtuous woman with considerable powers. As the agent of reform, Pamela has the power to emasculate B. She can compromise B.'s supremacy and authority as a man by her power to change his behaviour. Politeness itself – defined by Brean Hammond as 'attitudes and strategies of self-containment: internal sanctions, protocols of speech and behaviour calculated to eliminate conflict and oil the wheels of social intercourse' – might be seen as emasculating.[3] Michèle Cohen has argued that 'Politeness … is implicated in the problematization of masculinity, because it blurs gender boundaries'.[4] *Pamela* exposes the difficulties posed by the culture of politeness in terms of constructing a still-dominant masculinity, a dominance Richardson very much wanted to retain, despite the moral importance given to women in his work. The issue of what was, for men, an unwelcome new power and agency attributed to women in an increasingly secular society recurs in the novels I discuss in this chapter. If Richardson's 'personations' of women seem to promote female interests, his ability to take on a female character may have more to do in the end with his

---

[2]   On this aspect of Whig ideology, see Edmund Leites, 'Good Humor', 51–89.

[3]   Brean Hammond, 'Hackney for Bread', *Professional Imaginative Writing in England, 1670–1740* (Oxford: Clarendon, 1997), 151.

[4]   Michèle Cohen, *Fashioning Masculinity: National Identity and Language in the Eighteenth Century* (London: Routledge, 1996), 53.

own social position than with matters of gender. It may be that Richardson the printer, who was acutely conscious of his lack of education, and who in one letter constructed a fable about his lost gentility, actually found the female voice more congenial to him insofar as it spoke from a position of subordination. In a letter to his Dutch translator, Johannes Stinstra, Richardson gave an account of his parentage and early life in which he represented himself as having been deprived of gentlemanly status (*Selected Letters* 228–30). His father was a joiner, which Stinstra was to understand was something more than a mere carpenter. The elder Richardson was beloved, apparently, by the first Earl of Shaftesbury and the Duke of Monmouth and was forced, on account of his connection with the latter, to retire from London to Derbyshire after the failure of the Monmouth Rebellion in 1685. Richardson himself, apparently, had been destined for the clergy, but his father's business losses made it impossible for him to gain an appropriate education. As an apprentice to a printer, he became engaged in a correspondence with 'a Gentleman greatly my superior in Degree', who gave him, in effect, a version of a gentleman's education, and who, had he lived, intended 'high things' for the author.[5]

Pamela is coloured by these aspirations and sensitivities. Pamela's father, too, has had to endure downward social mobility, having been forced into the lowest kind of labour by debts and the failure of a little school he established. His poverty is constantly in Pamela's mind (albeit as, allegedly, a source of pride to her) and when he finds that Pamela is to marry B., and become a gentlewoman, he wonders if he and Pamela's mother 'ought to go into some far Country, to hide ourselves, that we may not disgrace you by our Poverty!' (*P* 295). Like Richardson's own father, though, Goodman Andrews is effectively upgraded in rank, being placed, by B., at the upper end of the table and being given a suit of B.'s clothes. He even fulfils one of Richardson's own ambitions by acting as a parish clerk at Sunday service.

If Richardson could identify with Pamela in terms of rank, though, he was still committed to the idea of female subordination, in and out of wedlock. B.'s power over Pamela is actually reinstated in terms of his male heterosexuality, despite the fact that this is the very quality that Pamela, as the exemplary virgin, seems designed to control. Patriarchy is reinvented in terms of an account of gender difference and heterosexual relationships in which male sexuality is permissible while, for the most part, female sexuality is not. Here Richardson very definitely parted company with any religious conception of the desired moral order. The extent to which masculine sexuality is regarded as acceptable may be seen in Pamela's acceptance of the illegitimate child B. has with Sally Godfrey into the household. Lawrence Stone argues that the sexual double standard made sense when the concern was to ensure legitimacy.[6] I would argue rather that the construction of masculine sexuality

---

⁵   *Selected Letters of Samuel Richardson*, ed. John Carroll (Oxford: Clarendon Press, 1964), 229.

⁶   Lawrence Stone, *The Road to Divorce, England 1530–1987* (Oxford: Oxford University Press, 1990), 7, 242–3.

as figured in *Pamela* and *Clarissa* was necessary to return the balance of power to men, when politeness seemed to invest so much power in women.

At points in the novel where B. either concedes, or is about to concede, Pamela's power over him, his control over her and over the situation, is reasserted in terms of his sexuality. At one point, for example, he rehearses her transgressions against his authority and considers conceding to feminine power, both in the sense that he will allow such transgressions and in the sense that he will concede to the feminine quality of forgiveness. Juxtaposed with these concessions is an assertion of his male sexuality:

> He said, as if he had been considering whether he could forgive me or not, No, I cannot forgive her neither—She has given me great Disturbance; has brought great Discredit upon me, both abroad and at home; has corrupted all my servants at the other House; has despised my honourable Views and Intentions to her, and sought to run away with this ingrateful Parson—And surely I ought not to forgive her all this!—Yet, with all this wretched Grimace, he kissed me again, and would have put his Hand in my Bosom. (*P* 187)

The moment of maximum feminization, as it were, when B. disguises himself as Nan, is also the point at which his heterosexuality is made most evident: he makes his most determined attempt on her chastity. B. hides in the closet and must hear Pamela's reproving dialogue with Mrs. Jervis: against the possible emasculation that this might entail is the subsequent assault where B. emerges from the closet and Pamela finds his hand on her breasts. The dialogue that revolves around the exact whereabouts, and extent, of Pamela's writings is another case in point. For B.'s reform to be complete, he must, in terms of the logic of the novel, see Pamela's letters in their entirety, since they are the agent of reform. At the same time as B. is about to give himself up to their feminizing power, he expresses his male heterosexuality in aggressive terms. He kisses her; takes both her hands; asks her about her pockets, stays and garters; unpins her handkerchief; and threatens to strip her. There are points where he seems to be moving towards a conversion to an affectionate code of manners. Pamela is 'confused at his so kind and unusual Freedom and Condescension' (*P* 212) when B. orders her to carve a piece of chicken and eat it. At these moments, though, there are also pointed reminders of his masculinity: we are told that he has just come from looking at his stud of horses in the stable. Riding and hunting function in the text as signifiers of an unfeminized 'authentic' masculinity. When Parson Williams weeps over the role of divine grace in B.'s reform, B. counterbalances an acknowledgement of his own reform with an oblique reference to his unaffected, and possibly transgressive, masculinity:

> You do well, said he, to remind me, that I owe all this to the Grace of God. I bless Him for it; and I thank this good Man for his excellent Lessons. I thank his dear Daughter for following them: And, I hope, from *her* good Example, and *your* Friendship, Mr. *Williams*, in time, to be half as good as my Tutoress. And that, said he, I believe you'll own, will make me, without Disparagement to any Gentleman, the best Fox-hunter in *England*. (*P* 308)

If Pamela has the power of sexual attraction over B., he also has this power over her. Since the story is told from her point of view, and Pamela, as exemplary modest woman, must be almost asexual, this must only appear implicitly. Just before the end of the first volume of the original two-volume first edition, B. asks Pamela directly if it is possible for her to love him after his attempts on her chastity:

> Since you so much prize your Honour and your Virtue; since all Attempts against that are so odious to you; and since I have avowedly made several of these attempts, do you think it is possible for you to love me *preferably* to any other of the Sex? (*P* 218)

Pamela's reply is at once evasive and telling:

> Ah! Sir, reply'd I, what can I say?—I have already said too much, if this dreadful *Hereafter* should take place. Don't bid me say how well I can—And then, my Face, glowing as the Fire, I, all abash'd, lean'd upon his Shoulder, to hide my Confusion. (*P* 218)

Here, the same heterosexuality that Pamela seems to be instrumental in controlling actually reinstates B.'s power over her because Richardson suggests that this is what Pamela really wants.

Male authority is also reinstated on 'natural' grounds by virtue of the fact that this, also, is what Pamela wants. Pamela represents a wish, on Richardson's part, for subordination willingly entered into. As the virtuous maiden, then (or, more accurately, the inner voice Richardson constructs for the virtuous woman), she finds ways of dissuading herself from leaving the scene of her ordeal. Sometimes this voluntary self-repression appears as a fear of the disorder beyond the world of the household, as when she decides not to leave for fear of being robbed. Crucially, though, when B. does allow her liberty to leave, Pamela finds herself drawn back by the dictates of her 'ungovernable' heart. As Chris Jones comments: 'Apparently an appeal to unconditioned natural feelings, [sensibility] was also a social construction which translated prevailing power-based relationships into loyalties upheld by "natural" feelings'.[7] B. underlines the necessity for this motivation when he remarks: 'I so much value a voluntier Love, in the person I would wish for my Wife, that I would have even Prudence and Interest, hardly nam'd, in Comparison with it' (*P* 270). The apparently involuntary passion of love means that Pamela herself 'chooses' a subordinate role.

The reinvention of patriarchy as figured in *Pamela* takes place, clearly, within the household and in terms of marriage. It is not mediated by the clergy. The role of the Church is marginal: the gentry are moral arbiters and control the action. Where the duties of husband and wife, matters of sexual reputation and defamation, and, more broadly, the parameters of acceptable sexual behaviour, previously fell

---

[7]   Chris Jones, *Radical Sensibility. Literature and Ideas in the 1790s* (London: Routledge, 1993), 7.

within the jurisdiction of the Church courts, they must now be regulated from within. Pamela has no outside agency to which she might have recourse in the matter of B.'s defamation of *her* sexual character.[8] However Richardson might express regret over the decline of clerical influence, it is for the clergy, in fact, to reform themselves in accordance with middle-class values: Richardson subscribed to the Whig conception of the Church as subordinate to the State. As B. tellingly observes: 'Mr. *Williams*, it is impossible that you and I should long live at Variance, when our Sentiments agree so well together, on Subjects the most material' (*P* 307). Parson Williams is an ineffectual character, applying to the gentry to help Pamela without result. B. holds sway. At B.'s instigation, Williams is attacked and arrested, and as he owes B. money, he is scarcely in a position to exercise any moral authority over the squire. In Volume II, Williams is acutely deferential towards B. He reproves Williams for not expostulating with him, B., to correct his moral behaviour. Williams consults with B. over the choice of text for church service and B. (generously perhaps) suggests, '*There is more Joy in Heaven over one Sinner that repenteth*' (*P* 310), to which Williams responds with the suggestion of a text which refers to his own gratitude and deference: '*Now lettest thy Servant depart in Peace* ' (*P* 310). In true Latitudinarian style, Williams gives a sermon on 'the Blessing attending the right Use of riches'.

The idea that the wedding should take place in church comes from Pamela, and the Church is really invoked only to solemnize, and make public, the institution of marriage. Pamela's fears about the sham marriage, and her scrutiny of the terms of B.'s articles, speak from a middle-class concern about the regularisation of the institution that would culminate in the Marriage Act of 1753. Under canon law, in fact, Pamela's acceptance of the conditional promise to marry, followed by sexual intercourse, could be construed as constituting a legal marriage, though common law refused to confer property rights on couples who had not gone through a public ceremony.[9] B.'s preference for a private and rather casual ceremony, to be performed in his or Pamela's chamber, perhaps reflects the middle-class perception that publicity was really necessary only to regulate the lower classes. In the end, Pamela and B. reach a kind of compromise about the matter of publicity: the ceremony is conducted in a chapel in B.'s house, which is recovered from the status of lumber-room only for the purpose of marriage. In an aside suggestive of the perceived remoteness of religion, B. assures Pamela that it was consecrated in his great-great-grandfather's time. He tells Mrs. Jewkes that they intend to wed

---

[8]   Martin Ingram notes that a high proportion of suits brought by women to the Church courts involved 'unspecific slanders', which usually meant the use of words signifying a sexually immoral female. See *Church Courts*, 302. Considering a later period, Anna Clark argues that in England, gossip about women's sexual reputations was used to control behaviour, as opposed to the seclusion used in Mediterranean countries. See 'Whores and Gossips: Sexual Reputation in London 1770–1825', *Current Issues in Women's History*, ed. Ariana Angerman *et al.* (London: Routledge, 1989), 231.

[9]   R.B. Outhwaite, *Clandestine Marriage in England 1500–1800* (London: Hambledon Press, 1995), 56.

'as privately as possible'. It is interesting to note, also, how little Pamela's consent, or the consent of her father – who is absent when the ceremony takes place – figures in the issue of the marriage itself. She is given away by the minister Mr. Peters. Pamela is permitted the illusion of choice by being allowed to procrastinate a little about the day. In fact, the ceremony could be construed as the kind of clandestine marriage the Marriage Act was devised to prevent.[10] The ceremony is a solemn one for Pamela, who approaches marriage with 'fear and trembling', while B. walks into the chapel inviting the opinions of Peters and Williams on the alterations he plans to make to it.

In *Pamela*, certain pleasures may be allowed, as long as Pamela does not acknowledge that she wants them. The reward may be gained, in other words, as long as it is not actively sought. After escaping from B.'s house into the garden, she thinks of drowning herself in the pond. She imagines how contrite her persecutors will be when they see her dead body dragged from the water, but having convinced herself of the sinfulness of despair, and, subsequently, *not* committing suicide, she is allowed the pleasure of spectating as those who would imprison and mistreat her repine at her apparent death: 'they all, *Swiss* among the rest, beat their Breasts, and made the most dismal Lamentations' (*P* 176). Similarly, *Pamela*, in its attempt to co-opt pleasure on the side of morality, enlisted the excitements of the amatory novel, except that Richardson would not, at least within the covers of the book, acknowledge that he had done so. He slyly alluded to the potentially erotic content in the teasing disclaimer on the title page:

> A Narrative which has its Foundation in TRUTH and NATURE; and at the same time that it agreeably entertains, by a Variety of *curious* and *affecting* INCIDENTS, is intirely divested of all those Images, which, in too many Pieces calculated for Amusement, tend to *Inflame* the Minds they should *instruct*.

As the author of *Pamela Censured* (1741) detected, the novel actually rehearsed the standard erotic gambits of the salacious tale: Pamela naked; Pamela in bed; Pamela seen through the keyhole, lying on her back; Pamela appearing in disguise; Pamela in a variety of dress. The last two might have been derived from the plot of Eliza Haywood's *Fantomina* (1725), in which the heroine disguises herself as a prostitute, a country girl and a mysterious widow to inspire and reinspire her lover's desire. In his correspondence, however, Richardson was rather more forthcoming. To George Cheyne's advice that he had better avoid 'Fondling … and Gallantry' (*Selected Letters* 46n.) he replied:

> I am endeavouring to write a Story, which shall catch young and airy Minds, and when Passions run high in them, to shew how they may be directed to laudable Meanings and Purposes, in order to decry such Novels and Romances, as have a Tendency to inflame and corrupt: And if I were to be too spiritual, I doubt

---

[10]   See Lawrence Stone, *The Road to Divorce, England 1530–1987* (Oxford: Oxford University Press, 1990), 96–7.

I should catch none but Grandmothers, for the Granddaughters would put my Girl indeed in better Company, such as that of the graver Writers, and *there* they would leave her. (*Selected Letters* 46–7)

As Richardson told Cheyne, he had taken human nature '*as it is*; for it is to no purpose to suppose it Angelic, or to endeavour to make it so' (*Selected Letters* 47).

Henry Fielding's *An Apology for the Life of Mrs. Shamela Andrews*, published in April 1741, was the first hostile reaction to *Pamela*. As one poetical essay, published in *the London Magazine* in June 1741 declared:

ADMIR'D *Pamela*, till *Shamela* shown,
Apperar'd in ev'ry colour—but her own:
Uncensur'd she remain'd in borrow'd light,
No nun more chaste, few angels shone so bright,
But now, the idol we no more adore.[11]

With his parodic version of the heroine, Fielding homed in on the novel's none too subtle appeal to acquisitiveness and social ambition as well as its links to erotic or pornographic fiction. *Shamela* levelled the charge of hypocrisy at Richardson and set the tone for other critical pamphlets, such as *Pamela Censured*, which appeared just 23 days after *Shamela*, and Eliza Haywood's *Anti-Pamela: or, Feigned Innocence Detected* (June 1741). It could be argued, though, that moral censure of *Pamela* provided Fielding with a vehicle for his own bawdy narrative. Perhaps in an attempt to legitimize his satire, and attest to its moral worthiness, Fielding framed the parody with the judgements of two clerics. Parson Tickletext accepts Pamela's innocence at face value, while the more worldly Parson Oliver undertakes to reveal her true character. Clerical commendation, we might recall, had helped to legitimize *Pamela*. A letter probably written by the Reverend William Webster, and published in *Weekly Miscellany*, a journal which he edited, on 11 October 1740, promoted sales of *Pamela* by praising it in advance of publication. The Reverend Benjamin Slocock gave the novel his seal of approval from the pulpit of St. Saviour's, Southwark in November or December 1740.

If *Shamela* subjected *Pamela* to moral censure, though, Fielding was not entirely motivated by an altruistic concern for public morality. *Shamela* and, subsequently, *Joseph Andrews*, began to exploit the market which *Pamela* had opened up, and at this time Fielding needed additional income. The passing of the Theatrical Licensing Act in 1737 had put a stop to his attacks on the Walpole administration in such plays as *The Historical Register*, *Eurydice Hiss'd*, and *Pasquin*, precisely as Walpole himself intended. Fielding's career as a dramatist came to an abrupt end. He continued as sometime journalist, contributing to *The Craftsman* and *Common Sense* whilst also preparing for the bar. In 1739,

---

[11]   Anonymous, 'To the Author of Shamela', *The Pamela Controversy. Criticisms and Adaptations of Samuel Richardson's* Pamela, eds Thomas Keymer and Peter Sabor (London: Pickering and Chatto, 2001), Vol. I, 183.

he re-emerged as Captain Hercules Vinegar, author of a new periodical called *The Champion*. In 1740–1741, Fielding was not in the happiest of financial positions: Martin Battestin describes this point as the 'nadir of his fortunes'.[12] In the spring of 1740, his worsening financial situation led him to acquiesce, reluctantly in Battestin's view, in the politicization of *The Champion*.[13] In the leader of 14 February 1739–1740, he represented himself as torn between 'two Parties', one of them offering 'Reputation, Honour, Fame and the like', with the other talking of 'Vacancies, good Things, snug Places, &c'.[14] On 4 October 1740, in a paper which allegorized his recent relations with Walpole, he speaks of suppressing a book whilst being in ill health for the payment of pills, that is, money. At the time, he was being pursued through the courts by two creditors. Possibly by December 1740, he ceased to write for *The Champion*, spending time on miscellaneous publications which might have been more remunerative.[15] One of these was a poem dedicated to his friend and patron, George Bubb Dodington, entitled *Of True Greatness*. In the Preface to the poem, Fielding defended his acceptance of money from Walpole. In January 1740–1741, he launched a new periodical, *The History of Our Own Times*, which only ran to four numbers, owing to Fielding's confinement in the bailiff's sponging house in late February or early March of that year. In January 1740–1741 his mock-epic poem *The Vernoniad* appeared, in praise of Admiral Vernon but once again satirizing Walpole, priced at 1s. 6d. a copy. Freed on bail, he produced *The Crisis: A Sermon*, in support of Lyttelton and Dodington's interests, at the time of a pending general election in April 1741. *Shamela* was also published in April 1741. Two months later, in June 1741, Fielding's father Edmund died, penniless and disgraced, having squandered the family estate and the emoluments of his position as a Lieutenant General. Fielding's final publication of 1741, appearing in December, was the anonymous pamphlet *The Opposition: A Vision*, a work which can confidently be attributed to Fielding since he acknowledged his authorship in the Preface to the *Miscellanies* (1743). In it, Fielding reversed his political views of the previous seven years and vindicated Walpole and his policies. His next piece of work to be published was *Joseph Andrews*, in February 1742, and for it he received from the bookseller Andrew Millar the then considerable sum of £183. 11s.

If *Shamela* was an opportunistic piece – besides being a funny and critically acute book – Fielding undertook a more thoughtful response to *Pamela* and to the threat to Anglicanism posed by Methodism in *The History of the Adventures of Joseph Andrews and his Friend Mr. Abraham Adams* (1742). Perhaps he also began to take the idea of himself as moral reformer more seriously. Like his contemporaries, Fielding held the Anglican clergy in low esteem, even though he pays lip service to the idea of respect

---

[12]   Martin C. Battestin with Ruthe R. Battestin, *Henry Fielding: A Life* (London: Routledge, 1989), 295.

[13]   Ibid., 282.

[14]   *Contributions to* The Champion *and Related Writings by Henry Fielding*, ed. W.B. Coley, The Wesleyan Edition of the Works of Henry Fielding (Oxford: Clarendon, 2003), 177.

[15]   Battestin, *Henry Fielding*, 289.

for the cloth and certainly valued the Church insofar as it might promote order. At the end of the Preface to *Joseph Andrews*, he rather self-consciously excuses himself for presenting a cleric involved in 'low' adventures, and declares:

> as the Goodness of his Heart will recommend him to the Good-natur'd; so I hope it will excuse me to the Gentlemen of his Cloth; for whom, while they are worthy of their sacred Order, no Man can possibly have a greater Respect.[16]

In 1740, Fielding wrote a series of four articles in *The Champion*, entitled 'An Apology for the Clergy', in reply to a pamphlet of which he had heard, and which he refers to as 'Reasons of the Contempt of the Clergy'. The pamphlet in question was probably John Hildrop's 'The Contempt of the Clergy Considered' of 1739. Ostensibly written in their defence, the articles really constitute a stinging critique of the clergy. Fielding expresses both resentment at the privileges the clergy still enjoy and a strong sense that the Church should be kept subordinate to the state. Fielding's most vivid portrait of a cleric comes in the fourth article (19 April 1740) where, having shown, he says, what a clergyman is, he will show what he is not and sketches a man of 'loose Morals, proud, malevolent, vain, rapacious, and revengeful' (*Contributions* 284).

Earlier, Fielding had undertaken to define how the clergy are regarded in law:

> the Law ... to remove all Difficulties and Discouragements from the due Execution of this Office, [the cure of souls] and to render its Institution most perfect, and its Influence most beneficial, hath wisely dignified it with the highest Honours, indulged it with the freest Immunities, rewarded it with the most plentiful Revenues, and secured it by the most wholesome Restraints. (*Contributions* 272)

In earlier times, Fielding declares, the clergy could commit treason, rape and murder without punishment and 'the Law still persists in allowing numberless Immunities ... to the Church which it regards with the affectionate and tender Care of a Parent or Guardian' (*Contributions* 274) – though he acknowledges that some of these immunities the law has 'wisely abridg'd'. The character of a cleric, Fielding insists, should be one of humility since Christ practised and taught contempt for worldly grandeur and honours. The clergy are not expected to live a life of poverty, but neither are they expected to get 'immense estates'. If the clergy are regarded with contempt, the reasons for this attitude can only be traced to their own 'bad Lives'.

To some extent, then, Fielding could make common cause with George Whitefield insofar as Whitefield criticized the worldliness of the Anglican clergy. One imagines Adams is speaking here for Fielding:

---

[16] Henry Fielding, *Joseph Andrews*, ed. Martin C. Battestin (Oxford: Clarendon, 1967), 10–11.

> I am myself as great an Enemy to the Luxury and Splendour of the Clergy as
> [Whitefield] can be. I do not, more than he, by the flourishing Estate of the
> Church, understand the palaces, Equipages, Dress, Furniture, rich Dainties, and
> vast Fortunes of her Ministers. (*JA* 82)

Where Adams, and Fielding, part company with Whitefield is when he calls on 'Nonsense and Enthusiasm' and preaches faith rather than works (*JA* 82). The Latitudinarian emphasis on works, particularly charitable works, has been well demonstrated by Martin Battestin, as has the place of such thinking in Fielding's fiction.[17] However, good works were also a more masculine alternative to the notorious Richardsonian identification of virtue with female chastity: a precursor, perhaps, of 'muscular Christianity'. Virtue as chastity is static and passive, a passivity one might associate, indeed, with the Calvinist diminution of human agency. As Pamela's brother, Joseph Andrews initially offers an example of a male chastity, a virtue much more commonly associated with women, but Fielding is quick to recuperate his hero's masculinity when it seems to be compromised. In the closing sentence of Joseph's letter to Adams recounting his refusal of Lady Booby's advances, Fielding underlines the fact that Joseph has normal heterosexual desires: 'But I am glad she turned me out of the Chamber as she did: for I had once almost forgotten every Word Parson *Adams* had ever said to me' (*JA* 46–7). Fielding also supplies Joseph with an alternative motive for his chastity, that is, love – which also means desire – for Fanny. When Joseph resists Betty, Fielding comments, rather self-consciously: 'How ought Man to rejoice, that his Chastity is always in his own power, that if he hath sufficient Strength of Mind, he hath always a competent Strength of Body to defend himself' (*JA* 87).

As Jill Campbell has pointed out, a recurring theme in Fielding's plays is the threat of female dominance, and *Joseph Andrews* 'corrected' *Pamela* by resituating a man at the centre of the moral order.[18] Over the course of the novel, what Anthony Fletcher has called 'ancient scriptural patriarchy' is replaced by a patriarchy based on distinctions of gender and a conception of the primacy of the heterosexual relationship. In *Joseph Andrews* we can see the importance of the older model waning in a very literal way. In the earlier part of the novel, Abraham Adams (a patriarchal figure if ever there was one) takes a more prominent role, and Joseph is usually seen deferring to him. In the latter part, from the point where Joseph and Fanny are reunited, and Joseph comes nearer to attaining the status of gentleman, Joseph becomes less deferential, emphasis on the heterosexual relationship becomes preeminent, and Adams's role becomes secondary.

In the chapter following the recognition scene in II, xii, where Joseph and Fanny are reunited, Adams falls asleep, leaving the lovers alone to enjoy an experience which edges towards the transcendent:

---

[17]   Martin Battestin, *The Moral Basis of Fielding's Art: A Study of* Joseph Andrews (Middletown: Wesleyan University Press, 1959).

[18]   Jill Campbell, *Natural Masques. Gender and Identity in Fielding's Plays and Novels* (Palo Alto: Stanford University Press, 1995), 21 *et passim*.

to enjoy by themselves during some Hours, an Happiness which none of my
Readers, who have never been in love, are capable of the least Conception of,
tho' we had as many Tongues as *Homer* desired to describe it with. (*JA* 160)

One condition for this happiness is the passivity of Fanny, who almost faints, and
another is a total possession voluntarily entered into by the woman: Fanny gives
up 'her whole Soul', and declares, 'I will be yours for ever'. At this point Joseph
wakens Adams so that they may marry immediately: Adams revives to insist on
the publication of the banns. This is a pattern that will be repeated in Books III and
IV. By Book III, Chapter ii, Adams voluntarily seats himself at some distance from
Joseph and Fanny, 'being unwilling to disturb them' (*JA* 205), and they embrace
under cover of darkness. Fanny is described as giving way to her passion – which
takes the form of lying beside Joseph and putting her arm around him. In Book
III, Chapter vi, Adams sleeps while a newly articulate Joseph delivers a sermon on
charity to Fanny and then begins a 'Dalliance' with her. By Book III, Chapter xii,
the cleric is urging the unmarried Joseph and Fanny to mount his horse together,
despite the fact that in Book II Chapter xvi he had a 'fierce Dispute' (*JA* 174) with
Joseph on precisely this subject. Here Parson Adams forbids such an arrangement,
with the strong implication that the erotic potential of this situation will be too much
for Joseph, telling Joseph that 'he was weaker than he imagined himself to be'.

By the latter half of the novel, also, Joseph begins to take over the more
masculine role. Avoiding the apparitions who turn out to be sheep-stealers, Adams
falls down the hill, while Joseph carries Fanny down. Fielding makes a point of
reminding the female reader, in particular, of Joseph's strength and 'lusty Arms'
(*JA* 194). As Jill Campbell has also observed, Adams is later identified with (and
mistaken for) the hare pursued by the 'roasting squire'.[19] The description of the
hare as silly, weak, innocent and defenceless suggests female vulnerability, and
Adams, here, is caught by his skirts (*JA* 236–7). Joseph, defending his friend,
takes over the preeminently masculine role of epic hero, and in the subsequent
chapter, Adams is asked to take the female part in a dance. Later, in the nighttime
confusion of gender identities, the parson is at a loss. On the evidence of the fop
Beau Didapper's soft skin, he rescues the man; on the evidence of Mrs. Slipslop's
beard, he attacks the woman. This episode too moves back towards the predominant
pattern of the latter half of the novel: Adams lies dormant at the foot of Fanny's
bed, until daylight, and order is restored with the entry of Joseph as the passive
Fanny's protector. Joseph, finally, acts as judge of innocence and guilt in sexual
matters – and as a more expert negotiator of matters of appearance and reality.

In his remarkably muted reaction to Wilson's story, Adams acts to legitimize an
account of male heterosexuality. Parson Adams is constructed, really, so as to validate
whatever Fielding wants the reader to find acceptable. When Wilson describes
how he contrived to have the reputation of affairs, Adams tells him to proceed
with his story, but not to swear. On hearing Wilson's account of theatre-going

---

[19]   Campbell, 103.

and relations with prostitutes, Adams merely concurs with the advice given by Wilson's surgeon: namely, a month's retirement and reflection. The parson reacts to Wilson's seduction of a young girl by getting out of his chair and walking across the room, but he still asks Wilson to proceed with his story while offering a pious hope that he has repented. He licks his lips on hearing Wilson's account of his embraces with Harriet. Adams asks to hear Wilson's 'obvious' remarks about the folly of vanity – the gentleman preaches to the cleric – whilst the parson's regret about losing his own sermon against vanity proves that he himself is susceptible to it. Wilson smiles at Adams's expense, and smiling, in *Joseph Andrews*, is always a sign of tacit superiority. In the 'disputation on schools', which forms a postscript to the Wilson story, Adams points Joseph in the direction of the moral of the tale, which is, in fact, that happiness and unhappiness are the criteria which have guided Wilson in his choice of life: '"And don't you think", says [Adams], "he was a very unhappy Man in his Youth?" "A very unhappy Man indeed", answered the other' (*JA* 229). Wilson's choice of the married life is the result of a series of tests by experience rather than any clerical prescriptions, and Fielding, no less than Richardson, believed in tangible rewards and punishments as incentives to virtue.

The approving reference Adams makes to the Low Church Bishop of Winchester, Dr. Benjamin Hoadly, in the dialogue with Parson Barnabas, implies that Adams himself subscribes to a subordinate role for the Church – another case of subordination willingly entered into – and to a Christianity, and an account of the sacraments, devoid of any mystery. Adams refers to Hoadly's work *A Plain Account of the Nature and End of the Sacrament of the Lord's Supper* (1735), and its excellence, for him, consists in its translation of the Eucharist into a purely social gathering, for the good of society. In Adams's comment on inappropriate luxury among the clergy – 'Surely those things, which savour so strongly of this World, become not the Servants of one who professed his Kingdom was not of it?' (*JA* 82) – there may also be an implied reference to Hoadly's sermon of 1717 on the text 'My kingdom is not of this world', which formed the starting point for the Bangorian controversy, so called because Hoadly was then Bishop of Bangor. From a distinction between Christ's kingdom and the kingdoms of this world, Hoadly elaborated the principle that Christ had left behind him no human authorities, no interpreters, and no judges in the matter of religion. It followed, then, that the priesthood had no claim to special authority. All that was left was unlimited private judgement.[20] The only opposition to Adams's arguments, presumably from a more High Church perspective, is represented by the lazy and hypocritical Barnabas, who reacts by ringing the bell with 'all the Violence imaginable', as opposed to Adams's offer of reasoned discussion. However, if Adams, at this point, subscribes to a Whig position on the subordination of Church to state, and to a rational religion, in terms of his relationship with the Joseph, who appears to be a servant, he approves of mystery. Fielding's characters really require clerical guidance only if they are children, servants, or women. Fielding is quick to enlist Adams to ensure

---

[20]		See the account by Sykes, *Church*, 292–3.

that Joseph, unlike his sister, has imbibed the right lessons from his reading – that is, not to repine at his lot, nor envy those above him. Joseph has read those works calculated to instruct in the matter of duty: *The Whole Duty of Man*, and *The Imitation of Christ*, a work first appearing in 1441 that retained an Anglican readership. He refers, also, to those parts of Sir Richard Baker's *Chronicle of the Kings of England* (1643) which involve supernatural interference: '*as how the Devil carried away half a Church in Sermon-time, without hurting one of the Congregation*' (*JA* 24). It was appropriate, then, for the servant to be instructed and informed of his duty by reading material which invoked a mysterious religion. Richardson, too, in his early didactic work *The Apprentice's Vade Mecum* (1734), had invoked a mysterious Christianity in the interests of exerting control over conduct.

Adams's subscription to the principle of absolute authority, as evidenced in his literal interpretation of the story of the sacrifice of Isaac lays him open, as Fielding and other Whig writers construed it, to the possibility of petticoat government.[21] Fearing that Squire Booby will prevent him from marrying Fanny, Joseph Andrews asks the parson to perform the ceremony with a licence, that is, without reading the banns. Adams counsels him against haste, 'excessive' love, and carnal desire, and uses the biblical Abraham's willingness to sacrifice his son Isaac as an example of proper submission. Just as he offers this lesson, someone rushes into the room with the news that his youngest son has been drowned, and Adams is inconsolable. Joseph attempts to comfort him with his own arguments, but to no avail. On either side of Adams's recommendation of absolute submission are instances of his wife's seeming domination. She reminds him of the duty he owes to the care of his wife and family and the chapter closes with Mrs. Adams's forceful refutation of his strictures about excessive love for wives. In the end, though, the episode undermines the claim of the clergy to any special authority in the very literal enactment of the impossibility of sacrificing Isaac. The authority of the clergy does *not* rest in any sacerdotal role. Adams's own claims to authority lie, in the end, in his masculinity and his responsibility for conducting the marriage service. Once more, the heterosexual relationship takes precedence over other systems of ordering society. The scene begins with Mrs. Adams pointing out to her husband that he has a wife and six children, whose interests should take precedence over his defiance of Lady Booby. Although Fielding's foregrounding of this speech appears to allow Mrs. Adams a dominant role, it actually reminds us that Adams is a patriarch by virtue of marriage and that his wife's concerns are properly domestic. The six children are a sign of Adams's otherwise invisible sexuality, to which Mrs. Adams makes oblique reference at the close of the chapter: 'I declare if I had not been convinced you had loved me as well as you could, I can answer for myself I should have hated and despised you – you have been a loving and a cherishing Husband to me, that's the truth on't' (*JA* 311). In reading the banns in the case of Fanny and Joseph, Adams actually defies the exercise of female authority by Lady Booby, which is here linked with a dominant female sexuality. There is a reminder of the

---

[21]   On this aspect of Whig ideology, see Campbell, 134 ff.

principle around which hierarchy in society is or should be based, when Adams remarks that he had just given his son his first lesson in '*Quae Genus*' (*JA* 309). Two sentences later we read that Mrs. Adams, in true 'feminine' style, is recovering from a swoon. When she corrects Adams's advice to Joseph not to love his wife too well, she is reinforcing (and proving that she remembers) the importance of the marriage service, and the proper forms of the Church, upon which Adams insists: 'Doth he [the husband] not promise to love her, and to comfort her, and to cherish her, and all that? I am sure I remember it all, as well as if I had repeated it over but Yesterday, and shall never forget it' (*JA* 311).

Sermons and preachers, however, are singularly ineffective in *Joseph Andrews*. In Fielding's novel Adams has, significantly, left at home the sermons he intended for publication, and so changes course from London, where he had hoped to sell them. When Adams does appear as a moral authority, he is always ineffectual, failing to console Joseph for the loss of the kidnapped Fanny or signally failing to live up to his own injunction to submission and resignation when it appears that his son has been drowned. As a preacher, Adams is pedantic and dogmatic, and dogmatism was precisely the tendency against which Latitudinarianism militated. In *Joseph Andrews*, it is Fielding, rather, who is able to hold together a narrative (or a society) in which there are diverse views and voices, of which he appears benignly tolerant. In his revisions of the novel for four subsequent editions in 1742, 1743, 1748 and 1751, we find Fielding also enhancing his own role as moral authority by augmenting the satire against female scolds, Trulliber and Peter Pounce, and adding to the appearance of learning.[22]

If it was no longer possible, or desirable, to base a theory of subordination on the rational interpretation of Scripture to which Whigs subscribed – Hobbes and Locke, among others, had shown that it was possible to wrest more libertarian political theories from selective or tortuous interpretations of Scripture – subordination may be reintroduced (as with *Pamela*) in terms of gender and sexuality. Eroticism, in the novel, is always linked to female passivity or submission. Even Lady Booby's fantasy of sex with Joseph seems to revolve round a wish for male dominance: 'I have trusted my self with a Man alone, naked in Bed … Must not my Reputation be then in your power? Would you not then be my Master?' (*JA* 30) – hinting that Lady Booby herself might be reincorporated into the natural social order by an appropriately dominant man. After the more overt sexuality of Lady Booby and the aggressive sexuality of Mrs. Slipslop, the 'natural' relationship between an active male sexuality and an almost inactive female sexuality is reinstated in the description of the relationship between Joseph and Fanny. However, if the relationship between Joseph and Fanny seems like a clear example of differential gendered identities, it might be argued that Fanny had to be constructed as a particularly yielding and minimal presence in order for Joseph's own compromised masculinity to seem strong, since Joseph is described, from the outset, in both

---

[22] See Martin C. Battestin, 'Fielding's Revisions of *Joseph Andrews*', *Studies in Bibliography*, XVI (1963), 81–117.

masculine and feminine terms. He plays the part of a scarecrow, which Fielding is careful to identify with the Greek god Priapus. Yet he has so musical a voice that birds and dogs are charmed by it: a sweet singing voice could be associated with the Italian castrati. He rides vicious horses with intrepidity and also sings psalms. He moves between the masculine world of the stables and the feminine world of the tea table. Crucially, he enacts a female role in turning down the sexual invitations of Lady Booby, Mrs. Slipslop and Betty.

Joseph Andrews constructs an image of masculinity in a feminized culture, that is to say, a culture in which masculinity as defined by aggression and combat is held in check by internalized or institutional restraints. While Fielding to some extent preserves the identification of masculinity with aggression, violence in the novel is always muted in some way by the standards of polite discourse. The scuffles which particularly recall *Don Quixote*, such as 'A dreadful Quarrel which happened at the Inn', or the 'Night Adventures', tone down the physicality and the humiliations of their models in Cervantes' work. On the other hand, Fielding seems concerned to absolve any episodes involving a lack of aggression, where it might be deemed appropriate, from the taint of emasculation. Following the sporting gentleman's castigation of the behaviour of British troops at Carthagena, Fielding has Adams vindicating temporary bouts of cowardice by reference to classical stories of male heroism, or the lack of it:

> [Adams] said, 'a Man might be a Coward at one time, and brave at another. *Homer*,' says he, 'who so well understood and copied Nature, hath taught us this Lesson; for *Paris* fights and *Hector* runs away'. (*JA* 136)

Similarly, a few chapters later, when Adams has no choice but to submit to the rulings of a drunken judge and the taunts of the company, the Latin phrases apparently randomly quoted juxtapose endurance and masculinity: 'Truly, as yellow gold is tested in fire, / So loyalty must be proved in times of stress' (*JA* 146n); 'Proper names that are assigned to the Male kind you may call masculines, / As are the names of the heathen Gods: Mars, Bacchus, Apollo' (*JA* 147n). When Joseph loses the fight over Fanny with the Captain, he is tied to the bedpost and temporarily rendered completely passive. He gives vent to his grief and consoles himself by citing Macduff's lines from *Macbeth*: '*Yes, I will bear my Sorrows like a Man / But I must also feel them as a Man*' (*JA* 267). The lines are drawn from a dialogue which itself revolves around questions of masculinity. Indeed, from Fielding's point of view, the play itself might offer an allegory about the danger posed by a dominant woman, in the shape of Lady Macbeth. Macduff, too, could offer a reassuring example of a feminized but unemasculated masculinity, since it is he who goes on to kill Macbeth.

Even the famous prefatory statement that defines the kind of fiction Fielding is writing implicitly distinguishes *Joseph Andrews* from a feminine tradition. The 'mere *English* reader' says Fielding, 'may have a different Idea of Romance with the Author of these little Volumes' (*JA* 3). Perhaps the 'mere English reader' might have drawn his or her ideas of romance from the most recent popular examples of it in English. Fielding might be thinking of *Pamela* here, but fictional writing in English in the eighteenth century before *Pamela* was predominantly female territory. Fielding also explicitly distinguishes *Joseph Andrews* from works with women as central characters, often written by women, in French: 'those voluminous Works commonly called *Romances*, namely, *Clelia*, *Cleopatra*, *Astraea*, *Cassandra*, the *Grand Cyrus*, and innumerable others'(*JA* 4). Fielding tries to place his novel in the securely masculine tradition of the epic, though his supposed model in the lost *Margites* is literally absent. Feminine writing is linked, in the chapter prefatory to Book III, with the delusive productions of the imagination:

> those Persons of surprizing Genius, the Authors of immense Romances, or the modern Novel and *Atalantis* Writers; who without any Assistance from Nature of History, record Persons who never were, or will be, and facts which never did nor possibly can happen: Whose Heroes are of their own Creation, and their Brains the Chaos whence all their Materials are collected. (*JA* 187)

This despite the fact that Fielding begins the chapter by conceding that the histories written by Tories such as the Earl of Clarendon or Laurence Eachard, or Whiggish historians like Bulstrode Whitelocke and Paul de Rapin, are so coloured by partisan politics that they may be considered as 'a Romance, in which the Writer hath indulged a happy and fertile Invention' (*JA* 186). Even the term *history*, then, which might seem to offer the security of a basis in an unmediated, essentialist truth, was suspect. *Fictional* writing by men, according to Fielding, offers access to a particular and universal truth, even if, in his rather uneasy ironic qualification, Cervantes, Scarron, Le Sage and Marivaux mistake the country in which the events they describe occurred. Cervantes' allegiance to this truth should compel our belief, apparently, in the shepherd Chrysostom who dies for love of Marcella, 'who hated him'. (In fact, Fielding distorts the import of this tale, which actually redounds to Marcella's good sense.) Included in the list of fiction which should compel belief is also the *Arabian Nights* – no more or less probable than Delarivière Manley's *New Atalantis* (1709). The boundaries Fielding tries to create between stories that debunk the idealized world of romance and those which rely on romance conventions prove to be difficult to sustain. At bottom, two principles are used to support the distinctions Fielding tries to make: gender and nature. Stories made up by men seem to be founded in nature, whereas those made up by women tend to emanate from chaos.

In the end, though, Fielding betrays an awareness of the provisionality of the ordering principles he might otherwise represent as 'natural'. There is an implication in the portrayal of Joseph that gender and sexuality are acquired rather than being given. His response to Lady Booby's invitation reinstates male moral authority and tellingly results in the silencing of Lady Booby for two minutes. Yet the mixed signals sent out by this episode – Joseph either as a dignified moral riposte to Lady Booby or as a laughably prim example of male chastity – and the mixture of feminine and masculine qualities with which he is endowed are indicative of an undecided sexuality. Gender is something Joseph grows into, given a proper tutor:

just as Adams reports that he had just begun to instruct his son in 'Quae Genus'. Moreover, gendered roles, being artificial, may be performed or misconstrued. In the 'Night-Adventures', a man who represents Fielding's conception of 'bad' effeminacy (Beau Didapper) seeks to gain power (here meaning sexual dominance) by impersonating a man representative of Fielding's conception of 'good' feminization: that is, Joseph. He is foiled by Slipslop, who as her name and her slippages of language might suggest, can slide between conceptions of the feminine and masculine. As soon as Didapper attempts to retreat, she assumes the persona of the modest and vulnerable woman. The gender of the participants, and the nature of the encounter, is misinterpreted by Adams. By the beau's soft skin, he recognizes a woman, and by the bearded chin of Slipslop, he recognizes a man. Order is partially restored when an asexual Adams lies dormant at the foot of Fanny's bed and is finally restored, in daylight, by the reunion of the 'correctly' gendered Joseph and Fanny.

Given that Fielding's concerns mirror Richardson's so exactly in terms of religion, a conception of gender, the perceived danger of feminization and a sense of the near-redundancy of the clergy, we might wonder whether Fielding's fable of social mobility, in *Joseph Andrews*, is also a reflection on lost gentility. Fielding's financial difficulties stemmed, ultimately, from the improvidence and the four marriages of his father. As the eldest son and heir of a man of rank, substance and noble connections – Fielding was related, through his father, to the Earls of Denbigh and Desmond – he might have expected a position of comfort and respectability, at the very least. Instead, he had to choose, as he famously and facetiously put it, between the life of a hackney-coachman or a hackney-writer. Unlike Richardson, Fielding had a gentleman's education and, as a barrister, being called to the bar in June 1740, a gentlemanly profession. Apart from his illustrious family connections, by 1741 he could number among his patrons his cousin Lady Mary Wortley Montagu, Dodington, Lyttleton, the Earl of Chesterfield and Ralph Allen. Fielding's anxieties about his social position, if he had any, were not likely to be identical to Richardson's. Nevertheless, *Joseph Andrews* tells the story of a servant who progresses to a position of autonomy, a dependent who becomes independent. Here, perhaps, is Fielding's fantasy of his situation as a writer, escaping the constraints or corruptions of patronage and service. A sense of his own possible importance had already been foreshadowed in *The Champion*, when, after the silence of two and a half years effectively imposed on him by the Licensing Act of 1737, Fielding reemerged in his periodical as Captain Hercules Vinegar, the censor and champion of Great Britain. His assumption of this role forms an ironic contrast with the situation of financial impecunity and compromised rank he actually occupied.

Fielding responded to the worldly and prudential ethic of *Pamela* by satirising its heroine in *Shamela*. He also responded to it in *Joseph Andrews* by creating an endearingly unworldly clerical hero. Adams's innocence and lack of calculation is set off against the venality of Trulliber, the malice of the Roasting-Squire and the worldly wisdom of the bookseller and the well-travelled innkeeper. Whether or not

Richardson read *Joseph Andrews* is unclear. There are a few fleeting references to it in his letters, but the information about the novel they contain could easily have been acquired secondhand, just as Richardson's knowledge of *Tom Jones* proved to be secondhand, even though he condemned the novel roundly in a letter to Astraea and Minerva Hill. It seems more likely that he at least read *Shamela*, and that it proved to be the most decisive influence on the composition of his second and greatest novel, *Clarissa*. *Clarissa* seems designed to address the very objections that Fielding had made, in *Shamela*, to *Pamela*.

Clarissa herself is a model of unworldliness and self-denial. Where Pamela was deemed ambitious and grasping, Clarissa preempts any such suspicions by rejecting money at every turn. Though her grandfather's bequest would allow Clarissa independence, she eschews it, arguing that even to take what is willed to her would suggest 'a want of moderation and graspingness that … are bad indications of the *use* that may be made of the power bequeathed' (*C* 104). *Pamela* has glowing accounts of clothes and jewellery: Clarissa, conversely, is struck with horror at talk of 'the richest silks' (*C* 110). Pamela seemed to revel in social acclaim: Clarissa would prefer privacy and retreat. In the first letter in *Clarissa*, Anna Howe remarks on how publicity must hurt her friend, so desirous is she of 'sliding through [life] to the end of it unnoted' (*C* 40). Where Pamela appeared to revel in the praise of the household, Clarissa asks Anna Howe to be sparing of praise. 'To avoid murder' she says, 'I would most willingly be buried alive' (*C* 142), and such proves an appropriate metaphor for her situation, even though murder, in the end, is not avoided. Her continuation of the prohibited correspondence with Anna Howe is a rare gesture of defiance – though very necessary for the story – and it is one which Richardson has Clarissa justify in terms of self-denial: 'what hurt could a letter now and then from each do? – mine occasionally filled with self-accusation too!' (*C* 409). When Anna's mother prohibits the correspondence again, Clarissa continues it with Hickman's approval, and because she may receive reproof and instruction from Anna (*C* 482). Pamela could be motivated by the desire for tangible rewards: such rewards are almost absent from *Clarissa*.

Where Pamela had power, including the crucial power to reform B., Clarissa has little agency. She performs exactly the role prescribed to women in terms of 'politeness', that is, softening masculine violence by preventing a possible duel between Lovelace and her brother James. This is a role that is forced on her, and she assumes it reluctantly. Yet she is punished for assuming any such influence over men. When Lovelace coerces her into running off with him, she reflects:

> I supposed it concerned me more than any other to be the arbitress of the quarrels of unruly spirits – and now I find my presumption punished! –punished, as other sins frequently are, by *itself*! (*C* 381)

Despite Clarissa's powers of reason and expression, the writing that proved so effectual in the case of Pamela has little or no power in Clarissa's hands. Her family often speak of her dangerous powers of 'moving', and yet her letters fail to move any of them to forgiveness or reconciliation. In *Pamela*, Richardson taught women that they might have the power to reform men: in *Clarissa*, any notions of agency or influence that a woman might derive from this idea of her role are severely punished. Clarissa admits that that the idea of reforming Lovelace gives her a 'secret pleasure'(*C* 183). No such pleasure is to be allowed. The reform of Lovelace's friend John Belford is purely accidental. She did not aim for it, so Richardson permits it. If Clarissa was conscious of herself as a possible exemplar, she is signally punished for any pride this might have given her. Now with Lovelace, she declares: 'How I am punished ... for my vanity in hoping to be an *example* to young persons of my sex!' (*C* 453). From now on she must be content to be a warning.

If women could not contain the disruptive power of male sexuality by reforming men, they might control it by not being attracted to rakes in the first place. *Clarissa* was aimed primarily at female readers who might reasonably have imbibed from Richardson's first novel the idea that 'a reformed rake makes the best husband'. The preface to *Clarissa*, which may have been written by William Warburton, speaks of gender-neutral 'children' who might prefer a rake to a virtuous man, but such caution could only be required in the case of women. In the closing pages of *Pamela ... In her Exalted Condition* (1742), Richardson's sequel to *Pamela*, which portrayed his heroine in her married state, Pamela inveighs against this 'sad, sad Notion', and Mrs. Towers, one of her coterie of female companions, points out that 'People will be apt to think, that you have less Reason than any of our sex, to be severe against the Notion you speak of'.[23] Richardson, characteristically, attributed the faulty conception to women themselves. The last few letters in *Pamela* II present three young women, two of whom have an unfortunate fondness for rakes, while the third is misled by a love of poetry and romance. Pamela wants to correct these false notions and is discovered to have been writing in a 'flighty vein', hoping to offer instruction adapted to the 'taste and temper' of such readers. Here, in outline, is *Clarissa*.

Critics have been reluctant to accept Richardson's formulation of the purpose of his dense and extensive fiction, which was repeated in his letters, or to accept that Richardson's avowed didactic purpose explains very much about the force or the form of the novel itself.[24] *Clarissa*, famously, is a work that offers the reader no definitive answers and no authoritative narrative voice. Yet if we reformulate Richardson's goal rather more globally, as nothing less than an attempt to reconstruct female desire, his aim is rather ambitious than banal and, in the newly gendered social order, more urgent. Although the form of *Clarissa* defers or denies closure, Richardson certainly did not revel in the liberating possibilities of uncertainty, as Sterne was later to do in *Tristram Shandy*. Thomas Keymer has argued that the novel's 'textual indeterminacy' is an environment created for the reader's education, in which he or she would ideally reach the conclusions

---

[23] Samuel Richardson, *Pamela, Or Virtue Rewarded ... and Afterwards in her Exalted Condition*, 4v. (1741–1742), Vol. IV, 445.

[24] See *Selected Letters*, 73, 81.

which Richardson 'at his most prescriptive' intended, though this could never be guaranteed.[25] However, Richardson's many revisions to the novel and his extensive commentary on it show how much he wanted to close down freedom of interpretation. From this perspective Richardson's approach is like that of Lovelace in relation to Clarissa, when he has her make the 'choice' of a house in London which was already made for her. Terry Castle has written of Lovelace's entrapment of Clarissa in a linguistic world of signs divorced from any objective referent.[26] Richardson, too, creates a world of gender distinctions and normative heterosexuality by the power of words alone. Lovelace's minute attention to methods of manipulation and control, regulating what Clarissa sees, hears and thinks, is a mirror for Richardson's concern with the manipulation of his female readers; and what Lovelace wants, as he repeats, is the *will*.

The point of *Clarissa*, as of *Pamela*, was not to reform masculine sexual morality, but rather to induce in women a conception of 'proper' female sexuality – which is to say, asexuality. Richardson was particularly careful to have Anna Howe articulate Clarissa's unconscious attraction to Lovelace: as a model of female asexuality, she cannot be conscious of it herself.[27] Women in the novel who do have a consciousness of sexuality are 'demons' belonging to the underworld of the brothel. Mrs. Sinclair is a grotesque monster. Despite the tragic conclusion, and the representation of Lovelace as a diabolic figure, *Clarissa* is never a critique of male sexuality. Anna Howe's dissatisfaction with the meek Hickman makes the point, whatever arguments Clarissa, or later, Richardson, offer in his favour. Patriarchy is reinstated in the shape of active male sexuality: Clarissa's revered but largely absent father symbolizes an idea of patriarchy which was becoming outmoded. Clarissa's attraction to Lovelace is the only power he has over her will. Where B., to Fielding's amusement in *Shamela*, failed to seduce Pamela, Lovelace finally imposes his will on Clarissa, albeit in a way which would not sully her 'virtue': as the almost unconscious victim of a rape, she could not be suspected of having consented to sex.

At one point in the novel, Richardson articulates the lesson through Lovelace:

> I will bring this charming creature to the strictest test that all the sex … may see what they ought to be; what is expected from them; and if they have to deal with a person of reflection and punctilio (*pride* if thou wilt), how careful they ought to be, by a regular and uniform conduct, not to give him cause to think lightly of them, by favours granted. (*C* 427)

The idea that women are ultimately at fault and that they are responsible for sexual continence is insistent and consistent. An attraction to rakes was a female failing Richardson was at pains to correct. The perverse tendency of women readers such

---

25   Thomas Keymer, *Richardson's* Clarissa, 72 *et passim*.

26   Terry Castle, *Clarissa's Ciphers: Meaning and Disruption in Richardson's* Clarissa (Ithaca: Cornell University Press, 1982), 81 ff.

27   See *Selected Letters*, 72.

as Lady Bradshaigh to go on liking Lovelace even after his full character was revealed was addressed in his revisions of the novel for the second, third and fourth editions. Lovelace's behaviour is an implied critique of female sexuality, since he found that women liked a rake:

> So dearly do I love the sex, that had I found that a character for virtue had been generally necessary to recommend me to them, I should have had a much greater regard to my morals, as to the sex, than I have had. (*C* 721)

Anna Howe, too, expresses the view that the fault lies with 'our eye-judging ... undistinguishing ... self-flattering ... too-confiding sex' who have not given Lovelace any reason to subdue his passions (*C* 747). Clarissa also believes that 'women are often to blame on this head' (*C* 1319) since few, if any, women look for virtue in men, and she admits that she too has been guilty in this respect. It is the immodesty of women rather than the licentiousness of men which is the problem, it seems. Nine women in every ten, says Lovelace, would have laughed off such physical intimacy as he has with Clarissa in the 'fire-scene' (*C* 728). Conversely, Clarissa's resistance to him is a model of female behaviour that is the exception to the norm:

> I never before encountered a resistance so much in earnest ... What a triumph has her sex obtained in my thoughts by this trial, and this resistance! (*C* 727)

Other women do not set the 'romantic value' on their honour that Clarissa does. Experience has taught Lovelace that women will ultimately succumb, and it is this knowledge which drives him to pursue Clarissa. He writes to Belford: 'dost thou think I could have held my purpose against such an angel as this, had I ever before met with one so much in earnest to defend her honour ... Why then were there not more examples of a virtue so immovable?' (*C* 972).

Moreover, Lovelace's faults can always ultimately be traced back to a woman. Here, we might say, Richardson secularized the Christian conception of Eve's fault. Lovelace's mother, writes Lord Morden, spoiled him (*C* 606). As a young man he was jilted by a lady, and debauching women is his revenge on the sex (*C* 143). Love of power is an 'infection' he has caught from women (*C* 790). The drugging of Clarissa, it turns out, was Mrs. Sinclair's idea (*C* 887), and after the rape it is actually Mrs. Sinclair of whom Clarissa is afraid, and she appeals to Lovelace not to 'set Mrs. Sinclair upon me again' (*C* 894). When she finally gives her account of the rape, it is the women of whom she has 'visionary remembrances' (*C* 1011). Lovelace often blames Clarissa for his intentions or actions: 'I only waited to see how *her* will would work, how *mine* would lead me on. Thou seest what bias hers takes – and wilt thou doubt that mine will be determined by it?' (*C* 424). The women in the brothel are always goading Lovelace and urging him to undescribed measures he would be unwilling to take, to 'worse than masculine violence'. At one point Lovelace is so awed by Clarissa he would have been 'a lost man', but fortunately for him Dorcas enters the room to give him a letter and involve him in a contrivance against Clarissa (*C* 651). When Clarissa is arrested in the street for debt – a humiliation Richardson imagines much more concretely than the rape – Dorcas, Sally and Mrs. Sinclair are responsible once again.

As an even more perfect Pamela, and a static example of virtue, Clarissa will always be Lovelace's moral superior. That is why he can never marry her, as he more than once reflects: 'My wife … to be so *much* my superior! – Myself to be considered but as the second person in my own family!' (*C* 734). Married to Clarissa, he would have been 'a penitent … dangling at her side to church' (*C* 970). The middle section of the novel, from the point when Clarissa runs off with Lovelace, enacts the nearly endless standoff between a man and a woman meeting on (as Richardson constructs it) equal terms. Although Clarissa, as we have seen, *does* almost nothing, Richardson represents her as having considerable powers over Lovelace. William B. Warner's controversial study of *Clarissa*, where he spoke of Clarissa's 'insidious will to power' in fact does rather more justice to this aspect of the novel than Terry Castle's better received *Clarissa's Cyphers*, even though Warner was charged by some with misogyny – and one might disagree with 'insidious'.[28] Clarissa, like Pamela, might have the power of 'witchcraft' (*C* 63). Lovelace continually reminds the reader of her alleged power by the numerous references to 'my charmer'. She is an angel or a goddess. Lovelace finds himself 'unaccountably overawed and tyrannized' (*C* 575) on many occasions. Clarissa has such power that Lovelace is more than once driven to propose marriage to her against his own will, and one of his 'attempts' is checked simply by her virtue (*C* 602). She can reduce him to a 'spiritless Hickman' (*C* 645). She 'half assimilates' him to her own moral code (*C* 658). Despite all the impersonations and plots that Lovelace is master of, all his seeming domination of the situation, he is desperately in search of Clarissa's approval. Lovelace is troubled by this very thought: 'love, which I hate … because 'tis my master' (*C* 148). The idea that Clarissa might prefer another man causes him deep disquiet. He is often defensive about the sheer effort that he devotes to his pursuit of Clarissa. When Clarissa's 'mantled cheek [and] downcast eye' indicate to Lovelace that his tentative talk about marriage is not unwelcome, he is exultant but betrays his (or rather Richardson's) consciousness that this makes him seem weak by parenthetically telling Belford not to let any women know that he feels like this (*C* 425). He hopes that she will have more confidence in him, and acknowledges himself 'bashful' with her (*C* 440). Her professed indifference to him provokes a passionate outburst (*C* 593). He resents her distance and haughtiness and longs for her forgiveness. He is willing to make himself temporarily ill to get Clarissa to express affection for him. The opinion of the women at the brothel also concerns him a great deal: at one point he calls Clarissa cruel for, as he sees it, exposing him to their derision (*C* 644). Lovelace's seeming triumph over Clarissa – the rape – signals, as Richardson styles it, the beginning of his own declining power over her. Clarissa, it seems, triumphs in

---

[28]   William B. Warner, *Reading* Clarissa: *The Struggles of Interpretation* (New Haven: Yale University Press, 1979).

death. Astonished and diminished by her refusal to marry him even after the rape, and by her perverse willingness to die, Lovelace reflects: 'has she not, from first to last, infinitely more triumphed over me than suffered from me?' (*C* 1308).

Richardson's conformation to 'politeness', made necessary by the reaction to *Pamela*'s lack of it, tame Lovelace even before the novel begins. He is the polite or 'decent' rake, couching his entrapment of Clarissa in terms of deference and repeated compliments. Although an atheist 'in practice' – which is to say, a libertine – he makes no unseemly jests at the expense of religion. Early in the novel, Anna Howe reflects on the surprising amount of time Lovelace spends in the more characteristically feminine activity of writing (Letter 12). Lovelace himself draws attention to his use of 'feminine' words, and he has a number of transsexual fantasies, though these always culminate in an assertion of his power over women. His strategies of control – inventing characters and stories, 'name-fathering', personation – are Richardson's own strategies as a writer and, as such, could be seen as compromising Lovelace's masculinity from the beginning. However much Lovelace plumes himself on his mastery of the situation, he is already a feminized man. Even his relentless pursuit of women could, in terms of the thinking about gender in the period, emasculate him. As Carolyn D. Williams notes, '[T]he use of effeminacy to denote both deficient masculinity and excessive heterosexuality fosters a tendency to connect these phenomena'.[29] Despite Richardson's disempowerment of Clarissa, she could be even more emasculating than Pamela. So Richardson constructed a masculine villain of diabolic proportions to overmatch her. Lovelace is a fantasy of male domination as a predatory virility in a period when, ostensibly anyway, women had to be accorded respect, and aggression and violence had been reined in by the middle-class ideology of politeness. He is also a fantasy of the dominant male as, above all, a writer.

The tragic conclusion of the novel seems to have been public knowledge long before the publication of the third and final installment in December 1748. The first reference to *Clarissa* in Richardson's correspondence occurs in a letter from the Reverend Edward Young in June 1744, and Young already knows the outcome.[30] The conclusion proved to be the most controversial, if least read, aspect of the novel. Sales of the final volumes of the first edition did not match that of Volumes I, II, III and IV.[31] In a letter to Aaron Hill, Richardson claimed that he had never intended that the outcome should be known in advance of publication but that 'one Friend and another got the Mss. out of my Hands' and had talked indiscreetly. It may be that Richardson, at least, did not discourage such 'leaks', as it allowed him to test reactions to Clarissa's death, preempt objections before actual publication and marshal his defences. Such considerations can be seen beginning to inform

---

[29]   Carolyn D. Williams, *Pope, Homer and Manliness: Some Aspects of Eighteenth-Century Classical Learning* (London: Routledge, 1993), 37.

[30]   T.C. Duncan Eaves and Ben D. Kimpel, 'The Composition of *Clarissa* and its Revision before Pulication', *PMLA*, 83 (1968), 416.

[31]   See Carroll, *Selected Letters*, 86n.

Richardson's thinking in the first edition. Belford tells Lovelace that Clarissa's suffering would be a good subject for a tragedy, were it not for that fact that her virtue is punished (*C* 1205). Even though he reconsiders, and talks of her reward in heaven, and how a marriage to Lovelace (the option preferred by a number of Richardson's readers) would be unworthy of her, Richardson adds a footnote pointing out that tragedies may indeed include unjust suffering. In the Postscript to the first edition, Richardson was again at pains to defend the absence of poetic justice in *Clarissa* and relied much more on literary than on religious precedents, citing the comments of Aristotle, as discussed by Addison and Rapin. Richardson's letter to 'Mrs. Belfour' (Lady Bradshaigh) in October 1748 answered his correspondent's disappointment with the ending by guiding her to reread certain key passages from the novel and emphasising Lovelace's unworthiness of her. Clarissa's death was also a punishment, apparently, for her 'execrable Relations' (*Selected Letters* 94). Richardson closed the argument by referring Mrs. Belfour to *Spectator* 40, where Addison derided poetic justice as 'ridiculous': 'In short Madam upon this Spectator might I have rested my cause' (*Selected Letters* 96). Taking up the argument with her again in December of that year, he cited the tragic conclusion of *Romeo and Juliet*, pointed again to Lovelace's unworthiness, and then ringingly pronounced: 'A Writer who follows Nature and keeps the Christian system in his Eye, cannot make a Heaven in this World for his Favourites; or represent this Life otherwise then as a State of Probation' (*Selected Letters* 108). This was a consideration which had not influenced him, apparently, when he wrote *Pamela*.

There is reason to suspect from Richardson's prioritization of literature, and from his comments elsewhere on religion, that Christian doctrine was not really uppermost in his thinking about Clarissa's death. Apart from the intermittent recourse to religion in his justifications of the conclusion and the religious coloration of the last third of the novel, there is little in Richardson's other writings to suggest close attention to matters of faith. That part of *The Apprentice's Vade Mecum* that cautioned the reader against scepticism and infidelity was only added, so Richardson claimed, at the instigation of an anonymous friend, and it was in his own words a 'cursory' treatment.[32] He promised Lady Bradshaigh that he would read Swift's sermon on the Holy Trinity, but he was afraid of raising doubts in his own mind on the subject that might prove difficult to resolve, emphasizing rather the importance of conduct.[33] He was resistant to the mystic or the enthusiastic in matters of religion without necessarily anathematizing those who were so inclined. On Hervey's *Meditations* in another letter to Lady Bradshaigh: 'A serious and good divine, of my acquaintance, sees [Hervey] as to his doctrines, too mystic; and I think him inclined to the enthusiastic part of

---

[32]   Samuel Richardson, *The Apprentice's Vade Mecum* (1734), ed. A.D. McKillop, *Augustan Reprint Society* 169–70 (Los Angeles: University of California Press, 1975), x, 56.

[33]   *The Correspondence of Samuel Richardson*, ed. Anna Laetitia Barbauld, 6v., (London: 1804), Vol. VI, 251.

Methodism. Yet I am sure he is a good and well-meaning man'.[34] Richardson printed works by the evangelicals William Law, John Byrom and George Whitefield, but as John A. Dussinger has shown, few conclusions can be drawn about Richardson's own beliefs from his eclectic practices as a printer.[35] The Postscipt to *Clarissa* acquired a more religious gloss in the third edition of 1751, a piece which may have been partially written by William Warburton or Edward Young, both clerics and friends of Richardson's.[36] *Meditations collected from the Sacred Books* (1750) built upon Clarissa's adaptations of scripture and would have reinforced the idea of *Clarissa* as a religious novel, but Richardson allowed this part of the lady's 'legacy' to be circulated only among a coterie of readers.[37] It never became common currency.

Whatever illusion of a coherent consciousness Richardson created in the shape of his heroine, he is always primarily interested in her usefulness to society. As a dishonoured woman, she is no longer useful, and so she disappears from society while dying an exemplary death. She had been an exemplar of chastity and duty; after leaving her father's house with Lovelace, she is a warning. Following the rape, her identity briefly fragments, and then she becomes Lovelace's nemesis. As a Christian version of Lucretia, she can offer an example of 'Holy Dying'. She is a female Job (*C* 1118), now an example of absolute submission without reproach. This was an aspect of Clarissa's character that Richardson particularly valued, both in relation to the tyranny and cruelty of her family and to her violation by Lovelace. In Clarissa's letter of Sunday, 23 July to Anna Howe (Letter 359), she speaks of 'strong resentments, but not unreasonable ones' that she has against Lovelace, which may have influenced her decision not to marry him. Edward Young evidently proposed some additions to this letter, which Richardson rejected, or held in reserve, as he wrote to Young:

> I am greatly obliged to you for your admirable additions to the letter I sent you; but believe I shall insert them rather nearer the hour of her death because in this letter I do not make her so fully able to die in charity with Lovelace, as she hopes she shall do. Such noble, such exalted sentiments and expressions, will adorn her last hours, when above the world, and above the resentments she acknowledges in this place. (*Selected Letters* 62)[38]

---

[34] *Correspondence*, Vol. VI, 13.

[35] John A. Dussinger, '"Stealing in the great doctrines of Christianity": Samuel Richardson as Journalist', *Eighteenth-Century Fiction*, 15:3–4 (2003), 458.

[36] *Samuel Richardson's Published Commentary on* Clarissa *1747–1765*, 3v., Introduction by Jocelyn Harris, ed., with head notes by Thomas Keymer (London: Pickering and Chatto, 1998), Vol. I, 46–7, 51–2.

[37] See Thomas Keymer, 'Richardson's *Meditations*: Clarissa's *Clarissa*', in *Samuel Richardson. Tercentenary Essays*, eds Margaret Anne Doody and Peter Sabor (Cambridge: Cambridge University Press, 1989), 89–109.

[38] See also the account in Eaves and Kimpel (1968), 418.

In the same letter Richardson expressed his dissatisfaction with additions suggested by the actor, poet and theatre manager Colley Cibber on the grounds that more than a month had passed since the rape and his other correspondent had attributed too much passion and warmth to his heroine. Richardson responded at length to Lady Bradshaigh's objection that he had 'given [his] willing Voice for every Trial, every Distress' that Clarissa suffered, and pointed again to the example the heroine sets:

> Meekness of Heart … intirely consistent with that Dignity of Mind, which on all proper Occasions she exerts with so much distinguishing Excellence, as carries her above the irascible Passions. (*Selected Letters* 116)

To Frances Grainger's objection that litigation against her father by Clarissa would have been justified, he responded: 'But then she would not have had the glorious Merit which she triumphed in, of a resigned and patient sufferer' (*Selected Letters* 149).

As the novel draws towards a close, Clarissa's attitude towards Lovelace gradually softens, so that on 27 July (Letter 368), she can pity him (*C* 1141). On 4 August (Letter 389), she can wish for his 'everlasting welfare' (*C* 1177). Four days later, in a letter to his family, she asks them to forgive him for the injuries done to her (*C* 1186). By 11 August (Letter 401) she can wish him happy, and by 5 September she tells Belford that she forgives Lovelace and prays that God may also forgive him. The construction of a normative heterosexuality already foreshadowed in Pamela's acceptance of B.'s illegitimate child into the household, and Abraham Adams's tolerance of Wilson's liaisons in *Joseph Andrews*, was becoming more emphatic. Men would transgress and women, the clergy and potentially the reader would forgive them.

For Richardson, Clarissa's forgiveness of Lovelace was proof of her exemplary Christianity. Fielding made this forgiveness of masculine sexual transgression even more overt in *Tom Jones*. This is not necessarily because Fielding was more tolerant than Richardson about sex, as has often been argued. There is probably just as much innuendo in Lovelace's letters as there is in *Tom Jones*, and perhaps rather more in the way of explicitly 'warm' scenes. Richardson insinuated the idea that male sexual transgression did not really stand in need of reform by aiming his novel at reforming female desire. However often Lovelace teeters on the brink of reform, he never does reform. If he did, as we have seen, he would be subordinate to Clarissa. The ambiguity of effect, with women readers persisting in admiring Lovelace, reflects the ambiguity of Richardson's own position. He wanted women to shun rakes so as to maintain sexual order, but he also wanted men to have more power than women. Fielding indicates that Tom Jones too needs to reform, but we never see him in his reformed state. A difficult balance had to be struck between pious hopes for moral reform and an implicit acceptance of masculine sexuality. Fielding struck that balance more confidently than Richardson, but the underlying idea is the same. In an increasingly feminized culture, where virtue was identified with a certain construction of womanhood, active masculine sexuality constituted a way of retaining, or reconstructing, male power over women, and this is a subordination which 'natural' women are constructed as wanting from *Pamela* to *Tom Jones*. At the end of *Tom Jones*, Sophia tells Tom that he must wait perhaps a year so that she can test his promise to reform. He protests that this is 'an eternity'. She responds:

> Perhaps it may be something sooner … I will not be teazed. If your Passion for me be what I would have it, I think you may now be easy.[39]

Jones takes her in his arms and kisses her 'with an ardour he had never ventured before'. A jubilant Western then enters the room and after some more deferring of the outcome, Sophia asks her father what he would have her do. He tells her to marry Tom, and Sophia replies 'Well, sir … I will obey you'. Female subordination, active masculine sexuality and patriarchy coincide.

In *Making the Novel* (2006), Brean Hammond and Shaun Regan argue that *Tom Jones* was conceived and written 'in conscious opposition' to *Clarissa*, with Fielding, in the end, defining virtue more ambiguously than Richardson.[40] The conception of Richardson and Fielding as opposites has a long history in criticism, going back to the influential remarks of Samuel Johnson and Samuel Taylor Coleridge. For Johnson, Richardson dived into the recesses of the human heart, while Fielding was only a superficial observer: for Coleridge, Richardson occupied a feverish hot house, while Fielding dwelt in the fresh open air. Certainly Fielding was aware of *Clarissa*'s plot and characters as he was writing *Tom Jones*. Martin Battestin judges that Fielding began work on *Tom Jones* in the Spring of 1745 and had completed perhaps a third of the book before August of that year.[41] His work on the novel may have been interrupted by the writing of anti-Jacobite propaganda, in the shape of three pamphlets published in October: *A Serious Address to the People of Great Britain*, *The History of the Present Rebellion in Scotland* and *A Dialogue between the Devil, the Pope, and the Pretender*. In November 1745 Fielding published the first number of *The True Patriot*, possibly sponsored by his friends in the 'Broad Bottom' Administration. Beginning work again on *Tom Jones* in 1746, Fielding gave the story a topical application, making his hero, now exiled from Paradise Hall, join the soldiers marching north to join the Duke of Cumberland. Volumes I and II of *Clarissa* were published in December 1747 and received a glowing review in *The Jacobite's Journal* of 2 January 1748. In March of that year, Fielding returned to the subject in the *Journal* not, he assured the reader, as 'puffing' but in order to bestow deserved praise. Whether or not Fielding intended the piece as a puff, it was good timing for the publication of Volumes III and IV, which followed in April 1748. The first three volumes of *Tom Jones* were printed in September 1748. By October 1748 Fielding had read

---

[39]   Henry Fielding, *The History of Tom Jones A Foundling*, The Wesleyan Edition of the Works of Henry Fielding, introduction and commentary by Martin C. Battestin, ed. Fredson Bowers (Hanover: University Press of New England, 1975), 974.

[40]   Brean Hammond and Shaun Regan, *Making the Novel: Fiction and Society in Britain, 1660–1789* (Houndmills: Palgrave Macmillan, 2006), 113–15.

[41]   Battestin, *Henry Fielding: A Life*, 391.

the fifth volume of *Clarissa*, evidently being one of those favoured readers who were given a copy in advance of publication as Volumes V and VI were not ready for the press until November of that year. On 15 October 1748, he wrote a letter to Richardson praising *Clarissa*'s power to move him.[42] By December 1748, the last three volumes of *Clarissa*, including Volume VII, were available to the public. The whole of *Tom Jones* was finally available in February 1749.

Although Fielding obviously admired aspects of *Clarissa*, there are certain critical glances at Richardson's novel in *Tom Jones*. When Sophia contemplates a marriage to Blifil under duress from her father and her aunt, just as Clarissa's family would force her to marry Solmes, she is almost persuaded to sacrifice herself by the workings of a combination of piety, religion, and 'filial Love and Duty' (*TJ* 360), aided by an 'agreeable Tickling in a certain little Passion', which is presumably her pride. All these are notable elements of Clarissa's character. However, 'natural' desire for Tom in the shape of 'Cupid, who lay hid in her muff', ensures that she carries out her resolution to leave Paradise Hall with her maid and travel to her cousin's in London. Perhaps Fielding felt that Clarissa's prostration before her family and her reluctance to accept Anna Howe's offers of help were implausible, perverse, or an unwelcome depiction of the suffering that might accompany filial duty. In contrast with Clarissa, Sophia tells her aunt that she 'will never run away with any Man' (*TJ* 793), though she does still run away. Later Fielding seems to take issue with the moral perfection of Clarissa and the seemingly unmitigated evil of Lovelace. In the prefatory chapter of Book X, he addresses the reader:

> If thou dost delight in ... Models of Perfection, there are Books enow written to gratify thy Taste; but as we have not, in the Course of our Conversation, ever happened to meet with any such Person, we have not chosen to introduce any such here. To say the Truth, I a little question whether mere Man ever arrived at this consummate Degree of Excellence, as well as whether there hath ever existed a Monster bad enough to verify that
> —nulla virtute redemptum
> A vitiis— [Whose vices are not allayed with a single virtue]
> in Juvenal: nor do I, indeed, conceive the good Purposes served by inserting Characters of such angelic Perfection, or such diabolical Depravity, in any Work of Invention: since from contemplating either, the Mind of Man is more likely to be overwhelmed with Sorrow and Shame, than to draw any good Uses from such Patterns.' (*TJ* 52–7)

Again, the objection lies in the unwelcome effect of such characterisations on the reader's perception and behaviour and Fielding goes on to recommend, rather, representing the foibles and vices of 'men in whom there is a great mixture of good'. Such representations, he claims, gravely, show such foibles and vices in a more glaring light and teach the reader to shun them. It could equally be argued, as Samuel Johnson later did argue in *Rambler* 4 (1750), that interesting the reader

---

[42]   See Eaves and Kimpel, 'The Composition of *Clarissa*', 426; Battestin, *Henry Fielding: A Life*, 442–3.

in the fortunes of a faulty character only served to make the faults less abhorrent, which was perhaps closer to Fielding's real intention. There is another glance at *Clarissa* in Book XVI when Sophia writes to Tom to tell him that she cannot receive letters from him. Fielding has her avoid the casuistical quibbles, or indeed the disobedience, of which Clarissa might be deemed guilty:

> One promise my aunt hath insisted on my making, which is, that I will not see or converse with any person without her consent. This promise I have most solemnly given, and shall most inviolably keep: and though she hath not expresly forbidden me writing, yet that must be an omission from forgetfulness; or this, perhaps, is included in the word conversing. However, as I cannot but consider this as a breach of her generous confidence in my honour, you cannot expect that I shall, after this, continue to write myself, or to receive letters, without her knowledge'. (*TJ* 755)

Similarly, the woman praised by Squire Allworthy for professing 'No dictatorial Sentiments, no judicial Opinions, no profound Criticisms' (*TJ* 882) might have been constructed as a rejoinder to a heroine long on moral reflections and perhaps too self-reliant in matters of moral judgement for Fielding's taste.

However, on those matters of gender and sexuality that distinguish the Whig ideology of manners, on politics and on religion, Richardson and Fielding were at one. Fielding has Tom partially absolved from responsibility for his sexual liaisons because they are always instigated by 'unnatural', dominant women. As in *Clarissa*, women take the blame. It is the masculine woman Moll Seagrim who triumphs, Fielding tells us, over Tom's 'virtuous resolutions'. At Upton, Tom is eating (natural behaviour) while the unnatural Mrs. Waters is not, unleashing instead 'the whole artillery of love' in a mock-epic battle which ends with her as the conqueror. Lady Bellaston pursues Tom and instigates a sexual relationship to which, it seems, he is disinclined. His subordination to dominant women only ends with his rejection of Mrs. Hunt: women should not be the pursuers. Sophia, as we hear earlier in the novel, does not enjoy foxhunting, as it is 'of too rough and masculine a Nature to suit with her Disposition' (*TJ* 199). Fielding also deflects blame from Tom by detailing the sexual history of the women who seduce him. The fact that they have such a history implies that they, rather than he, are at fault. Jones is let off the hook with respect to Moll Seagrim in the first instance by discovering her with Square, and secondly by finding out that Will Barnes was her first lover. Immediately after Mrs. Waters's seduction of Tom, we are given a brief account of her sexual history with Captain Waters and Ensign Northerton (*TJ* IX, vi), a narrative which is expanded in IX, vii. Lady Bellaston has 'a certain Imperfection' – perhaps the loss of her virginity? – which is 'above all others … most disagreeable to the Breath of Love' (*TJ* 724). It is Lady Bellaston, also, who persuades Lord Fellamar that he should rape Sophia. Aunt Western, rather than her brother, initiates the idea of a match between Blifil and Sophia. Bridget Allworthy it was, we discover, who brought illegitimacy into the household as it was she who had the infant deposited in her brother's bed, and the dénouement of the novel is made to turn on the matter of Tom's maternity rather than, as we might have expected, his paternity. The part played by the unseen Mr. Summer is relegated to the margins of the narrative. Even the Man of the Hill's problems seem to have begun with his domineering mother.

As critics have noted, Fielding deploys various rhetorical resources to have Tom forgiven for illicit sex.[43] Fielding induces approval of Tom's sexual behaviour by aligning it with generosity, charity, or bravery. While aiding Black George's family, he meets Molly. After rescuing Mrs. Waters from Northerton, he has sex with her. At the same time that he must perform sexual services for Lady Bellaston, Tom is acting most energetically to get Nightingale to marry the pregnant Nancy. Fielding also has characters in the novel preempt or guide the reader's reaction. By taking in the foundling child, Allworthy implicitly tolerates the sin of fornication. Both Allworthy and Sophia forgive Tom for (they believe) fathering a bastard child by Moll Seagrim. We are told that when Tom rushes to save Moll from being sent to the Bridewell and confesses his that he is the father, Allworthy gives him the same lecture that he had given Jenny Jones, but we do not read it as being applied to a man, as Fielding tells us that it has already been 'faithfully transcribed' and doesn't need to be repeated. Moreover, Tom's 'honour and honesty' in admitting that he has been guilty of sex outside marriage becomes, in Allworthy's mind, a virtue:

> But whatever Detestation Mr. *Allworthy* had to this or to any other Vice, he was not so blinded by it, but that he could discern any Virtue in the guilty Person, as clearly, indeed as if there had been no Mixture of Vice in the same Character. While he was angry, therefore with the Incontinence of *Jones*, he was no less pleased with the Honour and Honesty of his Self-accusation. He now began to form in his Mind, the same Opinion of this young Fellow which, we hope, our Reader may have conceived. (*TJ* 194)

Allworthy merely hopes that Tom will 'not transgress again'. The information that the child's father is probably one Will Barnes is never communicated to him or Sophia. When Sophia finds that Jones has had sex with Mrs. Waters at Upton, she leaves her muff (slang for female genitalia) in the bed. Far from blaming Tom for his inconstancy, she wishes she had been in Mrs. Waters's place. She later declares that she can 'forgive all rather than his exposing my *Name*' (italics mine), a statement which only reinforces the idea that the responsibility for women's reputations lies with men. Later, when Mrs. Miller is asking Tom to leave her house on account of his intrigue with Lady Bellaston, she also reminds Tom, and the reader, of how Allworthy loved him: 'had you been twenty Times his son, he could not have expressed more Regard for you' (*TJ* 759).

---

[43]   See Nicholas Hudson, 'Fielding's Hierarchy of Dialogue: "Meta-Response" and the Reader of *Tom Jones*', *Philological Quarterly*, 68 (1969), 177–94; Manuel Schonhorn, 'Fielding's Ecphrastic Moment: Tom Jones and His Egyptian Majesty', *Studies in Philology* 78 (1981), 305–23; Peter J. Carlton, 'The Mitigated Truth: Tom Jones's Double Heroism', *Studies in the Novel* 19 (1987), 397–409.

Like Mr. B., Joseph Andrews, Lovelace and even the be-frocked Abraham Adams, Tom Jones is a feminized hero. When assaulted by Northerton, his sense of honour demands revenge, but Fielding has Northerton escape before Jones can exact it from him. He *does* get revenge later, when he comes to Mrs. Waters's aid as she grapples with Northerton, but this time his motivation is the defence of a woman. Peter Carlton describes him as 'a Cavalier hero by intent, but a Christian hero by event'.[44] His honour is later redefined in sexual rather than militaristic terms: 'Gallantry to the Ladies was among his Principles of Honour; and he held it as much incumbent upon him to accept a Challenge to Love as if it had been a Challenge to Fight' (*TJ* 715). Fielding points up his hero's ambiguous gender when he likens Tom to Viola in *Twelfth Night*, sitting 'like Patience smiling on a Monument smiling at Grief' (*TJ* 204). When these words are spoken in the play, Viola is posing as the boy Cesario. One of Jones's most striking and persuasive characteristics is his physical beauty, an attribute typically accorded the heroine. The landlady of the inn on the road to Bristol, where Jones meets the soldiers, finds him 'irresistible' (*TJ* 414). At the same inn, Nancy the chambermaid falls in love with him in five minutes. Another landlady says he has 'the prettiest Eyes I ever saw, and he hath the prettiest Look with them' (*TJ* 645–6). Almost every woman in the novel is attracted to him. Fielding is careful to emphasize his hero's masculinity, though. At the same time that we are told that he has acquired the reputation of 'a pretty Fellow' among all the women in the neighbourhood, Fielding reminds the reader that Tom is often at Squire Western's house because of his great love of hunting (*TJ* 166). Similarly, just before his 'Battle of the amorous Kind' with Mrs. Waters, we read that 'his Face had a Delicacy in it almost inexpressible … which might have given him an Air rather too effeminate, had it not been joined to a most masculine Person and Mein' (*TJ* 510).

However, while Tom's gendered characteristics seem mutable and fluctuating during the course of the novel, there is still a desired endpoint, which is reached when Tom allows himself to kiss Sophia ardently. The hero's somewhat undecided gender could be seen as another rhetorical resource Fielding deploys to evade the question of defining masculinity. Men should, it seems, be the pursuers: Tom's tribulations are nearing an end when he rejects Mrs. Hunt. Yet men in the novel who are sexual aggressors appear only in the margins of the action, the most notable example being Will Barnes, who may have caused the death of a young woman. While both Richardson and Fielding want the reader to accept active masculine sexuality, neither can present it in an unmitigated form.

Given that women take the responsibility for sex in *Tom Jones*, they also have much of the agency. It could be argued, indeed, that *Clarissa* pushed Fielding further in the direction of feminization: certainly his next heroine, Amelia, gives her name to Fielding's last novel, and in contrast with that novel's many military figures, she offers an example of heroism defined in female terms. Despite his brave or charitable acts, Tom is a somewhat passive figure. He is expelled from Paradise

---

[44] Carlton, 404.

Hall; having no clear purpose in mind, he at first decides to go to sea, temporarily joins the army marching North, is sent in another direction by the discovery of Sophia's pocketbook, and having returned it, lingers in London waiting for Sophia whilst he is also Lady Bellaston's kept man. However, just as the feminized Joseph Andrews was contrasted with the yielding Fanny so as to make him more masculine, Tom, for the middle third of the novel, is contrasted with the henpecked and superstitious Partridge, who has been beaten by his wife and reduced from schoolteacher to barber-surgeon by his wife's false evidence. He has some of the same experiences as his companion. Like Jones, Partridge is wrongly suspected of fathering a bastard; he, too, is unjustly exiled; in the encounter with the gypsies, Partridge succumbs to female wiles and attractions. However, he is less active than Tom. Penalized by Allworthy for his crime, Partridge and his wife were:

> both obliged to submit to their Fate … for so far was he from doubling his Industry on the account of his lessened Income, that he did in a manner abandon himself to despair, and as he was by Nature indolent, that Vice now increased upon him, by which means he lost the little School he had. (*T* 103)

Partridge's favourite quotation is a line from the *Aeneid*: '*infandum, regina, jubes renovare dolorem*': 'Beyond all words, O Queen, is the grief thou bidst me revive'. The line recalls the circumstances and the choice of Aeneas. Escaping from Troy with the remnants of his army Aeneas arrives in Carthage and is made welcome by Dido. The line occurs as he tells her of the battle at Troy. His destiny is to found Rome, a destiny that could be frustrated by the love of Dido, and her offer of a realm in Carthage. Despite a brief sexual liaison with her, and despite her entreaties, he leaves her, she commits suicide, and he goes on to fulfill his imperial role. Partridge, we might say, is like a permanently backward-looking Aeneas, who would never choose to leave Dido. In a section of *Tom Jones* dominated by the theme of choice – the misguided choices of the Man of the Hill or Mrs. Fitzpatrick – Partridge functions as a femininely passive foil to Tom's more active role.

The dialogue between the novels of Richardson and Fielding began when Richardson deployed self-interest as a motivation to virtuous behaviour in *Pamela*. Fielding responded with the sharpest of satires in *Shamela* and provided one unworldly hero in *The Adventures of Joseph Andrews, and his Friend Mr. Abraham Adams*. In *Clarissa* Richardson corrected the offending principle, creating a heroine whose motivation for virtue is devoid of self-interest. In her eventually complete disregard for self, after she has been purged of any pride she might have had, Clarissa looks back to the old idea of salvation by faith alone. Bernard Harrison describes a 'true inward virtue' deriving from the Calvinist rejection of empty, because external, works, which would necessarily involve the 'denial of all passions and desires whatsoever, in favour either of obedience to a wholly abstract principle of rectitude, or a complete abjection of one's will and self before God'.[45] Clarissa's moral integrity is of just this kind. She can be rewarded but never in this life; otherwise, she might seem self-seeking. Richardson carried the principle of self-denial to its logical conclusion for his heroine, if not for the readers he hoped might imitate Clarissa. They, at least, might be persuaded by the pervasive praise Clarissa attracts. Fielding might have mocked the crudity of the appeal to self-interest in *Pamela*, but in fact he too always gives his readers tangible incentives to the life of virtue. In *The Champion* of 24 January 1740, he argued that virtue and ambition were compatible: 'Virtue and Interest are not, according to *Photinus* in *Lucan*, as repugnant as Fire and Water' (*Contributions* 140). It may be significant that this argument came two weeks after *The Champion* for 10 January 1740 had taken the form of a letter asking how he, Fielding, dared set himself up as a moral censor. In *The Champion* for 24 January he asserted: 'Virtue forbids not the satisfying our Appetites … she commands us no more than to be happy' (*Contributions* 140–41). In *Joseph Andrews* Fielding made marriage consonant with the satisfaction of sexual desire as Joseph rushes to marry the appropriately named Fanny. The Preface argues that pleasure in the form of laughter is conducive to the production of such virtues as good humour and benevolence:

> I will appeal to common Observation, whether the same companies are not found more full of Good-Humour and Benevolence, after they have been sweeten'd with entertainments of [the Burlesque] kind, than when soured by a Tragedy or a grave Lecture.

In the Dedication to *Tom Jones*, Fielding stated the argument directly:

> Besides displaying that Beauty of Virtue which may attract the Admiration of Mankind, I have attempted to engage a stronger Motive to human Action in her Favour, by convincing men, that their true Interest directs them to a Pursuit of her. (*TJ* 7)

He makes reference to a favourite image from Plato: 'a Kind of Picture, in which Virtue becomes as it were an Object of Sight and strikes us with an Idea of that Loveliness, which Plato asserts there is in her naked Charms'. The same formulation occurs in the issue of *The Champion* cited above and in his essays 'On Conversation' and 'On the Knowledge of the Characters of Men'. In fact, the idea of the naked charms of virtue is only implicit in Plato's *Phaedrus*: it could hardly be otherwise, when the whole Platonist ethos begins with the concept of Eternal Forms which exist above and beyond the mutable world of particulars, and which are only discernible by the eye of the mind. In Platonic philosophy, virtue and the good life are based on reason, not on the gratification of appetites. In Fielding's analogy, Tom's love of Sophia is *philein sophia*, the love of wisdom as well as love for a woman and the pursuit of sexual pleasure. Fielding encourages

---

[45]   Bernard Harrison, *Henry Fielding's* Tom Jones. *The Novelist as Moral Philosopher* (London: Sussex University Press, 1975), 78.

the reader to see a union between Tom and Sophia as an earthly goal of transcendent worth. In *The Providence of Wit*, Martin Battestin distinguishes between Fielding's conception of prudence in *Tom Jones* and debased versions of the concept in such works as William de Britaine's *Humane Prudence* (1680) and Thomas Fuller's *Introductio ad Prudentiam* (1731), where prudence is openly identified with self-interest.[46] Certainly, Tom Jones is not consciously self-serving: but Fielding's version of Platonism allowed him to reconcile self-interest with transcendence.

All the novels of Richardson and Fielding's published in the 1740s were written when the Anglican ethos was perceived as being under threat either by Methodism or by the possible resurgence of popery and tyranny in the form of the Jacobite Rebellion of 1745. Although *Clarissa* has no obvious topicality, Morris Golden and Thomas Keymer have found patterns in the novel which seem to allude to the broader context, with the in-fighting at Harlowe Place reflecting the factionalism of the post-Walpole period, Clarissa embodying the embattled nation, and Lovelace the absolutist adventurer Charles Stuart.[47] Whatever 'high-flying' sympathies Richardson might have had in the 1720s, *Clarissa* has an anti-Jacobite agenda.[48] As his riposte to the Jacobite threat, Fielding responded with an image of the natural religion to which eighteenth-century Anglicans subscribed. Every event in *Tom Jones*, however surprising, is given a natural cause. Squire Western's arrival just in time to save Sophia from Lord Fellamar can ultimately be traced back to his decision to ignore his sister's recommendation of certain formalities before meeting Lady Bellaston. The Irish peer's money, rather than any 'extraordinary ... or supernatural Means', effects Mrs. Fitzpatrick's escape from her husband. The mark of a truly religious man or woman, on Fielding's terms, is scepticism about the supernatural. When the sentinel guarding Northerton reports his sighting of an apparition, which is actually Tom in a blood-stained coat, he gains no credit with the officer who 'tho' a very religious Man was free from all Terrors of this kind' (*TJ* 390). The landlady, on the other hand, 'tho' not over religious ... had no kind of Aversion to the Doctrine of the Spirits'. Superstition is the hallmark of the papist and the Jacobite. To Partridge's prophecy of the miller with three thumbs, Tom answers that the cause of King George is the cause of liberty, true religion and common sense.

Where Richardson and Fielding are also united is in their belief in the persuasive power of fiction. Their methods are not as dissimilar as might at first appear. Both deployed characters in their novels as foils or guides, with Anna Howe and Belford helping to regulate the reader's reactions to Clarissa and Lovelace in Richardson's second novel. The need for more than a single letter-writer was another lesson Richardson no doubt learned from the response to *Pamela*. Both Richardson and Fielding aim to preempt the readers' reactions or close down divergent readings.

---

[46] Martin C. Battestin, *The Providence of Wit* (Oxford: Clarendon Press, 1974), 170 ff.

[47] Morris Golden, 'Public Context and Imagining Self in *Clarissa*' *Studies in English Literature 1500–1900*, 25 (1985), 575–98; Keymer, *Richardson's* Clarissa, 168–76.

[48] Keymer, *Richardson's* Clarissa, 170.

Richardson's efforts in this regard extend to his revisions, commentaries and selections from the novels, while Fielding intervenes constantly in his own narrative. He leaves the reader free to make certain well-premeditated errors: no reader has ever guessed that Bridget Allworthy is Tom's mother. However, Fielding only seems to allow room for readers to exercise their own judgement. Nicholas Hudson argues that our role as readers of *Tom Jones* is not really to judge but to respond to the text in ways that Fielding's masterly rhetoric has taught us to respond, all the while believing that our feelings are 'natural'. His dialogue with readers is really a smoke screen for more covert, and highly effective, methods of persuasion. To acknowledge that our responses are learned would be to undermine the presentation of certain ways of thinking and behaving as natural, a presentation crucial for both writers. 'Natural' equalled legitimate.

Richardson and Fielding both began somewhat defensively as writers of fiction, with Richardson initially offering *Pamela* to the public as the real memoirs of a servant. Even after his authorship became common knowledge, he wanted to keep up the idea that *Pamela* was a true story. In a letter to Aaron Hill, he wrote that the story of Pamela came to him via a nameless gentleman, now dead, who got it from the landlord of an (undesignated) inn, whom the gentleman met whilst on one of the summer tours which he always took alone.[49] The amount of back-covering in this formulation must invite scepticism. Fielding had written fiction before *Joseph Andrews*. *A Journey from This World to the Next* and *Jonathan Wild* probably both predate *Joseph Andrews* in terms of composition, though neither was published until the *Miscellanies* appeared in 1743, that is, after the success of *Joseph Andrews*. He justified the legitimacy of *Joseph Andrews* by contrived reference to Homer's lost *Margites* and the dubious precedent of a 'comic epic'. Both had grown in confidence after the success of their first novels. There is the indication of a provenance for *Clarissa* within the novel itself, as Clarissa plans to have Belford select letters and tell her story for her, but it is never confirmed that the novel *Clarissa* is the outcome of this arrangement. It stands as an acknowledged work of fiction. Fielding began *Tom Jones*, triumphantly, with 'An Author'. If he had to pay respects to his patron, or patrons, in the Dedication, he made them subservient to the triadic structure of the novel by including three. However, the opening sentence of the novel continues: 'An Author ought consider himself, not as a Gentleman ...'. Since the writer is not a gentleman, meaning a person of independent means, he must write for money. An author is like the keeper of a 'public Ordinary, at which all Persons are welcome for their Money'. As the novel proceeds, Fielding develops two parallel dialogues, one with the reader, whose 'Good and Advantage' he considers, and a much more adversarial one with the critic. He is the reader's equal: 'Let us e'en venture to slide down together'; and the reader is sometimes addressed as a 'worthy Friend'. Or, if the author is superior to the reader, he is a constitutional monarch rather than a *jure divino* tyrant. On the other hand, he is a better judge of what he is doing than 'any pitiful Critic whatever'. Should the critic object to the omission of long periods of time, the author is at

---

[49]   *Selected Letters*, 39.

liberty to make what laws he pleases. The only rules to which he must conform are those of probability. Critics have become so bold as to 'assume a Dictatorial Power'. These parallel dialogues could be seen as yet another of Fielding's rhetorical ploys, by means of which the reader is made feel that he or she is the author's intimate, a member of a favoured circle, despite the initial dismissal of the 'private or eleemosynary Treat'. The critics are the negative 'other'. When such a relationship has been cultivated, how much more likely is it that the reader will agree with Fielding when he issues a challenge: 'Examine your Heart, my good Reader, and resolve whether you do believe these Matters with me?' (*TJ* 271). Fielding's playful and shifting persona is one solution to the question of the relationship between the author of a fictional persuasive work and his readers. The author is not a preacher, even if he has something of the homilist about him. Battestin points to models for Fielding's 'Crust for the Critics' (*TJ* XI, i), for example, in Isaac Barrow's sermons on the folly of slander, censure and detraction (*TJ* 566n).

Fielding took the risk of making an illegitimate boy the hero of his novel, and Richardson, thinking of 'The History of a Foundling', thought it 'truly coarse-titled'.[50] It has been suggested that illegitimacy in *Tom Jones* quietly refers to the illegitimacy of the Hanoverian succession.[51] This is not to argue that Fielding was a Jacobite sympathizer. However strongly he supported the Protestant Succession, he could still recognize that the legitimacy of the Georges was a legal construction and not a matter of natural or divine right, just as Fielding also knows that the constructions of gender he promotes are highly mutable. Illegitimacy in *Tom Jones* also, surely, refers to the erstwhile illegitimacy of fiction. At the beginning of the eighteenth century, a writer to the *Athenian Mercury* asked whether or not it was lawful to read romances. By the 1740s prose fiction had achieved a certain stature and respectability, such that its practitioners could attempt works of considerable scope and ambition and gain a measure of fame by so doing. Richardson and Fielding used their novels to defend the Anglican ethos, the Whig supremacy and patriarchy. Given its growing legitimacy, fiction could also be used for other, rather different, purposes.

---

[50]   *Selected Letters*, 127.

[51]   John Allen Stevenson, 'Black George and the Black Act', *Eighteenth Century Fiction* 8 (1996), 379.

Chapter 2
Opposition and Persuasion:
From *Roderick Random* to *Humphry Clinker*

In their fiction, Samuel Richardson and Henry Fielding articulated the Latitudinarian and Whig ethos, in which self-interest was seen as compatible with virtue. The Opposition case, in which self-interest did not support virtue but rather undermined or destroyed it, found expression in, particularly, the early writings of Tobias Smollett. Among Smollett's earliest published work are two poems, 'Advice' and 'Reproof', which appeared in September 1746 and January 1747 respectively. Both poems recall Alexander Pope's verse dialogues *Imitations of the Satires of Horace* and *Epilogue to the Satires* (1738) both in form and in terms of political values and *ad hominem* attacks. Pope's satires exposed corruption in public life and the dominance of monied interest, the decline of literature and the nation. Among his targets in the *Imitations* were Peter Walter, an allegedly rapacious broker; Francis Charteris, a libertine; Whig poet Sir Richard Blackmore; the bisexual Lord Hervey (otherwise 'Lord Fanny'); Lady Mary Wortley Montagu, with whom he had a personal quarrel; Prime Minister Sir Robert Walpole (1676–1745); theatre manager Charles Rich; actor, theatre manager and Poet Laureate Colley Cibber; and sundry other 'Thieves, supercargoes, sharpers and directors'– 'directors' glancing at those responsible for the South Sea Bubble of 1720. For Pope, satire was a weapon both personal and political: 'Whoe'er offends, at some unlucky time/ Slides into verse, and hitches in a rhyme'. He styled himself as the scourge of otherwise uncorrected vice:

> Hear this, and tremble! you who 'scape the Laws,
> Yes, while I live, no rich or noble knave
> Shall walk the World, in credit, to his grave.
> (*First Satire of the Second Book of Horace Imitated* ll.118–20)[1]

Smollett had similar ambitions for himself:

> Th' indignant muse to Virtue's aid shall rise,
> And fix the brand of infamy on vice. ('Advice: A Satire' ll.129–30)[2]

Defending the practice of satire against the 'reproof' of the poem's title:

---

[1]   *The Poems of Alexander Pope*, ed. John Butt *et al.*, 6 vols (London: Methuen and New Haven. Yale University Press, 1940–1961), Vol. IV, 17.

[2]   Tobias Smollett, *Poems, Plays and* The Briton, ed. O.M. Brack, Jr., assisted by Leslie A. Chilton, with an introduction and notes by Byron Gassman (Athens: University of Georgia Press, 1993), 33.

P[oet].You deem it Rancour, then? – Look round and see
What vices flourish still, unprun'd by me:
Corruption, roll'd in a triumphant car,
Displays his burnish'd front and glitt'ring star
('Reproof: A Satire' ll.133–6)[3]

Smollett, in his turn, attacked contractors and money lenders, Peter Walter (now deceased), Charles Rich, homosexuality, the abuse of patronage and bad poets. He also named Whig politicians Newcastle, Grafton, Granville and Bath – Thomas Pelham Holles, Augustus Fitzroy, John Carteret and William Pulteney, respectively – as representative of the absence of virtue in public life.

By 1738, Pope could afford to ignore voices like those in the *Imitations* – voices constructed by Pope himself, of course – that would dissuade him from satire and personal attack. His reputation as a poet was established. He had made himself independent of patronage with the proceeds of his translations of Homer's *Odyssey* and *Iliad*, published between 1715 and 1726, and in any case he still had well-placed friends and patrons such as the Earl of Burlington, Lord Bathurst and Lord Cobham, dedicatees of three of the *Moral Essays* published between 1731 and 1734. Tobias Smollett had no such resources or connections, and his positioning of himself as the fear-inspiring scourge of corruption in public life was rather less plausible in his case than it might have been for Pope. He was born in Scotland, which immediately distanced him from spheres of influence, and would prejudice many Englishmen against him. His grandfather, James Smollett, had been active in the law and military affairs and was knighted in 1698 for his part in the Revolution, a line of descent that allowed Tobias Smollett to consider himself a gentleman. However, Archibald Smollett, father of Tobias, married a woman with no money, without parental consent. He died shortly Tobias's birth without leaving any income for his three children.[4] In a letter to Alexander Hume Campbell, third Earl of Marchmont, Smollett described himself as a 'person, who, as well as yourself, is a gentleman by birth, education, and profession', but as the rather defensive formulation itself might indicate, he could not lay claim to the more solid gentlemanly credentials of wealth deriving from land.[5] He attended Glasgow University without completing any degree, being apprenticed for three years to two prominent surgeons in the city. If he expected that this would grant him entry to the London medical establishment, he was to be disappointed. As a matter of necessity, perhaps, he turned to the Navy. From 1740–1741 he served on board the *Chichester* as a surgeon and witnessed the disastrous British siege

3   Ibid., 43.

4   Lewis Knapp, *Tobias Smollett. Doctor of Men and Manners* (Princeton: Princeton University Press, 1949), 4. I am indebted to Knapp for biographical details throughout this chapter.

5   Tobias Smollett, *The Letters of Tobias Smollett*, ed. Lewis Knapp (Oxford: Clarendon Press, 1970), 23. See also Ian Campbell Ross, 'Tobias Smollett: gentleman by birth, profession and education', *BJECS* 5 (1982), 18.

of Cartagena, an experience he drew on in *Roderick Random*. Between 1741 and 1744 he went back to the West Indies and married Anne Lassells, the heiress of a Jamaican planter, thus ameliorating his financial situation. Returning to England in the spring of 1744, he managed to establish a practice as a physician but was never really successful. Between 1741 and 1749, Smollett spent eight years trying, and failing, to have his play *The Regicide*, which dealt with part of the rebellion of Athol against James I of Scotland, performed in London. The humiliation wounded Smollett's pride. The saga of the author's trials with his play was commemorated in *Roderick Random* in the story told by Melopoyn, a debtor whom Roderick meets in the Marshalsea prison. It was rehearsed again in the preface to the published version of *The Regicide* (1749) and again in the story told by an unnamed author in *Peregrine Pickle* (1751). The lofty moral position to which Smollett aspired as a satirist and his social situation were distinctly at odds.

Rather than continuing his satire in a form modelled on Horace or Juvenal, Smollett resumed it in his prose fiction. It may be that he simply tried poetry and drama and found a form that was more congenial to him. On the other hand, fiction had certain advantages for an outsider in that the publication of a novel was less dependent on connections and patronage than the performance of a play. Fiction was far less respectable than poetry, however. *Roderick Random* was published in January 1748, just after Volumes I and II of *Clarissa* had appeared and before *Tom Jones* in 1749. The *Monthly Review*, which took fiction seriously enough to include reviews of novels, did not begin publication until 1749. The legitimization of fiction was at an early stage. In the preface to *The Adventures of Roderick Random* Smollett placed his work in the tradition of the romance that, while it might have had its origins in 'ignorance, vanity and superstition' (*RR* xliii) had been, in the author's view, reformed by Cervantes and Lesage and could now deal with the 'follies of ordinary life' (*RR* xliv). Invoking Cervantes might give Smollett some air of respectability, and the novel's episodic narrative could be said to resemble *Don Quixote*. *Roderick Random* owes more, however, to Alain-René Lesage's *Les Aventures de Gil Blas* (1715–1735). Smollett published his own translation of *Gil Blas* in October 1748, eight months after *Roderick Random*, and it is likely that he was working on both projects at the same time. Lesage's novel, set in Spain, is a more urbane, French version of the Spanish picaresque tradition, and it tells the story of the son of a squire and a chambermaid who serves many masters and experiences abrupt changes of fortune. Smollett's first novel, then, brought together some of his own experiences of misfortune, an attack on self-interest and monied interest characteristic of Opposition satire, in a form with picaresque origins. In this unlikely medium, Smollett satirized the breakdown of order and fixed standards.

Roderick Random begins with the circumstances of the hero's birth in Scotland, which in some ways resembles Smollett's: Roderick's father secretly marries a poor relation. In the novel, Roderick's grandfather disinherits his son. When his mother dies in childbirth, Roderick's father disappears, and the boy is given a home and education by his grandfather. Left with no money on his grandfather's death, he is temporarily supported by his uncle, Tom Bowling, a seaman. When this too fails, he is apprenticed to the surgeon Launcelot Crab. Roderick soon leaves Scotland for London with the aim of becoming a naval surgeon, carrying a letter of recommendation from Crab to the MP, Mr. Cringer. In London Roderick finds that he must pay a bribe before he can approach Cringer and that the MP was once his grandfather's footman.

Having passed his examinations at the Surgeon's Hall, Roderick must pay further bribes before he can gain a position onboard ship. Unable to do so, he becomes a journeyman apothecary and only gains a position as a naval surgeon on the *Thunder* thanks to the operations of a press gang. Surviving the siege of Cartagena in 1741, Roderick enjoys a brief reversal of fortune, where he has both money and the appearance of a gentleman. However, he is knocked unconscious during a duel and left destitute on a beach in England. Here he becomes a domestic servant in the household of a middle-aged woman and falls in love with her niece, Narcissa. After fighting with Narcissa's suitor, Sir Timothy, he is captured by smugglers and taken to France, where he enlists in the French army and fights at the Battle of Dettingen in 1743. Back in London, he tries to make himself independent by finding a rich woman to marry. On asking permission to marry Melinda, Roderick is forced to confess to her mother that he has no estate, and is rejected.

Still trying to find employment, Roderick thinks of a position working for the government and is recommended to Earl Strutwell, who is as corrupt as all the other possible patrons or figures of authority in the novel, corruption this time taking the form of homosexuality. His fortunes revived by winning at cards, Roderick pursues Miss Snapper, despite her grotesque appearance, and is diverted only by a chance reencounter with the beloved Narcissa. Losing money at cards, he fails to pay a debt to his tailor and is imprisoned in the Marshalsea, where he meets Melopoyn. His uncle, Tom Bowling, unexpectedly returns, pays Roderick's debts and gives him a position as a surgeon on the ship Bowling now commands. After making a large sum of money by selling slaves in South America, Roderick is unexpectedly reunited with his long-lost father. In the end, Roderick returns to Scotland with his new wife Narcissa and his father, to be greeted by an adoring peasantry.

Robert Irvine has argued that *Roderick Random* enacts what has been called country party ideology.[6] The chief exponent of country ideology was Henry St. John, Lord Bolingbroke, who was excluded from his seat in the Lords after the accession of George I because of his declared allegiance to The Pretender, James Stuart. In his contributions to *The Craftsman* in the 1730s and elsewhere, Bolingbroke argued that after the Revolution, the old divisions of Whig and Tory had been rendered meaningless. The real distinction was between court and country. Sir Robert Walpole, in particular, had used the financial resources of the Crown to buy the support of a court aristocracy by patronage or bribery. Ministers and members of parliament had been encouraged to neglect the real good of the

---

[6]   Robert Irvine, *Enlightenment and Romance. Gender and Agency in Smollett and Scott* (Oxford: Peter Lang, 2000), 41–51 *et passim*.

country for personal gain. Financial interests in the City had been allowed too much influence. In Bolingbroke's view, the only safeguard against the spread of corruption was the landed gentry, whose economic independence allowed them to act in a disinterested fashion. *Roderick Random* represents the world of Opposition or country nightmare: almost everyone is motivated by self-interest, and bribery is the only route to position. From the outset, money has a disfiguring effect on human relationships. Rejecting his own son because he has married a woman with no fortune, Roderick's grandfather is an 'unnatural' parent. Further, Roderick himself suffers what Irvine calls acute 'status inconsistency' because his birth should entitle him to a position of influence, but his status is actually dependent on his role as an employee. This is why he asks Launcelot Crab 'on what footing' he is to be entertained and fights to be perceived as something other than a servant.[7] The hero's status as a gentleman is confirmed by the unwavering, and disinterested, loyalty and deference of *his* servant, Hugh Strap – this despite the fact that Strap very often supports him financially, as Roderick bitterly reflects. Proper, meaning hierarchical, relationships are restored only at the end of the novel, when the Roderick is reunited with his father, now Don Rodriguez, who buys back the family estate.

A problem with *Roderick Random* as satire is that as a first-person narrative, the novel is written from a position of social and economic weakness. Yet, as spokesman for Smollett's exposure of corruption, Roderick assumes a position of moral superiority. His bitter resentment of his socially degraded status and his attempts to define himself as somehow superior to those who surround him are apparent throughout the novel. In Smollett's mind, no doubt, the difference between the hero who is a gentleman by birth and other, false gentlemen was clear, but for the reader, Roderick's unstable status is not dissimilar to that of a 'young prince' in London who is really a dancer and an ambassador who is really a fiddler. Smollett evidently expected the reader to share his belief that the hero was entitled to respect because of his birth. In the preface he writes: 'To secure a favourable prepossession, I have allowed [Roderick Random] the advantages of birth and education, which will, I hope, engage the ingenuous more warmly on his behalf' (*RR* xxxv). Where Pope wrote in a form with a prestigious classical lineage, Smollett's mode is the lower and more anarchic picaresque. Roderick, like the *picaro*, has many changes of fortune – to which the summary above scarcely does justice – and manages to survive them. Lesage's Gil Blas is philosophical about his many abrupt transitions from poverty to wealth and back again. There is no suggestion that the wheel of fortune is unjust. Gil Blas occasionally suffers pangs of conscience about his own trickery, indeed about his own pride and ambition. He reforms in the end and is rewarded with position and wealth. Smollett, on the other hand, would make the randomness of his hero's fate a comment on social injustice. Roderick is a self-confessed libertine and fortune hunter, but moral

---

[7] Tobias Smollett, *The Adventures of Roderick Random*, ed. Paul-Gabriel Boucé (Oxford: Oxford University Press, 1979), 27.

reform plays no part in his eventual social elevation. His exit from the corrupt society Smollett depicts is entirely arbitrary.

Random, like Smollett, has little agency, and for as long as that is the case, he can identify, quite literally, with women who are as powerless and marginalized as he is. A significant interpolation in the novel is the story of Miss Williams, a prostitute. Recovering from a venereal disease, Roderick hears a groan from the next room and rushes to the aid of a young woman. This is Miss Williams who, like Roderick, has had to endure downward social mobility and, like him, has been brought up as a Presbyterian. She tells him how she rejected this creed and became a freethinker and a philosopher whom, in typical Smollettian style, few people would face in argument. Roderick listens while Miss Williams tells her story of lost honour, projected revenge, the death of a father and the slide into prostitution. Like Roderick, she has been robbed and imprisoned and, like him, plans to find a rich spouse to escape from poverty. Later, when Roderick has been robbed of his money and gentlemanly clothes and left for dead on an English beach, he is saved thanks to the intervention of an old woman, Mrs. Sagely, who is ostracized as a witch by her neighbours. She was once an heiress but married secretly and was cut off by her parents. Mrs. Sagely (like Smollett) has a 'skill in curing distempers'. The same pattern recurs in Smollett's second novel, *Peregrine Pickle* (1751). The 'Memoirs of a Lady of Quality', the allegedly true story of Lady Frances Anne Vane's marriages and amours, of some 50,000 words long, interrupts the story of the eponymous hero's descent into dependence on a corrupt nobility. The content of the memoirs did not come from Smollett, but in a detailed and rigorous analysis, O.M. Brack has shown that Smollett certainly brought to the Memoirs his characteristic style and vocabulary and may have written, or rewritten, portions of them.[8] Smollett lent his voice, in short, to what Richardson called 'Women's Poison'.

Smollett explored the endangerment of the country ideal again in *The Adventures of Peregrine Pickle* (1751).[9] Peregrine is the eldest son of the owner of the family estate, Gamaliel Pickle. He is the landed country gentleman whose independence should provide a bulwark against corruption and tyranny. The early part of the novel sees young Peregrine rejected by his mother and taken into the care of his uncle, Commodore Trunnion. He is much given to elaborate and very physical practical jokes, among them the perforation of his aunt's chamberpot. This habit later becomes what Smollett calls 'practical satire', whereby Pickle humiliates the objects of his moral and social scorn. At Oxford, for example, he circulates satirical verses on the low birth of his tutor, Mr. Jumble. Peregrine's early attributes are promising, but he is also inordinately proud. As soon as he excels

---

[8]   O.M. Brack, Jr., 'Smollett and the Authorship of "The Memoirs of Lady of Quality"', in *Tobias Smollett, Scotland's First Novelist*, ed. O.M. Brack, Jr. (Newark: University of Delaware Press, 2007), 35–73.

[9]   For an analysis of the novel in terms of country politics, see Ian Campbell Ross, '"With Dignity and Importance": Peregrine Pickle as Country Gentleman', *Smollett: Author of the First Distinction*, ed. Alan Bold (London: Vision and Barnes and Noble, 1982), 148–69.

at school, he becomes even more ambitious and subjects all his fellow pupils by force. At Winchester, he leads a rebellion rather than submit to public punishment. He meets, and begins to court, Emilia Gauntlet but later fears that his passion for Emilia, who has no fortune, may detract from his own dignity. At Oxford he excels again but is also given to drinking, gaming and debauchery.

The prospect of travelling in Europe flatters his vanity and ambition, and once abroad he engages in a series of ill-advised sexual liaisons. Back in England after the Grand Tour, Peregrine courts the favour of noblemen, and they in turn perceive him as a 'young gentleman of fortune, who would make an useful and creditable addition to the number of their adherents'.[10] Halfway through the novel, Peregrine inherits £30,000 and property from his uncle, achieving a situation of independence which Roderick Random achieves only at the conclusion of the earlier novel. However, rather than living up to his responsibilities as an independent country gentleman, he takes up residence in London, purchases a new chariot and horses, and makes an appearance in the fashionable world. His vanity is pleased by the fact that his fortune is believed to be much larger than it really is, and he believes that he will be able to marry an heiress, or a rich widow, before his funds are exhausted. He attempts to seduce Emilia. By Chapter 93 he is spending a proportion of his time at 'nocturnal riots and revels' with profligate young nobles. Later he is 'in the protection' of a nobleman, at whose instigation he decides to contest an election for Member of Parliament with no other end in view than gain and social advancement. Attempting to buy victory in the election, he incurs a debt of £1200, and within a few chapters, with his fortune nearly exhausted, he is styled 'Minister's Dependent' (*PP* 618). With the discovery that the ten thousand pounds he had lent to a now deceased nobleman is irrecoverable, we find him, at the end of Chapter 100, in 'a state of the most deplorable dependance' (*PP* 636). Through his own pride and ambition, then, Peregrine Pickle has sacrificed the independence necessary, in terms of country ideology, for virtue.

In *Roderick Random* and *Peregrine Pickle* Smollett advanced the Opposition cause, and he also continued in the vein of his own, and Pope's poetry, by attacking literary and political foes. In *Roderick Random* Smollett had rehearsed the story of his failure to stage *The Regicide* in the story told by Melopoyn. Melopoyn relates how he approached Mr. Supple, a theatre manager, with a play, only to be put off for some weeks and then told that the manuscript had been accidentally burnt. Melopoyn writes another copy from memory, which Mr. Supple undertakes to revise and then stage the following season, the current season having 'slipt away insensibly' (*RR* 382). Resuming his applications to Mr. Supple, Melopoyn finds that his cause is to be taken up by Lord Rattle, who recommends revisions to the play. After a reading of the play by an actor whom Melopoyn finds 'excessively illiterate and assuming', more revisions are recommended, but by this time Supple has disposed of his patent to a Mr. Brayer, so that applications have to begin all over again.

---

[10]   Tobias Smollett, *The Adventures of Peregrine Pickle*, ed. James Clifford (London: Oxford University Press, 1964), 354.

Lord Rattle recommends the play to another actor, Mr. Bellower, and after having been kept waiting for an hour to meet him, Melopoyn is 'not a little astonished at the pert and supercilious behaviour of this stage-player' (*RR* 388). Told to call again in a week, he reflects that 'the dignity of a poet [is] greatly impaired since the days of Euripides and Sophocles' (*RR* 388). So the promises and delays go on, with Melopoyn's play being taken up (apparently) by Earl Sheerwit, and a 'celebrated player', Mr. Marmozet. However, the play is rejected by theatre manager Mr. Vandal as improper for the stage, an opinion seemingly derived from views privately expressed by Marmozet. A friend of Melopoyn's characterizes Marmozet thus:

> [Marmozet] had acted from first to last with the most perfidious dissimulation, cajoling with insinuating civilities, while he underhand employed all his art and influence to prejudice the ignorant manager against my performance; that nothing could equal his hypocrisy, but his avarice, which ingrossed the faculties of his soul so much, that he scrupled not to be guilty of the meanest practices to gratify that sordid appetite; that in consequence of this disposition, he had prostituted his honour in betraying my inexperience. (*RR* 394)

Although Melopoyn almost despairs of seeing the play performed, its cause is taken up by a 'lady of fashion', who recommends it (yet again) to Mr. Brayer, who promises to stage it the following winter, given certain alterations and amendments. However, by the time the next season arrives, Marmozet has become joint patentee with Brayer, and he prevents the play's performance once more. Turned out into the street 'naked, friendless and forlorn' (*RR* 396), Melopoyn is arrested for debts to his tailor and imprisoned.

In *A Study in Smollett* (1925) Howard Buck provided what remains the definitive key to Smollett's targets in *Roderick Random*, the preface to *The Regicide*, and *Peregrine Pickle*.[11] Mr. Supple, in Melopoyn's story, was Charles Fleetwood, manager of Drury Lane until 1745. 'Lord Rattle' was actually a composite of four of Smollett's patrons, the exceptions being Lady Vane (the 'lady of quality') and the Earl of Chesterfield, who appears as Earl Sheerwit. Mr. Brayer is the actor James Lacy, who succeeded Fleetwood as patentee of Drury Lane. Mr. Bellower, who in *Roderick Random* keeps Melopoyn waiting for an hour, and the 'excessively illiterate and assuming' actor are one and the same, being a representation of James Quin, successful actor and advisor to Charles Rich at Covent Garden. Rich himself appears as Mr. Vandal. The 'celebrated player, Mr. Marmozet', who influences Vandal, was David Garrick. The Earl of Chesterfield figures again in *Peregrine Pickle* as 'a certain nobleman of great pretensions to taste', who fails to live up to his promises of patronage.[12] A lengthy attack on David Garrick, easily identifiable from the catalogue of the roles he plays, appears in the form of the Knight of Malta's censure

---

[11]   Howard Buck, *A Study in Smollett* (New Haven: Yale University Press, 1925), 55 ff.

[12]   Tobias Smollett, *The Adventures of Peregrine Pickle*, ed. James L. Clifford (London: Oxford University Press, 1964), 646.

of the actor's want of decorum in tragic roles. James Quin is a vulgar buffoon whose 'action resembles that of heaving ballast into the hold of a ship' (*PP* 274).

George Lyttleton, though not directly involved in the matter of *The Regicide*, received the same searing treatment. Lyttleton's elegy to his wife was parodied, and Lyttleton himself was 'the universal patron, Gosling Scrag Esq; son and heir of Sir Marmaduke Scrag' (*PP* 658). As a patron, apparently, Scrag/Lyttleton expects 'slavish prostitution' (*PP* 659). The writer of the ridiculous elegy in *Peregrine Pickle* asks if:

> a few flimsy odes, barren epistles, pointless epigrams, and the superstitious suggestions of a half-witted enthusiast, intitle him to that eminent rank he maintains in the world of letters? (*PP* 658)

Lyttleton's offence, it seems, had been to suggest that Smollett try writing comedy, rather than tragedy – the suggestion may well have come after the publication of *Roderick Random* – and then to refuse to recommend his play, of which no trace now exists, for the stage.[13] Lyttleton had also helped James Quin to obtain royal patronage whilst he was secretary to the Prince of Wales.[14] Henry Fielding also appears briefly in *Peregrine Pickle* as Mr. Spondy, a man in danger of becoming Lyttleton's sycophant. The chairman of the College of Authors advises Spondy that 'when he is inclined to marry his own cook-wench, his gracious patron may condescend to give the bride away; and finally settle him in his old age, as a trading Westminster-justice' (*PP* 659–60). Here were references to Fielding's marriage to his deceased wife's chambermaid in November 1747 and his appointment, through Lyttleton's recommendation, as Commissioner of the Peace at Bow Street Court in December 1748. Until the publication of *Tom Jones* in 1749, Fielding was known primarily as a successful dramatist, with David Garrick producing one or more of his plays every year: here was reason enough, perhaps for Smollett's resentment.[15] Fielding had also, of course, dedicated *Tom Jones* (1749) to Lyttleton, drawing attention to the fact that he was supported by Lyttleton for most of the time he had spent writing the novel. Worst of all, perhaps, the authorship of the anonymous *Roderick Random* had been attributed to Fielding. In 1754 Lady Mary Wortley Montagu wrote to the Countess of Bute that she had 'guess'd R. Random to be his [Fielding's], thô without his name'.[16] A translation of the work into French was actually published under Fielding's name in 1761. Smollett's attack on Lyttleton and Fielding continued in the dark and scurrilous pamphlet *Habbakkuk Hilding* (1752), where Fielding/Hilding, after the administration of an elixir by Scrag, mounts a jackass, carries a mop aloft, mistakes a constable for Aristotle, and a shoe-black for Horace.[17] Although

---

[13]   Buck, *A Study in Smollett*, 101–3.

[14]   Ibid., 104–5

[15]   Ibid., 105.

[16]   Kelly, 101–2.

[17]   Anonymous, 'A Faithful Narrative of the Base and Inhuman Arts That were lately practised upon the Brain of Habbakkuk Hilding, Justice, Dealer, and Chapman, Who now

the pamphlet is anonymous, the charge that the character of Partridge, in *Tom Jones*, was a copy of *Roderick Random*'s Strap, and that the Miss Mathews of *Amelia* (1751) was actually Smollett's Miss Williams, might alone suggest Smollett's authorship.

Others who had found a place within the charmed circle of patronage or friendship were also caricatured in *Peregrine Pickle*. The republican Physician, who accompanies Peregrine Pickle as he returns from France, was based on Smollett's exact contemporary and fellow-physician, the poet Dr. Mark Akenside (1721–1770). The lines with which the doctor greets Peregrine on his release from the Bastille in Chapter 51 – '*O fool! to think the man, whose ample mind must grasp whatever yonder stars survey.*' – were taken from Akenside's 'Ode to the Earl of Huntingdon' (1748).[18] Lyttleton was also a friend and admirer of Akenside. Moreover, Akenside made some anti-Scottish remarks in the 'Ode' and Smollett wreaked a symbolic revenge: Akenside's lack of taste is enacted, very literally, in the memorable and indigestible banquet he provides in the manner of the Ancients in Chapter 48. Peregrine humiliates the doctor by pouring water into his bed, which the doctor then believes to be his own urine. Ronald Paulson has argued that Pallet the painter is actually a satirical portrait of William Hogarth.[19] An attack on him might have been justified, in Smollett's eyes, purely because of his association with Fielding and David Garrick.

Smollett, however, could always claim that his satirical portraits were representations of general types rather than specific individuals. Perhaps with objections to the personal satire in *Peregrine Pickle*, as much as *Roderick Random*, in mind, Smollett prefaced the fourth edition of *Roderick Random* (1755) with an Apologue.[20] Here he offered the allegory of a young painter who represents a bear, an owl and an ass with human characteristics, only to find that an old soldier, a physician and a politician apply the satire to themselves. '*In vain the astonished painter declared that he had no intention to give offence, or to characterize particular persons*', (*RR* xlviii) writes Smollett. Nevertheless, Smollett was still smarting about the issue of patronage, and George Lyttleton in particular, in 1753, when he dedicated *Ferdinand, Count Fathom* to himself as the only way of maintaining personal integrity:

> Whatever may have been the fate of other Dedicators, I, for my own part, sit down
> to write this address, without any apprehension of disgrace or disappointment;

---

lies at his House in Covent-garden, in a deporable State of Lunacy; a dreadful Monument of false Friendship and Delusion' (London: 1752).

[18]   Howard Buck, 'Smollett and Dr. Akenside', *JEGP* 31 (1932), 13.

[19]   Ronald Paulson, 'Smollett and Hogarth: The Identity of Pallet', *SEL* 4 (1964), 351–9.

[20]   Smollett had written to Alexander Carlyle in 1748 that he was 'not a little mortified to find the Characters [in *Roderick Random*] strangely misapplied to Particular Men whom I never had the least Intention to ridicule' (*Letters* 7). Smollett's schoolmaster, John Love, apparently believed the teacher in *Roderick Random* to be a portrait of himself.

because I know you are too well convinced of my affection and sincerity to repine at what I shall say touching your character and conduct.[21]

James Thomson, author of *The Seasons* (1730), *Liberty* (1735–1736), and *The Castle of Indolence* (1748) and a himself a Scot, was, on the other hand, was 'put to the blush for the undeserved incense he had offered' to a 'false Mæcenas' – that is, Lyttleton (*FCF* 1). Lyttleton had in fact given Thomson a sinecure.

Reviews of *Peregrine Pickle* in the *Monthly* and *The Royal Magazine* were not unfavourable, with John Cleland, in the former, offering a measured defence of Smollett's use of 'low' material. However, Cleland commented, urbanely, that 'to pronounce with an air of decision, that [Smollett] has every where preserved propriety and nature, would sound more towards interested commendation than genuine criticism'.[22] Smollett was to find that literary tastes had changed. Cleland extracted episodes involving Peregrine's satirical verses on the low birth of his tutor Jumble, and the perforation of Mrs. Trunnion's chamberpot, to allow readers to form their own judgement. The reviewer in *The Royal Magazine* gave an extensive summary of the plot, with the following comment on material in the first volume:

> Our author here fills several pages with a minute account of the many pranks play'd by Peregrine, till he arrived at the age of twelve years, the narration whereof can be no ways entertaining to those, who are older than Peregrine is said to have then been.[23]

Some of the episodes involving Peregrine's behaviour at university would also have been better left out:

> Peregrine ... is represented as guilty of such outrages, irregularities and indiscretions (some of which he acted against both his domestic and collegiate tutor) as tho' too frequently practiced by young gentlemen in the first outset from school, might have better been omitted in a work, which is likely to have the juvenile part of mankind, for the majority of its readers.[24]

Some of the narrative is 'tedious' or 'improbable', but the satire on affectations of taste, and the ridicule of excessive partiality for the customs and manners of other countries, received favourable comment.

The personal satire in the novel was thought generally inappropriate. John Cleland observed that there were several characters 'drawn so as cannot fail of giving offence to the supposed originals'.[25] Although apparently not recognising the physician as Mark Akenside, Cleland thought the character's extravagances

---

[21] Tobias Smollett, *The Adventures of Ferdinand Count Fathom*, ed. Damian Grant (London: Oxford University Press, 1971), 1–2.
[22] Kelly, 54.
[23] Ibid., 60.
[24] Ibid., 62.
[25] Ibid., 55.

'too sarcastically exposed, for good nature not to complain, however poetical justice may smile at the execution'. Thomas Gray, writing to Horace Walpole, recognized Gosling Scrag as Lyttleton. The reviewer in *The Royal Magazine* evidently identified James Quin:

> our hero commences author, and becomes a member of a college of writers, of whose proceedings we have here a tedious description, in which is introduced a severe criticism upon the improprieties of the dress, speaking and gesticulation of one of our celebrated actors, in the characters of Pierre, Othello and Zanga.[26]

Contemporary readers were more engaged by the scandalous 'Memoirs of a Lady of Quality' and were also more critical. Samuel Richardson wrote to Sarah Chapone of 'Womens Poison' (of which Lady V. was one exponent) two months before *Peregrine Pickle* was published.[27] Nevertheless, he subsequently sent the offending part to Sarah Chapone's son. Dr. John Hill's anonymous *The History of a Woman of Quality: or, The Adventures of Lady Frail* appeared two weeks before *Peregrine Pickle* was published and claimed to offer the authentic account of Lady Vane's amours. Thomas Gray gave his opinion of the work to Horace Walpole in March 1751:

> Has that miracle of *tenderness and sensibility* (as she calls it) *Lady Vane* given you any amusement? *Peregrine*, whom she uses as a vehicle, is very poor indeed, with a few exceptions.[28]

In March 1751 *The London Magazine* published some anonymous verses (which have been attributed to Richard Graves, author of *The Spiritual Quixote*) reflecting on 'The HEROINES: or, Modern memoirs'.[29] Still in the same month, Horace Walpole wrote to Horace Mann:

> There have been two events, not political, equal to any absurdities or follies of former years. My Lady Vane has literally published the Memoirs of her own life, only suppressing part of her lovers, no part of the success of the others with her: a degree of profligacy not to be accounted for; she does not want money, none of her stallions will raise her credit; and the number, all she had to brag of, concealed! The other is a play.[30]

Lady Henrietta Luxborough wrote to William Shenstone in May 1751:

> Peregrine Pickle I do not admire: it is by the author of Roderick Random, who is a lawyer: but the thing which makes the book sell, is the History of Lady V—[31]

---

[26]   Ibid., 67.
[27]   Ibid., 47.
[28]   Ibid., 69.
[29]   Ibid., 75.
[30]   Ibid., 76.
[31]   Ibid., 78.

More anonymous verses on Lady Vane appeared in *The Ladies' Magazine* of June 1751. From a more favourable point of view, but on the same subject, Elizabeth Montagu wrote to her sister Sarah Scott early in 1752, recommending that she read *Peregrine Pickle*, since 'Lady Vane's story is well told'.[32] Lady Mary Wortley Montagu was also sympathetic, considering that '[Lady Vane's] History, rightly consider'd, would be more instructive to young Women than any Sermon I know'.[33] Mary Granville Delany (a friend of Swift's), on the other hand, thought Lady Vane 'a wretch' – though she found the memoirs the only part of the novel worth reading.[34]

Smollett did not enjoy the independence of a landed country gentleman, but writing, even writing in the low form of a novel, might offer him the independence necessary to exercise the influence in public affairs that Smollett saw as his due. What we find in *Peregrine Pickle* are two versions of the gentleman: one in decline, and losing the independence so necessary, in the Tory view, to the continuance of national liberty; and another version of the gentleman as writer and critic, offering to correct moral and manners. Towards the end of the novel, the impoverished Peregrine takes on the latter role. In the literary arena, Peregrine exercises the power of patronage:

> he took the management of the pit into his direction, putting himself at the head of those critics who call themselves the town; and in that capacity chastised several players, who had been rendered insolent and refractory by unmerited success. As for the new productions of the stage, though generally unspirited and insipid, they always enjoyed the benefit of his influence and protection. (*PP* 576)

When he is penniless and excluded from fashionable society, he recommences as author and is invited to join the 'college of authors'. In this loose and argumentative federation, he sits at the right hand of the president. As member of the college, two chapters later, he is able to carry out the duties of a gentleman and earn the respect to which a gentleman would be entitled. He uses his acquaintance and influence with the creditor of an imprisoned writer to facilitate the writer's release. Despite Pickle's loss of integrity on the one hand, he has an alternative and apparently entirely stable career as moral censor and critic. The account of the 'practical satire' with which he exposes, and punishes, libertines, homosexuals, social climbers, card-sharpers, pedants, republican or High Church sympathizers, and pretenders to taste, is practically a separate narrative, apparently unimplicated in the story of the hero's own moral decline. In the character of Peregrine, then, the novel actually offers us a character split into two halves: a morally compromised gentleman by birth and a seemingly rootless but morally impeccable writer and critic. The critical reception of *Peregrine Pickle* made the latter less tenable as the site of virtue.

---

[32] Ibid., 80.
[33] Ibid., 88.
[34] Ibid., 89.

Given the contemporary response to the low material in *Peregrine Pickle*, we might feel that it was in defiance of the critics that Smollett made the circumstances of the hero's birth in his next work, *Ferdinand, Count Fathom* (1753), as ignominious as could be imagined. Ferdinand's mother is an English camp follower, and his father could be any one of the many soldiers in the allied army she has slept with. He is of no particular country, having been born in a wagon travelling between Holland and Flanders. I will cite at length here Smollett's imagining of the reader's possible response and his reply to it:

> And here it may not be amiss to anticipate the remarks of the reader, who, in the chastity and excellency of his conception, may possibly exclaim, 'Good Heaven! will these authors never reform their imaginations, and lift their ideas from the obscene objects of low life?'
>
> Have a little patience, gentle, delicate, sublime critic; you, I doubt not, are one of those consummate connoisseurs, who in their purifications, let humour evaporate, while they endeavour to preserve decorum, and polish wit, until the edge of it is quite wore off ... who extol the writings of Petronius Arbiter, read with raptures the amorous sallies of Ovid's pen, and chuckle over the story of Lucian's ass; yet, if a modern author presumes to relate the progress of a simple intrigue, are shocked at the indecency and immorality of the scene: who delight in following Guzman d'Alfarache, thro' all the mazes of squalid beggary; who with pleasure accompany Don Quixote and his squire, in the lowest paths of fortune; who are diverted with the adventures of Scarron's ragged troop of strollers, and highly entertained with the servile situations of Gil Blas; yet, when a character in humble life occasionally occurs in a performance of our own growth, exclaim with an air of disgust, 'Was ever any thing so mean! Sure, this writer must have been very conversant with the lowest scenes of life:' ...; who eagerly explore the jakes of Rabelais, for amusement, and even extract humour from the dean's description of a lady's dressing-room: yet, in a production of these days, unstampt with such venerable names, will stop their noses with all the signs of loathing and abhorrence, at a bare mention of the china chamber-pot: who applaud Catullus, Juvenal, Persius and Lucan, for their spirit in lashing the greatest names of antiquity; yet, when a British satirist, of this generation, has courage enough to call in question the talents of a Pseudo-patron, in power, accuse him of insolence, rancour and scurrility.
>
> If such you be, courteous reader, I say again, have a little patience; for your entertainment we are about to write. (*FCF* 7–8)

In fact, the promise to cater to polite taste is not ironic. However Smollett railed against his critics, and the standards that might be imposed upon him, *Ferdinand, Count Fathom* is very much shaped by the kinds of criticism that had been levelled at *Peregrine Pickle*. From Smollett's point of view, then, *Ferdinand Count Fathom* marked the point where fiction ceased to offer him the independence or agency it might hitherto have afforded, and which he did not really recover, in terms of fiction, until the publication of *The Expedition of Humphry Clinker* in 1771.

Ferdinand, Count Fathom is the first of Smollett's novels to be significantly shaped by a consciousness of female readers and politeness. There are Richardsonian plots of persecuted female virtue – the pursuit of the flawless Monimia is only the longest of these – which might have been designed to court the new taste. It is not insignificant that a subplot in the novel concerns the possible loss of honour by a pristine aristocrat, Don Diego de Zelos, Castilian, and head of an ancient family. Women, once again, are the root cause. On very strong evidence, Don Diego believes that his daughter has dishonoured him by marrying a man of low birth, the son of a Bohemian artisan. Since his wife connived at this, he gives them both poison to drink, and (apparently) they die. Later Don Diego finds that there was no such plot, and his wife and daughter survived. Still, he manages to 'kill' them, and (because of this?) his honour remains intact after all.

The need to court female approval to gain reputation, influence, or money is enacted in the novel itself. We see Ferdinand, even as a child, becoming adept at cards 'in the course of his assiduities and attention to the females of the house' (*FCF* 23). In the chapter entitled '*He meditates schemes of importance*' (*FCF* 23) Ferdinand courts – indeed, longs for – the favour of his patron's daughter, Mme Melvil. He declares his (pretended) love, but she does not respond quite as he would have wanted; even when he feigns illness, she does not rush to his assistance but orders her maid, Teresa, to help him. Ferdinand subsequently pursues an intrigue with Teresa – a much less daunting proposition – and enlists her help with the professed aim of robbing Mme Melvil of her fortune. In the end Ferdinand has to content himself with trying (unsuccessfully) to debauch her morals by having Teresa leave titillating books in her bedroom, manipulating her opinion of one of the other maids, and robbing her of some money and jewels. Two chapters later, Ferdinand is in Vienna and finds himself exiled from polite society due to the 'obscurity of his birth, and the want of a title' (*FCF* 44). The society of women, though, provides him with an alternative (if 'humbler') arena in which to exercise his powers. Lodging with a jeweller, he undertakes to manipulate the opinions of women by courting both the daughter and the stepmother and fostering their resentment of one another. Once again, his ultimate aim is pecuniary: he plans to defraud the jeweller. When he has succeeded in seducing the stepmother, she gives him jewels and trinkets. Both women give him money or jewels to pay off his (pretended) gambling debts. Finding himself treated with 'disregard and contempt' in an English stage coach, his first recourse is to court a young woman. He subsequently contrives to steal her purse before seducing her.

Feminized taste was not congenial to Smollett. From Smollett's point of view it is, in part, the pursuit of feminine approval that makes Ferdinand so obviously despicable. The pursuit of female approval tends to place him in humiliating or dangerous situations. Admitted to Wilhemina's room, he is overheard by her father and has to hide in a closet. On the brink of discovery, he hides inside the chimney. To meet with the stepmother, he has to hide in a wardrobe for three hours. In England, he conducts an affair with Mrs. Trapwell, only to find himself the victim of a plot by the husband to extort money from him. Discovered in bed with her, he is 'made prisoner … pinioned in such a manner that he could not stir' (*FCF* 170). He is subsequently involved in a lawsuit and imprisoned: 'deprived' as Smollett puts it, 'of his reputation, rank, liberty and friends; and his fortune reduced from two thousand pounds, to something less than two hundred' (*FCF* 181). Other women in the novel place him in situations of fear or degradation. Travelling through German woods at night in the middle of a storm, he takes refuge in a lonely cottage, the sole occupant of which is a seemingly hospitable old woman. When he retires to his room, he finds himself locked in with a corpse. The woman and her family conspire, it seems, to kill and rob passing travellers.

If *Ferdinand, Count Fathom* is shaped, in part, by the demands of a female audience, the novel also tries to make a sharp moral division between the faultless real gentleman (Renaldo de Melvile) and a rootless, illegitimate and manipulative villain. So far, then, the novel might be seen as morally respectable in that there were no 'mixed' characters. Yet, while the narrative is written in the third person, the action is seen from Ferdinand's point of view. Despite Smollett's prefatory moralisings, attempts at ironic framing, and the occasional pious interjection, the reader's sympathies might well be enlisted on Ferdinand's behalf, particularly as his career in many ways resembles that of Smollett's other heroes or, indeed, Smollett himself. Like Smollett, in relation to his characters, Fathom is master of various languages and dialects. In Paris, Fathom is believed to be, variously, from provincial France, Tuscany, Germany, Holland and England, and is supposed to be 'a personage of great consequence' (*FCF* 90). Always reconstructing himself for public approval, he adapts himself 'to the humour of each individual' (*FCF* 91). With an Italian he discourses on music, with a French abbé he talks of taste and genius, of industry with the Dutchman, and he endears himself to the Englishman by not talking to him at all. There is a certain poignancy in the picture of Fathom silent in the stagecoach, unwilling to venture a word in any of his various languages, and suspected of being a Jacobite: just as there is also a hint of Smollett's sense of his own importance in the belief, projected on to this cross-section of English society, that he is the Young Pretender. Like Smollett, or his heroes, Ferdinand has to fall back on one the ubiquitous 'letters of recommendation'.

John Barrell has suggested that Roderick Random might be understood as a parody of a gentleman: so too might Fathom.[35] He is briefly a soldier. Having travelled widely in Europe, he might be construed as having completed the Grand Tour. In England he cultivates the appearance of a gentleman, acquiring a coach with a coat of arms. He gains the approval of the nobility by expounding on mathematics, politics, military strategy, painting and music: there is a parallel here with Smollett's career as editor of and chief contributor to the *Critical Review*. Like Smollett in his career as critic, he cultivates the taste by which he himself might be appreciated. Once established in society, Fathom is able to sell diamonds of uncertain value at three times their cost. He counterfeits Cremona

---

[35]   John Barrell, *English Literature in History, 1730–1780. An Equal, Wide Survey* (London: Hutchinson, 1983), 206.

violins. '[H]e himself', writes Smollett, 'was astonished at the infatuation he had produced. Nothing was so wretched among the productions of art, that he could not impose upon the world as a capital performance' (*FCF* 151). In Bristol, he is at the centre of the fashionable society, devising parties and regulating diversions. He is an oracle in matters of punctilio. On the other hand, Ferdinand's reputation, like Roderick's (or Smollett's) is volatile. His association with a fraud committed by his confederate, Ratchkali, opens him to suspicion, and at the same time, he is recognized by the English card-sharpers who cheated him of his money (*FCF* 172–3). Once again, he finds himself excluded from society. Ferdinand's story is also Smollett's predicament.

Smollett's next response to the criticism of *Peregrine Pickle* was the abridged and revised second edition of the novel in 1758. In this edition, Smollett refined the language of the original and excised passages and episodes which had been deemed offensive or simply dull. The 'practical satire' at the expense of Peregrine's German schoolmaster Keypstick was cut, as was the matter of the perforated chamber pot. The tutor Jolter's assignation with a chambermaid was omitted. So, too, was the forming, whilst at Winchester, of a breakaway faction with Peregrine at its head. In the first edition Peregrine's friend Godfrey Gauntlet has an assignation with a married woman, and she is subsequently humiliated by Godfrey and Peregrine. These events were cut from the second edition. Where Peregrine enjoys 'the luscious fruits of his conquest' (*PP* 202) of Mrs. Hornbeck in the first edition, in the second his 'guilty passion was not gratified'.[36] Other excisions involved Pallet's misadventures whilst dressed as a woman, the doctor's bedwetting, the draper's wife's 'leathern convenience', and Peregrine's intrigue with a nun. The following passage was cut lest, we may assume, it offend female readers:

> And let the circumstances of this contention warn the reader, against all disputes with female politicians; unless he is desirous of incuring their animosity and implacable resentment; for, in matters of state, they are all, to a woman, enthusiasts, who believe that all those who differ from them in opinion, are in a state of reprobation; and far from laying any stress upon probability, in the articles of their faith, like believers of another class, disdainfully reject the evidence of reason, and trust to the revelation of their own fancy. (*PP* 292)

Lady Vane's 'Memoirs' underwent certain revisions which tended to place her in a more creditable light – whether by her own hand or Smollett's is not clear. The attack on Garrick was changed into a short compliment, and the satire at the expense of Lyttleton and Fielding was also omitted.

One reason for the revision of *Peregrine Pickle* is clear. At last, in 1757, Smollett finally gained access to the theatre. David Garrick, no less, had agreed to stage Smollett's patriotic farce, *The Reprisal*, and in a letter of January of that year, Smollett wrote to Garrick of 'former animosities, which, on my part, are forgotten and self-condemned' (*Letters* 53). A reconciliation had evidently taken place, and

---

[36] Clifford (ed.), *Peregrine Pickle*, 787n.

Smollett made his earlier work inoffensive to a man who had lately become his benefactor. It could be argued that the revision of the work was simply pragmatic, making *Peregrine Pickle* more saleable in the current climate of critical opinion. As a journalist, living by the pen, Smollett always seems to have made all of his copy work as hard as it possibly could. Still, the concessions to criticism of the novel are fairly comprehensive, and particularly striking if satire, both personal and 'practical', granted Smollett a position of power to which he could not otherwise lay claim. Perhaps, then, Smollett had found another position which granted him authority and independence. Concerned with *Ferdinand, Count Fathom* rather than the revisions of *Peregrine Pickle*, Frank Donoghue contends that 'almost immediately after founding the *Critical* in 1756, Smollett ceased to think of himself as primarily an author and began to think of himself as the editor of a major Review'.[37] In fact, the sharp distinction Donoghue makes between Smollett as author and as reviewer is misleading. As James Basker's study of Smollett as critic makes clear, Smollett never lost sight of the fact that a journal which was going to succeed in the marketplace had to entertain, however serious its didactic intentions.[38] He had to please a broad and diverse reading public, especially those readers who might never open the pages of a learned journal. He modelled the *Critical* on the already successful *Monthly Review*, making extensive use of quoted material – but in Smollett's hands, quotation tended to serve an analytic and evaluative purpose. The *Critical Review*, then, was really an extension of a project upon which Smollett had embarked as soon as he made his fiction serve the cause of moral standards, albeit for partly personal reasons.

Perhaps by the late 1750s, the range of the literary activities in which Smollett was involved might have allowed him to feel that he had, as a writer, achieved that moral and indeed financial independence which characterized the true gentleman: the revision of an earlier piece of work might then have been less injurious to his sense of personal integrity. He had translated from the French a collection of scientific essays, which were published anonymously and entitled *Select Essays on Commerce, Agriculture, Mines, Fisheries, and other Useful Subjects* in February 1754. In the winter of 1753–1754, he was working on the preparation for the press of a book of travels by Alexander Drummond and the second volume of Dr. William Smellie's *A Treatise on the Theory and Practice of Midwifery* as well as his own 'History of the German Empire', which appeared later in the *Universal History* (1759–1765), and a translation of *Don Quixote* which was published in 1755. In March 1756 the first number of the *Critical Review* appeared. In April 1756 *A Compendium of Authentic and Entertaining Voyages* was also published in seven volumes, edited by Smollett. The *Complete History of England*, on which he had been working since 1755, was published in four quarto volumes in the period 1757–1758.

[37]   Frank Donoghue, *The Fame Machine. Book Reviewing and Eighteenth-Century Literary Careers* (Palo Alto: Stanford University Press, 1996), 125.

[38]   James Basker, *Tobias Smollett, Critic and Journalist* (Newark, University of Delaware Press, 1988).

The revised version appeared in 1758 in six-penny weekly numbers, and Smollett told John Moore: 'You will not be sorry to hear that the weekly Sale of the History has increased to above Ten thousand' (*Letters* 73). Sales of the *History* and its *Continuation* (1760–1765), Knapp maintains, freed Smollett from any acute financial difficulties: he may have realized £2000.[39] Smollett himself wrote to John Moore in January 1758 that he had 'for some time done very little in the Critical Review' (*Letters* 65) as he had been finishing his *History*.

The publication of *The Life and Adventures of Sir Launcelot Greaves* (1760–1761) in the *British Magazine* (also founded by Smollett) suggests that Smollett's sense of himself as, on the one hand, a gentleman who fulfilled his role by upholding moral standards, and, on the other, as a professional gentleman who worked for a living, were beginning to cohere. As James Basker observes, the decision to publish the novel in serial form made sound commercial sense.[40] Smollett had written *Roderick Random* in eight months in 1747–1748 by devoting himself exclusively to that task, but by 1759–1760 his numerous other commitments made it impossible to take such a single-minded approach to the composition of a novel. By serializing the work, he could realize an income from *Launcelot Greaves* as he wrote it. He could gauge the public's response before committing himself to a protracted piece of writing. Less text was required, and Smollett was even able to send his instalments by post whilst on a journey to Scotland. Publication in a magazine meant access to a wider readership, and initial printing costs were avoided. It is telling, then, that the narrative itself is shared by the eponymous hero, a quixotic baronet who is on a quest to right wrongs and expose corruption, and a group of professional men: Mr. Fillet, a surgeon and midwife; Captain Crowe, a naval officer; and Thomas Clarke, an attorney.

In the second installment, Launcelot describes his aims:

> I do purpose … to act as a coadjutor to the law, and even to remedy evils which the law cannot reach; to detect fraud and treason, abase insolence, mortify pride, discourage slander, disgrace immodesty, and stigmatize ingratitude.[41]

As it turns out, though, he is far from self-sufficient or completely effectual: he needs professional assistance, and it is the group of professional gentlemen who appear first, in the first instalment. Finding himself unjustly imprisoned and his servant Crabshaw tied in the stocks, Launcelot is about to use force to break out, but the attorney Tom Clarke offers a plan whereby he can gain revenge on Justice Gobble without a breach of the peace. Again, when he is moved to assist a woman who has been driven into bankruptcy, imprisonment and madness by Gobble's machinations, he first consults with Clarke about the steps he should take (*SLG* 91). Clarke even controls the narrative presentation of Greaves's character: it is he who

---

[39]   Knapp, 192.
[40]   Basker, 206–8.
[41]   Tobias Smollett, *The Life and Adventures of Sir Launcelot Greaves*, ed. David Evans (London: Oxford University Press, 1973), 14.

relates the story of the baronet's earlier life. When Greaves appears before Justice Gobble, Fillet and another lawyer, Mr. Fenton, offer to provide bail for him, and Clarke advises the judge on the letter and interpretation of the law. Sir Launcelot admonishes Gobble, but Fenton completes his 'terror and mortification' by assuring him that the actions of the knight will be 'reinforced with divers prosecutions for corrupt practices' (*SLG* 99). Fillet even uses his medical skills to conjure up the appearance of a ghost, and Gobble duly falls insensible on the floor. When Sir Launcelot is imprisoned for a second time, now in a madhouse, it is Clarke who discovers his whereabouts by placing an advertisement in a daily newspaper. In the retrospective tale, Launcelot's rank and wealth allow him to exercise the prerogatives of the country gentleman: he is able to donate a living to an indigent cleric and force a rich farmer's son to marry the cottager's daughter he has debauched. He acts as a 'general redresser of grievances', usually by means of lawsuits. However, when the narrative moves to the present, his power exists primarily in the form of rhetoric. By 1761, the dream of independence, status and a social role that is Sir Launcelot Greaves had less to do with the by now anachronistic ideal of the country gentleman than it had with a conception of the role of the writer: hence the importance of Launcelot's use of language. The fact that Smollett used *Don Quixote* as his model suggests that he himself recognized the anachronism. It is the professional gentlemen, rather, who cohere around the ethic Greaves proposes.

Yet the fact remains that at the same time Smollett ceased to satirize his former targets, among whom were the Whigs Lyttleton and Fielding, he also adopted more of the aesthetic of 'politeness', an aesthetic which was Whig in nature, and one which aimed at social cohesion by virtue of consensus rather than hierarchy. It was not that he had dropped the practice of personal satire altogether: far from it. The character of Ferret in *Sir Launcelot Greaves* was a portrait of pamphleteer John Shebbeare. Nor did Smollett entirely desist from his characteristic physicality: Launcelot's squire, Timothy Crabshaw, receives some punishing beatings. Yet there are very definite concessions to a feminized taste. The full title of Smollett's periodical – the *British Magazine, or Monthly Repository for Gentleman and Ladies* – made explicit the consciousness of a female readership, and Sir Launcelot himself is a feminized man, very much in the Grandisonian mode. His morals are exemplary: there is no question of intrigues or sexual misadventures. Although he wears armour and carries a lance, he generally does not engage in physical combat. In the retrospective tale, he proves to be a capable swordsman, but when the narrative moves to the present, we often see him refraining from force, as when Ferret is reduced to 'a temporary privation of all his faculties' (*SLG* 13) by the power of words alone. In Chapter 18, he declines a challenge to a duel by Squire Sycamore, and he is more likely to serve his antagonists with a writ than engage them in combat, especially in the latter half of the work. The romantic plot involving Launcelot and Aurelia Darnel and his effusions about her occupy a much greater proportion of the work than comparable plots in *Roderick Random* or *Peregrine Pickle*. Aurelia herself is a conventional and exemplary heroine, and this time there are no Lady Vanes or Miss Williamses to complicate the picture.

In fact, with a quixotic hero, a group of characters who diverge and meet again, subdued violence, inconclusive arguments, and the thwarted romance plot, *Sir Launcelot Greaves* in many ways resembles *Joseph Andrews*. There is even a dropped pocketbook which gives Sir Launcelot a reason to pursue the heroine, after the manner of *Tom Jones*, and a providential meeting at an inn at the end of Chapter 14. 'Was it not Providence that sent me hither, to guard and protect the injured Aurelia?' Launcelot asks (*SLG* 124). In *Roderick Random* the hero feels himself to be 'no ways comprehended within the scheme or protection of Providence' (*RR* 25–6): the hero of *Sir Launcelot Greaves* sees himself as an agent of it. The contrast is striking. *Sir Launcelot Greaves* is the most pious of all Smollett's fictional works.

It is also a work which pays much greater attention to the issue of the reader's response. This was a feature of Smollett's fictional writing which received greater attention from *Ferdinand Count Fathom* onwards. At the same time that Smollett began to address this issue, he also began to develop his ideas of what a novel might actually be and do. In the preface to *Ferdinand Count Fathom*, he defined a novel as 'a large diffused picture, comprehending the characters of life, disposed in different groups, for the purposes of a uniform plan'. As John Valdimir Price has argued, Smollett took particular pains in *Sir Launcelot Greaves* to manage, or cultivate, a relationship with the reader, and even those chapter headings which do not directly address the reader reflect a sense, on Smollett's part, of ways in which the material might be perceived.[42] It could be argued, of course, that the fact that *Sir Launcelot Greaves* was serialized over a two-year period called for special consideration to be paid to the reader: Smollett often refers ironically to the reader's possible expectations or impatience. Yet this new attention to the reader's response also marks a change in Smollett's rhetoric. Smollett expected that the hero's gentlemanly status, in *Roderick Random*, would generate sympathy on his behalf, but he left his readers to judge of moral matters for themselves in his first novel and in *Peregrine Pickle*. In a letter to Alexander Carlyle (himself a Presbyterian minister), Smollett spoke of his 'Antipathy to Sermons' (*Letters* 4), and in *Peregrine Pickle*, he offered a reflection on the practice of moralising which was surely aimed at Fielding:

> I might here, in imitation of some celebrated writers, furnish out a page or two with the reflections he made upon the instability of human affairs, the treachery of the world, and the temerity of youth; and endeavour to decoy the reader into a smile by some quaint observation of my own touching the sagacious moralizer: but, besides that I look upon this practice as an impertinent anticipation of the peruser's thoughts, I have too much matter upon my hands to give the reader the least reason to believe that I am driven to such paultry shifts, in order to eke out the volume. (*PP* 682–3)

---

[42]   John Valdimir Price, 'Smollett and the Reader in *Sir Launcelot Greaves*', in *Smollett: Author of the First Distinction*, ed. Alan Bold (London: Vision and Barnes and Noble, 1982), 193–208.

Sir Launcelot Greaves is not *Pamela* or *Clarissa*, but it does concern itself rather more with the business of persuasion than Smollett's earlier works – hence the emphasis on language and rhetoric. As Price observes: 'To a certain extent, comedy has given way to morality, sometimes too much so'.[43] In 1747 Smollett mocked his own aversion to sermons as 'a vulgar prejudice' (*Letters* 4), but by 1761 he had modified this along with many of his other 'vulgarities'. On the title page of early editions of *The Expedition of Humphry Clinker* (1771) indeed, were lines taken from Horace's *Sermones*, lines which pointed to a rhetorical purpose: – 'Quorsum haec tam putida tendunt, / Furcifer? ad te, inquam [To what object are these disagreeable facts directed, you rogue? To you, I said]'.[44] The publication of the letters which comprise the novel are vindicated on the first page of *Humphry Clinker* as tending 'to the information and edification of mankind' (*HC* 1), by a cleric who seems, by his language, to be of the most precise and proper character.

In the 10 years which elapsed between the publication of *Sir Launcelot Greaves* and *Humphry Clinker*, Smollett's fortunes had undergone reversals. By 1762 his health was deteriorating, but he was nevertheless persuaded to write the *Briton*, a sheet defending the Bute administration, which appeared once a week for some 10 months.[45] As a result, Smollett became embroiled in bitter political controversies involving Bute and John Wilkes and found himself the target of vituperative anti-Scottish writing. In April 1763 the Smolletts' only child died at the age of 15, and in June 1763 Smollett left for France. In the epistolary *Travels through France and Italy* (1766), Smollett represented himself, on leaving England, as 'traduced by malice, persecuted by faction, [and] abandoned by false patrons', and his bitterness about politics was aired again in the anonymous and scatological *The History and Adventures of an Atom* (1769).[46] Historical writing and editorial work continued. Between 1760 and 1765, he worked on the five-volume *Continuation of the Complete History of England* and acted as joint editor of the *Works of Voltaire*. In 1768 the eight-volume *The Present State of All Nations* was completed, although, as Louis Martz argues, it is unlikely that all of it was written by Smollett himself.[47] It was in many ways a work of compilation. In *Humphry Clinker*, then, came together Smollett's experience of writing in the epistolary form, his experience of history and travel writing, an expression of political disillusionment in the shape of the satire at the expense of politicians Cumberland and Newcastle, a desire to inform an ignorant English readership about Scotland, a wish to vindicate his own native country, a much more developed sense of a relationship with readers, and all of these in a form which had proved to be successful in reaching an audience.

---

[43]   Price, 206.

[44]   Tobias Smollett, *The Expedition of Humphry Clinker*, ed. Lewis M. Knapp (London: Oxford University Press, 1966), 355n. Translation is from this edition.

[45]   Knapp, *Tobias Smollett*, 245.

[46]   Tobias Smollett, *Travels Through France and Italy*, ed. Frank Felsenstein (Oxford: Oxford University Press, 1979), 2.

[47]   Louis Martz, *The Later Career of Tobias Smollett* (New Haven: Yale University Press, 1942), 106.

Travel writing was enjoying a particular vogue, as the bookseller Henry Davis does not fail to point out to Jonathan Dustwich, and epistolary fiction too seems to have been prevalent in the early 1770s.[48] Martz also suggests that Smollett may have wished to satirize England and praise Scotland so as to reconcile himself with his own countrymen who were offended by the favourable account of England offered in *Present State*.[49] Fallen women like Miss Williams and Lady Vane do not appear in *Ferdinand, Count Fathom* and *Sir Launcelot Greaves* because a polite code of manners would not allow them to be represented sympathetically. They do not appear in *Humphry Clinker* because Smollett no longer identified with their lack of agency.

Smollett has his Welsh and English correspondents, Matthew Bramble and Jery Melford, make the case for Scotland, in part by representing it as a location where standards once held in common still prevail. The ancient virtue of hospitality survives in Scotland, and even the Scottish accent preserves classical values: 'It is a sort of Doric dialect, which gives an idea of amiable simplicity' (*HC* 221). When different ranks mingle, at the ball after the Leith races, Jery sees them 'as the slaves and their masters were in the time of the Saturnalia in ancient Rome' (*HC* 227). Dr. John Gordon, a Glasgow merchant, is 'a patriot of a truly Roman spirit' (*HC* 246). As Lismahago explains, the Scots have not, unlike the English, lost the sense of the true meaning of the word *gentle*: it means '*noble, high-minded*' (*HC* 200). Where there is actual poverty, it can be characterized as an ancient and healthful virtue:

> Our landlord's housekeeping is ... rough and hospitable, and savours much of the simplicity of ancient times. At night, half a dozen occasional beds are ranged on each side along to wall. These are made of fresh heath, pulled up by the roots, and disposed in such a manner as to make a very agreeable couch, where they lie, without any other covering than the plaid—My uncle and I were indulged with separate chambers and down beds which we begged to exchange for a layer of heath. (*HC* 242)

In Edinburgh Matthew Bramble finds that he can 'eat like a farmer, sleep from mid-night till eight in the morning without interruption, and enjoy a constant tide of spirits, equally distant from inanition and excess' (*HC* 219): Scotland is the location, then, of the golden mean. Patriarchy survives here. Campbell, a Highland laird, appears at an open window to be greeted by the prostration of his 'vassals and dependents', who 'worship his first appearance' (*HC* 242). And Loch Lomond is the 'Arcadia of Scotland' (*HC* 248). One reader, at least, got the point. John Gray wrote to Smollett: 'I have read the *Adventures of Humphry Clinker* with great delight, and think it calculated to give a very great run, and to add to the

---

48 Paul-Gabriel Boucé gives a brief account of the currency of travel writing in the 1760s and notes that 27 epistolary novels were published in 1771 alone. See *The Novels of Tobias Smollett*, trans. Antonia White (London: Longman, 1976), 191–3.

49 Martz, 130.

reputation of the author, who has, by the magic of his pen, turned the banks of Loch Lomond into classic ground'.[50]

Smollett is careful to inform the English reader that Scotland is in some ways more like England than he or she might have imagined. Writing in the month of August, Jery Melford comments on the availability of apricots, peaches, nectarines and other soft fruits, a circumstance which should be less surprising were the reader conscious of 'how little difference there is, in fact, betwixt this climate and that of London' (*HC* 223). English points of reference are often used. All the correspondents usually refer to 'South Britain' and 'North Britain' rather than England and Scotland. The case for the inclusion of Scotland within an expanded sense of Britain is also suggested in Lismahago's assertion that 'what we generally called the Scottish dialect was, in fact, true genuine old English' (*HC* 199).

The Lowland Scots are, it seems, likely to be derived from the same stock as the English. In part, Smollett might hope to secure the sympathy of English readers by catering to their anti-Scottish and pro-English prejudices. Micklewhimmen, the first of the Scottish characters whom the party encounter, is revealed to be a hypocrite (he disguises his claret as '*stomachic tincture*') who is concerned only for his own safety when there is a fire at an inn in Yorkshire. Lismahago, a more complex case, is characterized by Jery at one point as 'a self-conceited pedant, aukward, rude, and disputacious' (*HC* 190). On the other hand, the request by the actor James Quin (with whom Smollett was now also reconciled) that Jery take a drink in Edinburgh with his friend Robert Cullen, a Scottish lawyer, provides what we might now call a celebrity endorsement. Flattery could also be persuasive. When Jery and Bramble hear of the veteran Lismahago's sufferings at the hands of the American Indians, Jery remarks: 'There is no hold by which an Englishman is sooner taken than that of compassion' (*HC* 189), a sentiment with which it is difficult to imagine Smollett himself concurred.

The Scottish reader, though, might be pleased by the fact that what seems to be criticism of Scotland often turns out be oblique praise. The unexpected prosperity of Scotland – unexpected to the English reader, that is – is exemplified in Matthew Bramble's 'censure':

> I must observe, that their weak side seems to be vanity. – I am afraid that even their hospitality is not quite free of ostentation. – I think I have discovered among them uncommon pains taken to display their fine linen, of which, indeed, they have great plenty, their furniture, plate, house-keeping, and variety of wines, in which article, it must be owned, they are profuse, if not prodigal. (*HC* 234)

The juxtaposition of praise and criticism is possibly the most frequent ploy, with Bramble's reservations, in the following, taking little away from another vindication of Scottish prosperity:

---

[50]   Kelly, 212.

> In the neighbourhood of Haddington, there is a gentleman's house, in the building of which, and the improvements about it, he is said to have expended forty thousand pounds: but I cannot say I was much pleased with either the architecture or the situation; though it has in front a pastoral stream, the banks of which are laid out in a very agreeable manner. (*HC* 216)

If Edinburgh can be convicted of mingling the good with the bad, then so too can London:

> Considering [Canongate's] fine pavement, its width, and the lofty houses on each side, this would be undoubtedly one of the noblest streets in Europe, if an ugly mass of mean buildings, called the Lucken-Booths, had not thrust itself, by what accident I know not, into the middle of the way, like Middle-Row in Holborn. (*HC* 217)

What starts as criticism can lead into the apparently casual inclusion of more praiseworthy features of the metropolitan landscape:

> In all parts of the world, we see the force of habit prevailing over all the dictates of convenience and sagacity—All the people of business at Edinburgh, and even the genteel company, may be seen standing in crowds every day, from one to two in the afternoon, in the open street, at a place where formerly stood a market-cross, which (by the bye) was a curious piece of Gothic architecture, still to be seen in lord Sommerville's garden in this neighbourhood—I say, the people stand in the open street from the force of custom, rather than move a few yards to an Exchange that stands empty on one side, or to the Parliament-close on the other, which is a noble square, adorned with a fine equestrian statue of king Charles II. (*HC* 218)

Smollett thus underlines the presence in Edinburgh of commerce and gentility as well as loyalty to the British monarch.

Smollett was concerned, also, to counter the prejudices of the English against manners and customs with which they were unfamiliar or against which they might have an almost automatic bias. '[T]heir looks, their language, and their customs, are so different from ours', writes Jery from Edinburgh, 'that I can hardly believe myself in Great-Britain' (*HC* 214). The hundred pages or so of *Humphry Clinker* which deal with the journey through Scotland serve to make these customs familiar: everything from the 'unconscionable' height of the houses in Edinburgh to the clan system. If the lean and shabby Scottish peasants should come off worst in a comparison with their English counterparts, then Matthew Bramble assures Jery that they could compete well with the peasants of France, Italy and Savoy, not to mention those of Wales, and, lastly, Ireland. In Matthew Bramble's letter of August 8th, we have some account of the distinctive practices of Scottish law and the method of teaching medicine in the University of Edinburgh. Discovering that the peasants near Alloa scatter large stones across the fields they are cultivating, Bramble finds that there may be viable reasons for this practice. Four weeks into his journey through Scotland, Jery Melford finds himself 'insensibly sucked into the channel of their manners and customs' (*HC* 221). The letters of Bramble and Jery Melford invite sympathy for difference.

On the face of it, the epistolary form of *Humphry Clinker*, with five correspondents, and no single authoritative voice also exemplifies the tolerance of differing views. The representation of Win Jenkins's unique way with language could itself suggest a willingness to countenance individuality. There is frequent acceptance, within the letters themselves, of the principle of relativism. Lydia writes to her friend Miss Willis: 'People of experience and infirmity, my dear Letty, see with very different eyes from those such as you and I make use of' (*HC* 93). Opinions may change. Jery gives Matthew Bramble the benefit of the doubt in the matter of his temperament: 'Indeed his being tortured by the gout may have soured his temper, and, perhaps, I may like him better on further acquaintance' (*HC* 8). Bramble himself, writing to Dr. Lewis, acknowledges that his own views have no absolute authority:

> You must know, I find nothing but disappointment at Bath; which is so altered, that I can scarce believe it is the same place that I frequented about thirty years ago. Methinks I hear you say, 'Altered it is, without all doubt; but then it is altered for the better; a truth which, perhaps, you would own without hesitation, if you yourself was not altered for the worse.' The reflection may, for aught I know, be just. (*HC* 34)

For Bramble, the mingling of ranks in Bath and London and the rapid growth of towns and consumption in general are deplorable. Jery, on the other hand, finds that: '[T]his chaos is to me a source of infinite amusement' (*HC* 49). For Bramble, those partaking of the amusements at Ranelagh are like 'blind asses in an olive-mill' (*HC* 89), while for Lydia, Ranelagh is a place of enchantment. Her evident naïvete makes her no less reliable a witness than the infirm Bramble or the rather self-satisfied Jery.

In the last quarter of the century, according to Neil McKendrick, a consumer boom reached 'revolutionary proportions', and an uneasy response to luxury was articulated in a number of novels, of which *Humphry Clinker* is one.[51] Among the works of this type are Charles Johnstone's *Chrysal, or the Adventures of a Guinea* (1760–1765); Oliver Goldsmith's *The Vicar of Wakefield* (1766); Henry Brooke's *The Fool of Quality* (1765–1770); Henry Mackenzie's *The Man of Feeling* (1771), *The Man of the World* (1773) and *Julia de Roubigné* (1779); Richard Graves's *The Spiritual Quixote* (1773); Thomas Day's *Sandford and Merton* (1783–1789); and William Beckford's *Vathek* (1786). It is Matthew Bramble who articulates a critique of this development, and Smollett is careful to engage the reader's sympathy for him from the very beginning. In his first letter, dated 2 April, we find Bramble concerned with the efficient and benevolent management of his estate but refusing

---

[51]   Neil McKendrick, 'Introduction, The Birth of a Consumer Society.' *The Commercialization of Eighteenth-Century England*, by Neil McKendrick, John Brewer and J.H. Plumb (London: Europa, 1982), 9.

to engage in litigation for his own profit. A widow is to be given an Alderney cow and 40 shillings to clothe her children. This contrasts with Tabitha Bramble's concern, in the her letter of the same date, with her 'rose collard neglejay' and her desire to know what price the Alderney calf fetched at market. Praise for Bramble comes indirectly and via an unbiased source. Jery Melford, who finds his uncle so unpleasant that he would rather resign his claim to the Bramble estate than keep him company, reports that Matthew Bramble's servants and neighbours 'are fond of him, even to a degree of enthusiasm, the reason of which I cannot as yet understand' (*HC* 8, 9). Lydia Melford also relates how her uncle, unlike Tabitha Bramble, was moved by her 'tears and distress' (*HC* 10). Matthew Bramble begins his splenetic account of England in his second letter to Dr. Lewis – the same letter in which we hear Bramble's irritable account of his family, but also how he prevented a duel between Jery and Wilson, Lydia's suitor, and feared for the death of Lydia. By 18 April, Jery Melford has begun to change his mind about his uncle: 'I think his peevishness arises partly from bodily pain' (*HC* 17). By 24 April: 'Mr. Bramble's character, which seems to interest you greatly, opens and improves upon me every day' (*HC* 28). Sometimes Jery Melford's letters simply contain a report of his uncle's encounters. Even when he is not writing, Bramble's views and actions dominate the book, and Jery's view of him becomes affectionate from a very early stage. Bramble presents a view of the breakdown of social order in Bath:

> Every upstart of fortune, harnessed in the trappings of the mode, presents himself at Bath, as in the very focus of observation—Clerks and factors from the East Indies, loaded with the spoil of plundered provinces; planters, negro-drivers, and hucksters, from our American plantations, enriched they know not how; agents, commissaries, and contractors, who have fattened, in two successive wars, on the blood of the nation; usurers, brokers, and jobbers of every kind; men of low birth and no breeding, have found themselves suddenly translated into a state of affluence, unknown to former ages; and no wonder that their brains should be intoxicated with pride, vanity, and presumption. Knowing no other criterion of greatness, but the ostentation of wealth, they discharge their affluence without taste or conduct, through every channel of the most absurd extravagance; and all of them hurry to Bath, because here, without any further qualification, they can mingle with the princes and nobles of the land. (*HC* 36–7)

If the reader should find this view, and others like it, extreme, it comes from a man who in a postscript to the same letter is concerned, once again, with charitable acts, and the welfare of his servants and even an old horse. Jery's account of the entertainments at Bath might be said to reinforce rather than undermine his uncle's view. He is every bit as aware as Bramble of disparity of rank:

> I was extremely diverted, last ball-night, to see the Master of the Ceremonies leading, with great solemnity, to the upper end of the room, an antiquated Abigail, dressed in her lady's cast-clothes; whom he (I suppose) mistook for some countess just arrived at Bath. The ball was opened by a Scotch lord, with a mulatto heiress from St. Christopher's; and the gay colonel Tinsel danced all the evening with

the daughter of an eminent tinman from the borough of Southwark—Yesterday morning, at the Pump-room, I saw a broken-winded Wapping landlady squeeze through a circle of peers, to salute her brandy-merchant, who stood by the window, prop'd upon crutches; and a paralytic attorney of Shoe-lane, in shuffling up to the bar, kicked the shins of the chancellor of England. (*HC* 49)

The accounts of the breakdown of order are almost interchangeable. Jery does not deny that there *is* chaos, and his detached amusement could strike the reader as merely shallow. He subsequently gives an account of another breakdown of order and decorum in Bath, in the shape of the ladies' scramble for sweetmeats and nosegays, which, as he concedes, 'seems to confirm the view of those two cynic philosphers' (that is, Quin and Bramble) (*HC* 51). Bramble charges Paunceford with ingratitude to his patron, Serle, and the letter is written by Jery. The satire at the expense of Newcastle and Cumberland comes via Jery's letter of 5 June. It could be said, then, that the seeming tolerance of diversity is actually rather superficial and that Jery subscribes to Bramble's values, whose voice actually dominates the novel.

The Methodist preacher Humphry Clinker represents the disinterest of which Smollett approved because he is not motivated by money, refusing the financial reward Bramble offers him for saving his life. Clinker unceremoniously dumps Winifred Jenkins, whom he has just dragged from the stream, when he finds that Bramble's life is in danger: he is on the side of patriarchy, hierarchy and subordination. Ultimately he is discovered to be Bramble's illegitimate son. Dissent, then, might be tolerated if it posed no threat to order. As Aileen Douglas argues, the space given to challenges by women is minimal.[52] Tabitha is the ageing spinster, desperate for a man, straight out of Restoration comedy. Lydia is an entirely conventional picture of a young woman who is always suitably grateful to her uncle. Although her letters may qualify Bramble's, they are few in number, and the letters of Tabitha and Lydia actually confirm the preoccupation of the female mind with matters of romance. Lydia's purchase of souvenirs from Bath also tends to confirm her uncle's opinion of the corrupting effects of luxury: 'I send you two dozen of Bath rings. I don't know how you will approve of the mottoes; some of them are not much to my own liking; but I was obliged to take such as I could find ready manufactured' (*HC* 58). When Matthew Bramble and Jery Melford leave for the West Highlands, the women remain behind at Cameron. The connection between excessive female influence, luxury and national decline is made explicit later in the novel when the party returns to England. Bramble discovers that his old friend Baynard has been ruined (and therefore robbed of his independence) by his wife's ostentatious consumption. The same pattern is repeated by Baynard's neighbours, from the wife of Sir Charles Chickwell, who is vying for grandeur with a peeress, to the wives of Mr. Milksan and Mr. Sowerby, and it only begins to be reversed with Mrs. Baynard's fortuitous death. The praise of female novelists

---

[52]	Aileen Douglas, *Uneasy Sensations. Smollett and the Body* (Chicago: University of Chicago Press, 1995), 165–6.

in Jery Melford's letter is surely undermined by its juxtaposition with the lot of a male author, entertained at the home of Dr. S——, who hopes his tragedy will bring him fame and money:

> as for little Tim Cropdale, the most facetious member of the whole society, he had happily wound up the catastrophe of a virgin tragedy, from the exhibition of which he promised himself a large fund of profit and reputation. Tim had made shift to live many years by writing novels, at the rate of five pounds a volume; but that branch of business is now engrossed by female authors, who publish merely for the propagation of virtue, with so much ease and spirit, and delicacy, and knowledge of the human heart, and all in the serene tranquillity of high life, that the reader is not only enchanted by their genius, but reformed by their morality. (*HC* 127–8)

Criticism of women, in the new dispensation, had to be buried.

Smollett's fundamental allegiance, always, was to an older idea of social order as figured in the representations of Baynard and Dennison. Towards the end of the novel, Bramble orders that roots, leaves and pebbles be cleared so that a stream which had been reduced to a rivulet in Baynard's estate may be allowed to run in its old channel: the old order can be restored. Dennison, writes Bramble, has 'really attained that pitch of rural felicity, at which I have been aspiring these twenty years in vain' (*HC* 320). Dennison (like Smollett's father) is a younger son who marries for love and has to exist for some years in relative poverty. However, with the death of his older brother, he inherits the family estate and takes up a life in the country of exemplary moderation, reviving the neglected house, garden and lands. Lydia's suitor, Wilson, turns out, in true romance style, to be a gentleman by birth and Dennison's son. Jery finds the society at Dennison's to be 'enchanting', with even Tabitha pacified and Lismahago less severe. For once, Bramble has no desire to move on. However, while *Humphry Clinker* is certainly strongly informed by Smollett's conservative instincts, it is, in the end, tolerant of difference. The novel concludes with the party dividing. Bramble, Tabitha, Lismahago, Baynard, Humphry Clinker (now Matthew Loyd) and Win Jenkins (now Winifred Loyd) return to Wales, while Jery, Lydia and young Dennison go to Bath. Smollett might view the growth of consumption and the breakdown of traditional standards with disquiet, but by 1771 he was prepared to live on 'dissent terms of civility' (to borrow Win Jenkins's language) with those who felt otherwise (*HC* 353). For that view, he found the novel an appropriate form of expression.

From the beginning, Smollett's political values belonged to a cause that was in decline: that is, Toryism as defined by opposition to Walpole. Walpole left office in 1742 and died in 1745. Jacobitism ceased to be an option for Tories with the crushing of the '45 Rebellion at Culloden, an event commemorated in Smollett's own poem of 1746, 'The Tears of Scotland'. Bolingbroke, chief architect of country ideology, died in 1751. In the 1750s, Tories in Parliament could find little to oppose in the policies of the Pelham administration.[53] By 1760, when George III succeeded to the throne, there was little to distinguish Tories from 'Old Whigs' who were themselves independent country gentlemen. Old fault lines of party that dated back to the Exclusion Crisis of 1679–1681 were disintegrating, a disintegration that may well be reflected in the many images of disruption in Smollett's fiction. Smollett himself subscribed to a restricted and increasingly outdated definition of a gentleman. While his contemporaries might not consider trade and gentility mutually exclusive, Smollett, in *The Present State of All Nations* (1768), placed those who got their fortune by trade fourth in line behind the nobility, gentlemen (knights and esquires) and yeomen (freeholders and copyholders). Ownership of land and inherited rank, rather than wealth, distinguished the gentleman. Such conservatism could only find an uneasy home in the democratising milieu of a novel. Nevertheless, Smollett showed that it was possible to use fiction to oppose the dominant ideology. Opposition of a more radical nature is to be found in fiction written by women in the mid-eighteenth century. These novels, and their critique of self-interest and duty, are the subject of the next chapter.

---

[53]   See Geoffrey Holmes and Daniel Szechi, *The Age of Oligarchy, Pre-Industrial Britain 1722–83* (London: Longman, 1993), 268.

Chapter 3
Rewriting Ethics:
David Simple, *The Female Quixote*, and *Memoirs of Miss Sidney Bidulph*

In their fiction of the 1740s, Samuel Richardson and Henry Fielding worked to support the Latitudinarian ethos, in which self-interest was seen as compatible with virtue. Pamela's economic and social self-interest would be served by preserving her chastity. Fielding's *Shamela* questioned that identification, but by the time of writing *Joseph Andrews* the author had resolved the issue in another way. Masculine self-interest, in the form of Joseph Andrews's sexual desire, could be satisfied by marriage to the virtuous woman, Fanny. Clarissa only seems to be an anomaly here. From a purely abstract point of view, Clarissa's death is irrelevant. She gains a reward in heaven for her resistance to Lovelace, and Richardson is clear, at least, that she deserves to be so rewarded. Tom Jones's pursuit of Sophia is a metaphor for the pursuit of wisdom and so aligns sexual desire with a Platonic ideal – and this quest involves having sex with the wrong women so as to realize Sophia's true worth. The problem for women was that all these resolutions of the possible conflict between self-interest and virtue positioned them as the preservers of transcendent values, transcendence here being conceived of as feminine asexuality, duty and self-denial.

The novels to be considered in this chapter – Sarah Fielding's *The Adventures of David Simple* (1744); Charlotte Lennox's *The Female Quixote, or, The Adventures of Arabella* (1752); and Frances Sheridan's *Memoirs of Miss Sidney Bidulph* (1761) – can be, and have been, seen as representative of the kinds of codes and restrictions that inhibited women's fiction after 1740.[1] The austerity of *David Simple*, for example, forms a striking contrast with the amatory fiction of Delarivière Manley and Eliza Haywood. The fact that Arabella, heroine of *The Female Quixote*, ends the novel not only 'cured' of her belief in salon romances, but also married and submissive, has been read as indicating the imperative to reject the 'authentic' female self-expression of the romance.[2] *Memoirs of Miss Sidney Bidulph* places

---

[1]   Examples of this approach are Mary Poovey, *The Proper Lady and the Woman Writer, Ideology as Style in the Works of Mary Wollstonecraft, Mary Shelley and Jane Austen* (Chicago: University of Chicago Press, 1984); Jane Spencer, *The Rise of the Woman Novelist. From Aphra Behn to Jane Austen* (Oxford: Basil Blackwell, 1986); Janet Todd, *The Sign of Angellica. Women, Writing and Fiction 1660–1800* (London: Virago, 1989); and Patricia Meyer Spacks, *Desire and Truth. Functions of Plot in Eighteenth-Century English Novels* (Chicago: University of Chicago Press, 1994).

[2]   See below, pp. 115–16.

at its centre a heroine who is even more dutiful and selfless than Richardson's Clarissa. Sidney acquiesces to her mother's rejection of one suitor and choice of another, without question, and suffers her husband's infidelity without complaint. Yet Sarah Fielding, Charlotte Lennox and Frances Sheridan all participate in the debate about ethics, either questioning the validity of self-interest as a basis for moral or social order, as does Sarah Fielding in *David Simple*; or by reimagining transcendence in terms that could serve female interests, such as friendship in *David Simple*, or constancy in *The Female Quixote*; or by showing, as Frances Sheridan's *The Memoirs of Miss Sidney Bidulph* does, that duty and self-denial are not only not in women's interests, but not in the public interest either.

Feminist criticism of the later twentieth century saw women as acquiescing in the powerful middle-class ideology that would confine them to the domestic sphere: Nancy Armstrong's *Desire and Domestic Fiction* (1987) is one of the most influential expositions of this argument in literary studies.[3] More recently, doubts have been expressed about the validity of the 'separate spheres' argument. In *The Gentleman's Daughter, Women's Lives in Georgian England* (2006), Amanda Vickery has argued that the explanatory power given to the conception in women's studies is unwarranted and that the 'separate spheres' ideology was a reaction against the increasing opportunities for women in the public sphere: 'a cry from the embattled *status quo* rather than the leading edge of change'.[4] Novels, by the very fact of their publication, gave women a voice in the public sphere, a voice that Sarah Fielding, Charlotte Lennox and Frances Sheridan used to articulate a protest against, and offer alternatives to, the injunctions to self-denial and duty. They also worked to provide a literary career for women who were typically in the same position of impoverished gentility as most of their male counterparts, and dependent, like most writers of the period, on connections and patronage.

Sarah Fielding's point of departure, in terms of a literary career, was the same as that of her brother: that is, an improvident father.[5] Edmund Fielding married a Roman Catholic widow, Anne Rapha, some nine months or so after the death of his first wife, also called Sarah. Although the income from the family estate

---

[3]   Nancy Armstrong, *Desire and Domestic Fiction. A Political History of the Novel* (Oxford: Oxford University Press, 1987). This view is still influential. See Susan Staves, *A Literary History of Women's Writing in Britain, 1660–1789* (Cambridge: Cambridge University Press, 2006), 230 *et passim*.

[4]   Amanda Vickery, *The Gentleman's Daughter, Women's Lives in Georgian England* (London: The Folio Society, 2006), 8. See also Amanda Vickery, 'Golden Age to Separate Spheres? A Review of the Categories and Chronology of English Women's History', *The Historical Journal* 36 (1993), 383–414; Lawrence E. Klein, 'Gender and the Public/Private Distinction in the Eighteenth Century: Some Questions about Evidence and Analytic Procedure', *ECS* 29.1 (Fall 1995), 97–109; and Betty A. Schellenberg, *The Professionalization of Women Writers in Eighteenth-Century England* (Cambridge: Cambridge University Press, 2005).

[5]   I am particularly indebted to Martin Battestin's *Henry Fielding: A Life* for biographical details about Sarah Fielding.

at East Stour had been willed by Edmund Fielding's father-in-law, Judge Gould, to the Fielding children, Sarah's father continued to receive it. After investing in South Sea stocks, Edmund Fielding sold part of the estate in 1720. Lady Gould, Henry Fielding's maternal grandmother, objected to this flouting of the terms of the will and also feared that the children could be brought up as Roman Catholics. She subsequently brought a suit against Edmund Fielding in Chancery, seeking legal custody of the children and establishing their right to what was left of the property at East Stour. She won the case in 1722, when Sarah was 11 years old. Thereafter Sarah, her three sisters and their younger brother lived with Lady Gould in Salisbury, Henry Fielding having been sent to Eton in 1719.

David Simple, published anonymously in 1744, reflects on its author's own circumstances. The Frenchman Mr. Orgueil, whom the eponymous hero meets in London and whom he regards for some time as a moral guide, points out a man whose father was 'one of those sort of Men, who, tho' he never designed any Ill, yet from an indolent, careless Disposition, and trusting his Affairs entirely to others, ran out of a very good Estate'.[6] Spatter, another of David's guides through London, also speaks of men who have '*extravagant Fathers*, who took no Care to provide for them' (*DS* 73). This remark was excised from the second edition by Henry Fielding, no doubt with family sensitivities and the impropriety of criticising fathers in mind, although he himself reflected bitterly on precisely the same events in *The Crisis: A Sermon*.[7] *David Simple* begins with David's disinheritance at the hands of his brother: the children of Edmund Fielding's first marriage were themselves disinherited.[8] The bitterness felt by Camilla, a woman whom David Simple rescues from destitution and possible social disgrace, towards her stepmother may well reflect Sarah Fielding's feelings about Edmund Fielding's second wife. In Camilla's story, she and her brother Valentine are ejected from their father's house thanks to the machinations of their stepmother, Livia, who seals their fate by accusing them of incest: the charge of 'indecent actions' with his youngest sister Beatrice was in fact levelled at Henry Fielding by Frances Barber, a nursery maid who testified for Edmund Fielding when he lodged a complaint of his own against Lady Gould. From the loss of her mother, Camilla dates 'all the Miseries of my Life' (*DS* 106–7). Later, in London, she is found thinking:

> in all that number of Houses they passed, how many miserable Creatures there were tearing one another to-pieces, from Envy and Folly; how many *Mothers-in-Law*, working under-hand with their Husbands, to make them *turn their Children out of Doors* to *Beggary* and *Misery*. (*DS* 148)

---

[6]   Sarah Fielding, *The Adventures of David Simple*, and *The Adventures of David Simple, Volume the Last*, ed. Pater Sabor (Kentucky: The University Press of Kentucky, 1998), 47.

[7]   Battestin, *Henry Fielding*, 300.

[8]   Ibid., 18 ff.

Lady Gould died in 1733, and in 1739 the now run-down property at East Stour was finally sold, and the proceeds were divided among the six siblings.[9] Little is known about Sarah Fielding's circumstances between 1737 and 1754, when she moved to Bath, but money was undoubtedly a problem. Where Henry Fielding might have expected the status, and the income, of a landed gentleman, Sarah Fielding might have expected an at least respectable marriage and the financial security that went with it. None of the Fielding sisters ever married, though, and Linda Bree suggests that their lack of a sufficient dowry may have precluded marriage to a man of their own class.[10] '[T]here is no Situation so deplorable', reflects Camilla, 'no Condition so much to be pitied, as that of a Gentle-woman in real Poverty' (*DS* 132). *David Simple* expresses a sharp sense of social humiliation and exclusion when it focuses on the dependent situation of David and, later, of Cynthia. David finds Cynthia in the situation of a Lady's companion or, as she styles it, a 'Toad-eater'.

Sarah Fielding augmented her income by writing, presumably with her brother's approval. She may have contributed the letter from Leonora to Horatio in *Joseph Andrews* (1742) and the fictional autobiography of Anne Boleyn, which formed the last chapter of Henry Fielding's *A Journey from this World to the Next*, included in the *Miscellanies* of 1743. *David Simple*, like *Joseph Andrews*, was published by Andrew Millar, to whom we may suppose her brother provided an introduction. In the preface Fielding added to the second edition of *David Simple*, he speaks of having given '*some little Direction as to the Conduct of the second Volume*' (*DS* 344) (that is, Books III and IV) and having corrected some grammatical errors and '*Errors in Style*'. Some of these corrections took the form of cutting Sarah Fielding's extensive use of the dash.[11] The preface made it clear that *David Simple* was not authored by him, as its anonymity, and, presumably, something about the style, had led at least two readers to suppose.[12] Nevertheless, Henry Fielding promoted the novel by adding his name to the title page. The still-anonymous second edition told the reader that this was 'THE SECOND EDITION, *Revised and Corrected*. With a PREFACE *By* HENRY FIELDING Esq.'[13] Undoubtedly Henry Fielding impressed his own concerns about gender and the legitimacy of fiction on *David Simple*. In his revisions of *David Simple* he lost no opportunity to stigmatize the romance. Where Cynthia speaks of having anything beyond the 'most silly Story' (*DS* 80) removed from her, Henry Fielding added 'the most silly Story or Romance' (*DS* 358). No wonder he gave Charlotte Lennox's *The Female Quixote* (1752), ostensibly a satire on romances, a long and glowing review in *The*

---

    [9]   Ibid., 248–9.

    [10]   Linda Bree, 'Introduction', *The Adventures of David Simple*, by Sarah Fielding, ed. Linda Bree (London: Penguin, 2002), xiv.

    [11]   See Janine Barchas, 'Sarah Fielding's Dashing Style and Eighteenth-Century Print Culture', *ELH* 63 (1996), 633–56.

    [12]   Battestin, *Henry Fielding: A Life*, 663n.

    [13]   Ibid., 379.

Covent Garden Journal.[14] Henry Fielding also censored one of his sister's more acid reflections on masculine vanity:

> I have known some [men], from the most desperate State of ill Health occasioned by the want of a few Yards of Lace, when they have attained them by half starving themselves for a considerable time, immediately recover, chirp, and perch about on all their usual Haunts, like little warbling Birds at the Return of Spring. (*DS* 73)

Henry Fielding, then, acted as his sister's mentor, patron and editor. His position as omniscient narrator in *Joseph Andrews* also offered her a model of the author as moral authority, a role that Sarah Fielding adopted and adapted for her own purposes. *David Simple* echoes the cadences of *Joseph Andrews* on more than one occasion. We might take, for example, Henry Fielding's account of Parson Trulliber's reaction to Adams's request for money:

> Suppose a Stranger, who entered the Chambers of a Lawyer, being imagined a Client, when the Lawyer was preparing his Palm for the Fee, should pull out a Writ against him. Suppose an Apothecary, at the Door of a Chariot containing some Great Doctor of eminent Skill, should, instead of Directions to a Patient, present him with a Potion for himself. Suppose a Minister should, instead of a good round Sum, treat my Lord—or Sir—or Esq;—with a good Broomstick. (*JA* 165)

To describe David's feelings when Camilla agrees to marry him, Sarah Fielding writes:

> And now, Reader, if you are inclined to have an adequate Idea of *David*'s Raptures on that Confession,—think what Pretty Miss feels when her Parents wisely prefer her in their Applause—to all her Brothers and Sisters;—Observe her yet a little older, when she is pinning on her first Manteau and Petticoat; —then follow her to the Ball, and view her Eyes sparkle. (*DS* 230)

Interestingly, David's reaction is described in terms of female experience and in terms which might reflect a low opinion of marriage itself.

At the beginning of Sarah Fielding's novel, David Simple is the loving brother of Daniel, but Daniel's only concern is 'in some shape or other to promote his own interest' (*DS* 8). On the death of their father, Daniel contrives to disinherit David. The deceit is soon discovered, but a disillusioned David begins a quest to find 'a friend that he could live with, who could throw off all separate interests; for where selfishness reigns in any of the Community, there can be no happiness' (*DS* 20). His first stop on his quest is the Royal Exchange, where he sees:

> Men of all Ages and all Nations ... assembled, with no other View than to barter for Interest. (*DS* 22)

---

[14]   See *The Covent Garden Journal*, 24 March 1752.

In a pattern that recurs throughout the novel, David is advised by one man to buy stock and then warned off by another, only to find that neither is offering him disinterested advice. Both are motivated by greed or envy. We might recall, by way of contrast, how Joseph Addison wept tears of joy during his visit to the Royal Exchange, to see men 'thriving in their own private Fortunes, and at the same time promoting the Publick Stock' (*Spectator* 69). However, the real significance of this point of departure for David Simple seems to be that it allows the reader to form a link between bartering for interest and bargaining for daughters. In the next chapter, David stays at the house of Mr. Johnson, a jeweller, and is attracted to his youngest daughter, Nanny. Knowing that David has received an inheritance, Johnson encourages his addresses. At the same time, a rich Jew is prepared to buy Nanny's elder sister from the father without marrying her. Under the guise of morality, her father rejects this plan, whilst considering that his own fortune will be better served by allowing the Jew to marry her without a dowry. The girl must, in consequence, convert to Judaism. When the old, ugly and 'immensely rich' Mr. Nokes proposes to marry Nanny Johnson, whom it has been understood David will marry, her father tells her to accept the offer or walk on foot while her sister rides in a coach. Nanny is persuaded by vanity and the desire for money to accept the latter. Still, for the author, female frailties are understandable. Women are no less 'mixed', morally, than men:

> I hope to be excused by those Gentleman, who are quite sure they have found one Woman, who is a perfect *Angel*, and that all the rest are perfect *Devils*, for drawing the Character of a Woman who was neither: for Miss *Nanny Johnson* was very good-humour'd, had a great deal of Softness, and had no Alloy to these good Qualities but a great Share of Vanity, with some small Spices of Envy, which must always accompany it. And I make no matter of doubt, but of she had not met with this Temptation, she would have made a very affectionate Wife to the Man who loved her. (*DS* 29)

David overhears Nanny weighing his merits against the promise of a fortune, but he never blames her: 'instead of resolving to be her Enemy, he could not help wishing her well' (*DS* 30).

Continuing on his quest, David meets a Frenchman, Mr. Orgueil, who appears to represent the disinterestedness David is looking for, though his name actually means 'pride'. Orgueil introduces him to witty and pleasant company, only to reveal that none of his new acquaintances are what they seem. The man who descants on envy and covetousness is a miser; one who castigates extravagance spends lavishly on himself. Orgueil's exposure of the true nature of a man who inveighed against treachery and ingratitude takes the form of a brief interpolated tale, in which, once again, the real sufferer is a woman. The unnamed gentleman had been left to fend for himself at the age of 15 by an improvident father and was fortunate to be raised by a benevolent neighbour. He was attracted to this man's daughter, seduced her and left her pregnant. In *David Simple*, the fault is not seen as lying with the woman. Through her narrator, Sarah Fielding describes the girl as 'naturally warm in her Passions, and inclined to love every body, who endeavoured to oblige her' (*DS* 47).

The emphasis here is on male selfishness: '*he found it was in her power to give him Pleasure, and he gave himself no trouble what Price she paid for gratifying his Inclination*'. The girl reveals her secret to her father, who assures her 'he would never upbraid her', accusing the man, rather, of 'Baseness'. The girl and her father die in misery, and the seducer goes on to marry a rich woman. The real vanity of another gentleman of apparently 'good understanding' has been hidden from David because there were no women present. 'You could observe nothing of this,' says Mr. Orgueil, 'because there were no women amongst us' (*DS* 50). If there had been, David could have witnessed the gentleman's love of self-adornment and his pleasure in making conquests. Again, the male hypocrite is responsible for female misery. In a reversal of the more familiar conception of the disruptive effects of female misbehaviour, Sarah Fielding has Mr. Orgueil extrapolate the threat posed to social stability by the masculine wish for female approval:

> this Man's Vanity produces as many real Evils, as Ill-nature, or the most cruel Dispositions could do. For there are very few Families, where he has ever been acquainted, in which at least there is not one Person, and sometimes more, unhappy on his account. As the Welfare and Happiness of most Families depend in a great measure on Women, to go about endeavouring to destroy their Peace of Mind, and raise such Passions in them, as render them incapable of being either of Use or Comfort to their Friends, is really taking a pleasure in a general Destruction. And I myself know at this present time several young Ladies, who used to be the Comfort and Joy of their Parents, and the Delight of all who conversed with them, that are become, from a short Acquaintance with this Spark, negligent of everything; their Tempers are changed from Good-humour and Liveliness, to Peevishness and Insipidity, and each of them languishes away her days in fruitless Hopes and chimerical Fancies, that her superiour Merit will at last fix him her own. (*DS* 50)

Mistreatment and exploitation of women are the hidden realities in polite society in *David Simple*.

In due course, Orgueil's own apparent disinterestedness in acting as David's moral guide proves to be illusory. Orgueil's acquaintance, Mr. Spatter, reveals that Orgueil's vice is pride, as his name has indicated to the reader from the outset, and that he is devoid of sympathy and compassion. Guided by Spatter through London society, David finds, again, that everyone he meets is self-serving. At this point he meets Cynthia in the role of lady's companion, and his quest now becomes a vehicle for stories of female suffering. David encourages Cynthia to tell the story of her life, and she relates how as a child she was discouraged from trying to educate herself. Refusing the man her father tells her to marry, she is disinherited and so becomes almost a domestic servant in the house of the Lady or, as she describes it, a 'slave'. This servitude is made worse by taking place under 'the pretence of *Friendship*'. Where Cynthia, as the recipient of the lady's charity, might be expected to express a dutiful gratitude, she relates instead how the Lady has abused her position of power, and in the end Cynthia rebels against her. With

David's help, she escapes to lead an independent life. Another 'undutiful' woman is Camilla, whom David finds in a situation of near destitution, caring for her brother. Camilla's father was alienated from his daughter by the manipulations of his second wife and, in the end, strikes Camilla. She then decides to leave her father's house, with her brother's support. Two other episodes in *David Simple* contrasting the lots of an indolent and an exemplary wife intimate that the role of dutiful and affectionate spouse is a damaging choice for women. In Book I, Chapter viii, one woman refuses an exemplary domestic role: she lies in bed, does not prepare the dinner, drinks tea and indulges in other expenses. She is even ugly. She is vindicated by the husband, who declares himself 'the happiest of all Mortals; for he certainly had the best Wife in the World'. Sarah Fielding's commentary suggests that questions of masculine and feminine superiority are really quite arbitrary. They are merely states of mind:

> there could be no other Reason assign'd for this poor Man's being such a willing Slave, but her great Pride and high Spirit, which imposed on him, and made him afraid to disoblige her; together with a sufficient manner of talking, which made him imagine her much more capable than she really was. (*DS* 40)

Female acceptance of a subject role leads not to a harmonious and mutually beneficial order, but to female misery:

> I think it very likely, if she had known her own Deserts, and been humble in her Behaviour, he would have paid her no other Compliment, than that of confessing she was in the right, in the mean Thoughts she had of herself. He then would have been Master in his own House, and made a Drudge of her. (*DS* 40)

Three supposedly dutiful daughters mourning for their father are discovered by David, the next day, fighting over the inheritance of a carpet. The apparent inconsistency is explained in terms of arbitrary authority, the prevalence of custom, the privilege granted by society to good looks, and seduction by men:

> The Behaviour of these Sisters to each other, and that lately shown to their Father, may appear perhaps very inconsistent, and difficult to be reconciled. But it must be considered, that as the old Man had always preserved all the Power in his own hands, they had been used implicitly to obey his Commands, and wait on him ... And it being usual for Families to cry and mourn for their Relations, till they are buried, there is such a Prevalency in Custom, that it is not uncommon to see a whole House in Tears, for the Death of those very People they have hated and abused while living ... But these three sisters had an inveterate Hatred to each other; for the eldest being much older than the others, had, during their Childhood, usurped so unreasonable an Authority over them, as they could never forgive; and as they were handsomer when they grew up than she was, they were more liked by the rest of the World, and consequently more disliked and hated by her. The other two, as they were nearer of an Age, in all appearance agreed better; but they had met with one of those fine Gentlemen, who make Love to every Woman they chance to be in company with. (*DS* 37–8)

Through Sarah Fielding's own commentary, and through David's response to women's stories, we learn that female frailties are, in the main, an understandable consequence of corrupt social custom. Preoccupation with courtship and romance makes women stupid and frivolous. The married life of 'fine ladies', as we see later, is one of card games and plays. Spatter suggests, at one point, that the custom which dictates that unmarried women should be silent unless spoken to is a plot devised by parents to encourage their daughters to accept any match, so that they may at least have the privilege of speaking (*DS* 68).

Although the novel ends with the marriages of David and Camilla, and Cynthia and Valentine, the thrust of *David Simple* is against marriage as an institution, and indeed against any participation in what we might call the heterosexual economy. David's point of departure is a quest for friendship. Cynthia refuses suitors who are always her moral and intellectual inferiors. Camilla's story can also be read as an account of sexuality as disempowerment: an idyllic happiness ends, significantly, when Camilla reaches the age of puberty. Later in the novel, in the longest of the interpolated tales, we hear the story of Isabelle, a French acquaintance of Cynthia. The group of friends which now comprises David, Cynthia, Camilla and her brother Valentine, meet her on their journey through England. Sexual passion in Isabelle's story works against friendship. Isabelle has spent most of her childhood in a nunnery and is to be married at the age of 14 to Monsieur Le Buisson with her father's approval. This immediately leads to a conflict between Isabelle and her friend Julié, who is in love with Le Buisson but conceals her feelings. Since by Isabelle's account, it seems, marriages in France are not freely chosen on the basis of sincere mutual affection, Monsieur Le Buisson must be manipulated into marrying Julié. To oblige her friend, Isabelle treats Le Buisson badly enough to 'work him into a Rage' (*DS* 156) while Julié uses 'mild and gentle Methods' to calm him. By these artificial means, Le Buisson is persuaded to marry Julié, but the match does not end in happiness. Le Buisson grows indifferent, then angry and reproachful, and Julié languishes in 'greater Misery than I can express', as Isabelle puts it, and then dies.

Filial obedience and French custom persuade the young and inexperienced Dorimene to agree to marry Isabelle's brother, the Marquis de Stainville, though her affections, or passions, have not been engaged. The depth and sincerity of the Marquis de Stainville's friendship with one Chevalier Dumont are emphasized in two episodes interpolated into the tale. Both Isabelle and Dorimene are in love with Dumont – Dorimene's being now an adulterous love – but neither declares it. Dorimene's brother Vieuville conceives a passion for Isabelle that leads to conflict between Isabelle and Dorimene, who threatens a relapse into illness if Isabelle rejects her brother. When marriage is arranged between Isabelle and Dumont, Dorimene succumbs to a fever. She later declares her love to Dumont and threatens to kill Isabelle if Dumont proceeds with the marriage. Dorimene, 'past all Sense of Shame' (*DS* 190) later follows Dumont to his chamber and is discovered by her brother. De Stainville kills Dumont and is immediately reproached with a reminder of friendship: '[Y]ou have murdered the faithfullest Friend that ever Man was blessed with' (*DS* 191). De Stainville attempts suicide, Dorimene poisons herself and Isabelle vows to enter a convent.

In the end, Sarah Fielding seems unable to imagine a heterosexual relationship in which men and women are equal, a position not very different from that advanced by Mary Wollstonecraft half a century later. A situation in which female sexuality confers power is enacted only in a kind of coda to the novel, in which Cynthia relates the story of Corinna. Corinna is married but has many admirers and manipulates and plays them off against each other. In a Hobbesian scenario in which man and woman, husband and wife, vie constantly for power over the other, Corinna gains the upper hand by playing the coquette. Sarah Fielding qualifies this account by briefly setting against it the apparently superior happiness of the modest, soft, good-natured, submissive (and perhaps satirically named) Sacharissa, a method she also adopted in her later work, *The Lives of Cleopatra and Octavia* (1757). The autobiography of the powerful and unconventional Cleopatra occupies some 70 pages, while the 'mild and gentle' and morally exemplary Octavia gets a rather derisory 18 pages. The only way Sarah Fielding can put men and women on an equal footing is to represent both as sexless – or, as Betty Rizzo sees it, as equally rational.[15]

The object of the hero's quest is friendship, and Sylvia Harcstark Myers has argued for the central importance of friendship, both male and female, for women of the bluestocking circle, a group which might include Sarah Fielding, although the term itself did not appear until 1756.[16] The 'first generation' of bluestockings was represented by Elizabeth Carter, who translated Epictetus (1758); Elizabeth Montagu, who published an *Essay on the Writings and Genius of Shakespeare* (1769); Catherine Talbot, author of *Reflections on the Seven Days of the Week* (1770) and *Essays on Various Subjects* (1772); and Hester Chapone, who wrote *Letters on the Improvement of the Mind* (1773). Sarah Fielding too ventured into classical scholarship, by translating Xenophon's *Memoirs of Socrates* (1762). Elizabeth Montagu helped Sarah Fielding financially at several points in her career, and Sarah Fielding was also involved in a network of friendships and contacts with such figures as Samuel Richardson and Frances Sheridan.[17] Friendship in *David Simple* forms an alternative to marriage and subordination. In *David Simple* a woman, it seems, must opt out of marriage to avoid subordination; and there is really no conception of an enjoyment of heterosexuality outside of marriage. A life of independence and equality requires money, but this too seems to be scarcely imaginable. A situation in which financial independence offers complete freedom of action is briefly considered in the novel. It seems to produce a deep unease and

[15]   Betty Rizzo, 'Renegotiating the Gothic', *Revising Women. Eighteenth-Century "Women's Fiction" and Social Engagement*, ed. Paula R. Backscheider (Baltimore: The Johns Hopkins Press, 2000), 67.

[16]   Sylvia Harcstark Myers, *The Bluestocking Circle. Women, Friendship, and the Life of the Mind in Eighteenth-Century England* (Oxford: Clarendon Press, 1990).

[17]   Myers, 135.

uncontainable energies. At the point in the narrative where Cynthia has collected an unexpected inheritance and thus gained financial independence, she is described as 'being, like People in a burning Fever, who, from finding themselves continually uneasy, are in hopes by every Change of Place to find Relief' (*DS* 137).

In 1744, when Sarah Fielding published *David Simple*, a young Charlotte Lennox was surviving thanks to the patronage of Lady Cecilia Isabella Finch and her sister, Lady Rockingham. According to Duncan Isles's account, Lennox (née Ramsay) was born in Gibraltar around 1729 or 1730 and moved to New York in 1739.[18] The date surmised for her birth would agree with Samuel Richardson's description of her as 'hardly twenty-four' in a letter of 1753.[19] Miriam Rossiter Small's biography, however, has her born in New York in 1720 and leaving for England in 1735.[20] Isles, on the other hand, suggests that she did not leave for England until around 1742. The reasons for her departure from America are unclear. The account given in Lennox's obituary in the *Gentleman's Magazine* for January 1804 coincides with circumstances in her partly autobiographical first novel, *The Life of Harriot Stuart, Written by Herself* (1750), and Small suggests that this was a version sponsored by Lennox herself.[21] According to this account, she was sent over to live with a wealthy aunt, but on arrival found that the aunt was incurably insane, and no provision had been made for her. She may, alternatively, have been sent to complete her education, which was interrupted by the death of her parents, who left no property. Duncan Isles agrees that her father, a military officer, died around 1743–1746. This, too, was an event which was commemorated in *Harriot Stuart*:

> A short illness deprived me of the best of fathers, and the world of the best of men ... His death opened the door to those cruel adventures in which I have been since engaged, and from this fatal period my numberless misfortunes took their rise.[22]

Charlotte Lennox's father was James Ramsay, Captain of an Independent Company of Foot serving in New York Province in 1738, though Lennox, in information she herself provided, seems to have promoted him (falsely) to the position of Lieutenant-Governor of New York.[23]

---

[18] Duncan Isles, 'A Chronology of Charlotte Lennox', *The Female Quixote*, ed. Margaret Dalziel (Oxford: World's Classics, 1989), xxxvi. I follow Isles's chronology here, and in the rather more detailed version he gives in 'The Lennox Collection', *Harvard Library Bulletin*, 18–19, 1970–1971. This is a collection of Charlotte Lennox's extant correspondence.

[19] Samuel Richardson, *Selected Letters*, 223.

[20] Miriam Rossiter Small, *Charlotte Ramsay Lennox. An Eighteenth Century Lady of Letters* (New Haven: Yale University Press, 1935), 2–4.

[21] Small, 4.

[22] Charlotte Lennox, *The Life of Harriot Stuart, Written by Herself*, ed. Susan Kubica Howard (Madison: Fairleigh Dickinson University Press, 1995), 124.

[23] Small, 2.

By the mid-1740s, Charlotte Ramsay was in England, courting the favour of Lady Cecilia Isabella Finch, to whom she dedicated *Poems on Several Occasions* (1747). Her connection with Lady Cecilia and Lady Rockingham may simply have ceased with her marriage to Alexander Lennox, an employee of William Strahan, the London printer, in 1747, though again the circumstances are somewhat unclear. Charlotte Ramsay may have been planning to go to live with Lady Rockingham, with the relationship coming to an end because of a love affair between Ramsay and a young male visitor to the Rockingham household. In *Harriot Stuart*, though, what we find are scheming and faithless patrons who are responsible for Harriot's misfortune. A friend of the eponymous heroine gives one Lady Cecilia some of Harriot's poems in manuscript, and Lady Cecilia gives an 'absolute promise' to find her a 'genteel place about the princess' (*HS* 172). This may refer to Lady Cecilia Isabella's intention to use her own position as first Lady of the Bed-chamber to the Princess Amelia to find Charlotte Ramsay a place.[24] Yet the Lady Cecilia of *Harriot Stuart* grows uneasy at the compliments paid to the beautiful and talented Harriot in her presence, and the heroine realizes, in due course, that she was 'capable of meditating the blackest designs against me' (*HS* 182). Moved to the home of Lady Cecilia's sister, Harriot finds herself, humiliatingly, relegated to the nursery, but she still manages to attract the attentions of (among others) the chaplain of the household. Lady Cecilia's sister, though married, is a rival for this young man. In the end, Lady Cecilia finds a reason not to carry out her promise when another suitor is discovered in the innocent Harriot's room. If the identical names did not make the identity of Lady Cecilia Isabella Finch clear enough, Lennox included in *Harriot Stuart* a poem 'To Flavia', which had also appeared in the *Poems on Several Occasions* presented to Lady Cecilia. In a letter of 1752, Lady Mary Wortley Montagu criticized *Harriot Stuart* for maligning 'one of the very few women I have a real value for, I mean Lady BF' (Belle Finch).[25]

Charlotte Lennox found, then, that fiction was a vehicle for protest. Writing also gave her a degree of power. In the manner of one of Tobias Smollett's fictional alter egos, we find Harriot aiming to correct false taste by writing verses, or 'amply revenged' by poetry her friends write to defend her. Later, a poem she has written is instrumental in liberating her from the convent where she is imprisoned. Publication could grant Lennox a certain amount of independence, even if any money she earned from her writings legally belonged to her improvident husband. Her marriage to Alexander Lennox, whom Duncan Isles characterizes as 'indigent and shiftless' was neither happy nor prosperous, and they separated sometime between 1792 and 1803. However, while Charlotte Lennox attacked her erstwhile patrons in *Harriot Stuart*, this was by no means indicative of a freedom from the need for patronage in a broader sense. By 1750, when *Harriot Stuart* was published, Lennox had met Samuel Johnson, who promoted her interests with John Payne, a London bookseller, and Edward Cave, founder and proprietor of the

---

[24]   Howard, 283n.
[25]   Cited by Small, 6.

Gentleman's Magazine. The review of *Harriot Stuart* in the *Gentleman's Magazine* for December 1750 duly accorded Lennox's work the highest of praise:

> These volumes contain a series of love-affairs from 11 years of age, attended with a number of her adventures and misfortunes, which were borne with the patience, and are penn'd with the purity of a *Clarissa.*[26]

The review may even have been written by Johnson himself.[27] Johnson, in turn, introduced Lennox to Samuel Richardson, and Richardson was closely involved in the writing, printing and publication of *The Female Quixote* (1752). Johnson wrote the dedication of the novel, addressed to the Earl of Middlesex, while Richardson read and criticized the work in manuscript, helped to persuade Andrew Millar to accept it for publication, and printed the first edition.[28] The shift from aristocratic to 'professional' patronage in Charlotte Lennox's literary career is indicative of the decline of the traditional model.[29] Richardson had evidently seen a substantial draft of the work by November 1751, when he wrote to Charlotte Lennox with advice about a point of detail in Sir George Bellmour's facetious autobiography, which occupies all of Book VI, and approving comments on material in Book VII. In January 1752, Richardson wrote to Lennox again, advising her to complete her heroine's 'cure' within the present two volumes rather than extending *The Female Quixote* to three volumes, as Lennox must have considered. (Her own letters on this matter have not survived.) From the terms of Richardon's reply, the resolution Lennox envisaged involved using *Clarissa* as a model in some way:

> Dear Madam,
>   It is my humble Opinion, that you should finish your Heroine's Cure in your present Vols. The method you propose, tho' it might flatter my Vanity, yet will be thought a Contrivance between the Author of Arabella, and the Writer of Clarissa, to do Credit to the latter; and expecially if the Contraste … would … take up much Room in the proposed 3d Volume. If it will not take up much, it may be done, if you *will* do it, that way (which I beg you to consider, and to consult Mr. Johnson before you resolve) at the latter End of the Second Volume.[30]

One wonders how, exactly, *The Female Quixote* was to follow *Clarissa* in Lennox's original plan: could she have decided to have Arabella die rather than marry?

In Lennox's novel, the heroine's father has fallen out of favour at court and retires to a remote castle. There, with the death of her mother, he must bring up his daughter alone. In this seclusion, Arabella largely educates herself by reading

---

26   *Gentleman's Magazine,* 20, 575.
27   Howard, 283n.
28   Isles, *IILB* 18 (1970), 335n.
29   See Brian Hanley, 'Henry Fielding, Samuel Johnson, Samuel Richardson and the Reception of Charlotte Lennox's *The Female Quixote* in the Popular Press', *ANQ* 13.3 (2000), 28.
30   Isles, *HLB* 18 (1970), 340–41.

French romances, and from them she derives all her ideas of proper female, and male, behaviour. Arabella expects to make conquests, a view confirmed by the admiration of most men she meets. She believes that she has the power of life and death over her lovers, and when her admirers do *not* die when she rejects them, she finds another way to make their actions fit her construction of the world. For her, Edward the gardener is a man of high birth *incognito*, disguised so that he has the opportunity to see her every day. She does not expect to submit quietly to marrying her father's choice for a husband, her cousin Glanville. Marriage should only happen after '… an infinite deal of Trouble … her Lover should purchase her with his Sword from a Croud of Rivals'.[31] Arabella's father dies early in the novel, and a provision in his will stipulates that Glanville will be given one third of her estate if she does not marry him. Arabella is unmoved by this consideration and only gradually allows Glanville to profess his liking for her: unlike more conventional women, she will not accept kisses, love letters, or ready declarations of love.

The comedy in *The Female Quixote* derives from the mismatch between Arabella's romantic notions and commonplace reality. She meets Miss Groves, a young woman with a scandalous history who gave birth to two illegitimate children. For Arabella, this is like the situation of the 'unfortunate' rather than disreputable Cleopatra, whom she believes was privately married to Julius Caesar. She articulates a wish for adventures, which shocks the more conventional Miss Glanville, Glanville's sister. Arabella can call upon the 'Authority of Custom' (*FQ* 44) to prove that, by one set of conventions, it is an unpardonable crime for a man to tell a woman that he loves her. She and Miss Glanville interpret the word *criminal* in such different ways as to lead to complete mutual misunderstanding. There are also situations that provoke alarm, as when the heroine believes that Edward the gardener is going to force his way into her apartment and flees the castle, only to throw herself on the protection of a complete stranger, who may well take advantage of her plight. When Glanville rescues her, she believes that he is Edward's accomplice, and some time elapses before he is restored to her favour.

A young baronet, Sir George Bellmour, visits the castle at Arabella's invitation: boundless hospitality is another rule in romance, but Sir George is evidently willing to exploit the heroine's unconventional notions and begins to court her in 'romance' style. At Arabella's command he tells her his own 'history' – reinventing himself as the dispossessed Prince of Kent – and in suitable style relates his own amours with a milkmaid, 'Sydimiris' (who marries another man) and 'Philonice', who is carried off by a man and disappears. Sir George is disconcerted to find that rather than being charmed by his conformity to the romance style, Arabella strongly disapproves of his inconstancy and his failure to die of disappointed love.

The company takes a trip to Bath, where Arabella's unconventional dress and behaviour attract generally admiring attention, much to the dismay of Miss Glanville, who is jealous of Arabella and wants Sir George Bellmour for herself.

---

[31] Charlotte Lennox, *The Female Quixote*, ed. Margaret Dalziel (Oxford: Oxford University Press/World's Classics, 1989), 27.

In Bath she meets a countess who understands her devotion to romance while offering her an example of an unadventurous life and a conventional marriage. The countess tries to show Arabella that manners and morals may change:

> Custom, said the Countess smiling, changes the very Nature of Things, and what was honourable a thousand Years ago, may probably be look'd upon as infamous now. (*FQ* 328)

Arabella is impressed by the countess but not persuaded.

In the last book, Book IX, the party goes to London. In the gardens at Vauxhall, Arabella encounters a prostitute disguised as a boy and, to Glanville's horror, tries to engage him to rescue the girl from the attentions of a group of men. Sir George Bellmour hires an actress to pose as the princess Cynecia, to whom Sir George's rival, Glanville, has been unfaithful. Jealous and furious on Cynecia's account, Arabella banishes Glanville from her sight. Whilst walking through Twickenham with a group of young women in search of Cynecia, she sees men in the distance who she fears will carry her off and imitates another romance heroine, Clelia, by throwing herself into the river (Thames rather than Tiber) to defend her honour. She succumbs to a fever and almost dies. Meantime Glanville discovers Sir George's deception and almost kills him in a sword fight. Arabella is cured of her belief in romances thanks to a dialogue with a clergyman who convinces her that such works are absurd, and dangerous, fictions. In a very brief concluding chapter, she accepts Glanville as her husband.

The Female Quixote has been read as a satire on outmoded ideas and ideals, with reality showing the folly, or danger, of reading romances. In his review of *The Female Quixote* for *The Covent Garden Journal* of March 1752, Henry Fielding interpreted it in this way, opining that the book offered 'very useful lessons' for young women who would 'peruse it with proper attention'. In *The Progress of Romance* (1785) Clara Reeve also judged that 'the passion for the French Romances … and the effect of them upon the manners is finely exposed and ridiculed', though she thought the satire on romances came 30 or 40 years too late, such works having gone out of fashion well before the novel's date of publication.[32] In criticism of the late-twentieth century, *The Female Quixote* has more often been read as covertly pro-romance, with Arabella's 'cure' reflecting the increasing restrictions placed on female expression and female behaviour after 1740. For Laurie Langbauer, Lennox faced a dilemma: whether to continue working in the 'insubstantial world of romance, the only realm in which the woman [writer] is given a place, however illusory', or to follow the 'imperative' to leave it behind.[33] *The Female Quixote* ultimately revealed women's dispossession, exposing 'the lack of stable ground on which women might situate their stories'.[34] While critics have acknowledged that Arabella's unconventional beliefs and behaviour in the novel allowed Lennox

---

[32]   Clara Reeve, *The Progress of Romance* (1785) (New York: Garland, 1970, Vol. II), 6.

[33]   Laurie Langbauer, *Women and Romance. The Consolations of Gender in the English Novel* (Ithaca: Cornell, 1990), 62.

[34]   Langbauer, 63.

to challenge prevailing social customs, *The Female Quixote* has been read as an example of a dying tradition. In a survey of women's writing from 1660–1800, Janet Todd's analysis of *The Female Quixote* emphasized the heroine's reform.[35] Focusing on the heroine's reform, Deborah Ross, too, was forced to conclude that the novel's didactic message was ultimately one of obedience to authority.[36] On the other hand Arabella's obsessive chastity and her fear of forced entries into her apartment invited a Freudian reading in which the heroine's very active sexual desires could be symbolically, but only symbolically, revealed. Arabella is in fact a type of the coquette: a woman who likes amatory conquests. In late-twentieth century feminist interpretations, the romance becomes a specifically female genre articulating a female sexuality that had, later, to be repressed. As Patricia Meyer Spacks put it: 'Romances tell the truth of female desire'.[37] As stories that give women central importance romances are empowering for women, providing an alternative to a 'socially-defined state of meaningless and powerless activity'. This reading of the romance makes Arabella's reform at the end of *The Female Quixote* all the more poignant, and significant. Scott Paul Gordon has argued, however, that such an understanding of the romance is reductive and neglects the ideal of disinterestedness that the romance really valued.[38] Answering those who argue that Arabella wants power, and that romance gives her that power, Gordon points out that the heroine never seeks it: her 'fatal beauty' has, she believes, effects she herself cannot control. The self-seeking woman in the novel is the real coquette, Miss Glanville, who competes with Arabella for male attention, and relishes her humiliations. *The Female Quixote* actually works against the Hobbesian or Mandevillean belief that all human actions are really prompted by self-interest.

Gordon's argument is suggestive and could be carried further. Self-interest as compatible with or supporting virtue was, as we have seen, the Anglican and Whig ethos of the late-seventeenth and early eighteenth centuries. Insisting that everyone is motivated by self-interest has the benefit, from the Whig point of view, of making the operations of the market seem natural and inevitable. Latitudinarianism reconciled the competing aims of self-interest and virtue by arguing that virtue brought rewards. Those who felt excluded by the Whig definition of self-interest – that is, the self-interest of male, middle-class, property-owning, Protestant Englishmen – had to draw on values and traditions other than those of the Established Church and other than those of the 'middling sort'. For most eighteenth-century British writers, the romance was aristocratic, foreign and Roman Catholic. As Tobias Smollett put it in *Roderick Random*: '[W]hen the minds of men were debauched by the imposition of priest-craft to the most absurd

---

[35]   Todd, *The Sign of Angellica*, 151–60.

[36]   Deborah Ross, 'Mirror, Mirror: The Didactic Dilemma of *The Female Quixote*', *SEL* 27 (1987), 455–73.

[37]   Spacks, *Desire and Truth*, 14.

[38]   Scott Paul Gordon, 'The Space of Romance in Lennox's *The Female Quixote*', *SEL* (1998), 499–516.

pitch of credulity ... the authors of romance arose' (*RR* xxxiv). Romances were full of 'the marvellous', inimical to a Protestant natural religion, and inimical to the Whig idea of liberty.

Followers of the romance tradition in England often had Tory and Jacobite sympathies and, like Smollett, associated self-interest with the Whigs. Mary Delarivière Manley's *The Secret History of Queen Zarah and the Sarazians* (1709) was an attack on her Whig opponent Sarah Churchill, Duchess of Marlborough, whom Manley characterized as 'cut out purely for the Service of her own Interest, without any Regard to the strict Rules of Honour or Virtue'.[39] Manley's more famous *The New Atalantis* (1709) attacked the Duke of Marlborough, who was 'excessive in nothing but his love of riches'.[40] Still in the tradition of Tory romance was Eliza Haywood's *The Fortunate Foundlings* (1744), which may well have influenced Henry Fielding's Whig-inflected *History of a Foundling*, otherwise *Tom Jones*. *The Fortunate Foundlings* advertises its politics from the start, beginning in the year 1688, with the departure of 'the unfortunate king James'. Lennox's first heroine, Harriot, is significantly named 'Stuart', hardly an accidental choice five years after the '45 Rebellion. *The Female Quixote* opens with Arabella's father being banished from the court as the result of plots, after having 'in a manner governed the whole Kingdom' (*FQ* 5). The reading he provides for his daughter belongs to a dispossessed group.

Samuel Richardson and Henry Fielding, Lennox's Whig contemporaries, published novels that while expressing pious hopes for the reform of rakes actually underwrote the sexual double standard that was in male self-interest. Lennox wrote in a romance tradition that valued disinterest and self-denial. Arabella herself is not motivated by self-interest, as shown by her indifference to the possible loss of one-third of her estate if she does not marry Glanville. Suspecting that Glanville's conversion to the romance code of manners is only superficial, she recounts how Mazares, a character in Mlle de Scudèry's *Artamenes; or, The Grand Cyrus* (1690–1691), was forced by the princess Mandana to fight on the side of his rival Cyrus, thus giving a 'glorious Instance of Self-Denial' that proved his repentance was real. Unlike the novels of Richardson and Fielding, the romance privileges male constancy and draws on a code of values in which women are treated with enormous respect. Sir George Bellmour loses Arabella's favour forever by betraying his inconstancy. From this point of view, the romance *does* serve women's interests, but not in the narrowly sexual terms some critics have suggested.

It could be argued that the clash with reality in *The Female Quixote* ridicules the romance, exactly as Henry Fielding and Clara Reeve believed. Certainly Lennox derives some expert comedy from episodes of mutual misunderstanding and Glanville's mortification at Arabella's sometimes very public eccentricity.

---

[39] Mary Delarivière Manley, *The Secret History of Queen Zarah and the Zarazians* (New York: Garland, 1972), 40.

[40] Mary Delarivière Manley, *The New Atalantis*, ed. Rosalind Ballaster (London: Penguin, 1991), 17.

She knew that the romance could not survive in its 'pure' form, in mid-eighteenth-century England. With the publication of *Harriot Stuart*, Lennox showed that she was capable of treating an obsession with amatory conquest with a certain amount of humour. Rescued from a burning theatre by a male admirer, Harriot writes that she thought herself of 'prodigious importance', and 'nothing less than a Clelia or Statira' (*HS* 66). Clelia and Statira are the heroines of, respectively, De Scudéry's *Clélie* (1654–1660) and La Calprenède's *Cassandra* (1644–1650). The author already had in place a sense of the parallels with the French salon romances which she was to exploit to a much greater extent in *The Female Quixote* as well as a sense of the possible irony of these comparisons. However, Lennox manipulates the plot of *The Female Quixote* so that 'reality', rather than challenging Arabella's construction of the world, actually plays it out, albeit in more prosaic terms. Arabella expects Glanville to endure 'numberless Misfortunes, infinite Services, and many dangerous Adventures' (*FQ* 48) on her behalf, and he does. He has to suffer embarrassment, protect her reputation, and fight to defend her honour when Hervey, a former admirer, laughs at her. When Glanville falls ill, his recovery fortuitously coincides with her command to live. On many occasions, Lennox manages events so that the heroine does not suffer contradiction. To take one minor, but typical, instance: in an early part of the novel Arabella tells her maid Lucy to command Glanville not to follow her. Failing to understand the obedience expected of him, Glanville is going to follow her anyway, but the Marquis calls Glanville away, and so Arabella's sense of her own rights and privileges remains unchallenged. Like Cervantes' Don Quixote, Arabella is alternately ridiculed and revered, but unlike Don Quixote she does not have to suffer the burning of her beloved volumes of romance because Glanville saves them. She *is* 'cured' or converted by the end of the novel, but so is Glanville. Rather than being a merely conventional and rather complacent suitor, he becomes a version of the romance hero. In fact, his conversion takes up a great deal more space in the novel than Arabella's, and we see more of him as a 'reformed' character. *The Female Quixote* is not the last expression of a dying tradition but a new mutation of it. The plot, in which an initially unpromising suitor overcomes obstacles and adopts, or adapts to, the heroine's values, and she too learns to reform, is a template for Jane Austen's enduringly popular and influential work, *Pride and Prejudice* (1813).

Arabella's anticipations of forced entries into her apartment in the novel need not be read as symbolising a repressed female sexuality, but rather as Lennox's quite conscious *double entendres*. The heading of Book VIII, Chapter iv: '*In which* Mr. Glanville *makes an unsuccessful Attempt upon* Arabella' – he is actually trying, once again, to correct her romance values – does not suggest coyness about sex, and neither do Lennox's other works. One of the author's earliest literary productions was a poem some 105 lines long entitled 'The Art of Coquetry', which appeared in the *Poems of Several Occasions* of 1747. Here the author provided rules, not for those 'Who in their faces show their yielding mind', but rather for women who 'unsubdu'd controul the world by love'.[41] It should be said that women's beauty as power was not an idea that female contemporaries necessarily found attractive. On 1 December 1750, Mrs. Elizabeth Carter wrote to her friend, Miss Talbot, that Lennox's poem offered a 'doctrine indeed by no means to be admired'.[42] She added: 'It is intolerably provoking to see people who really appear to have a genius, apply it to such idle unprofitable purposes'. Lennox never really found favour with the 'blues'.[43]

Male readers, however, were more susceptible. One responded in verse to 'The Art of Coquetry' in the *Gentleman's Magazine* for January 1751, offering to arm 'honest wretches' against the 'tutor'd fair inspir'd by Charlotte's pen'. Samuel Johnson hosted a famous all-night party at the Ivy Lane club to celebrate the publication of *Harriot Stuart*, and an engraving by Richard Samuel which appeared in the *Ladies' Pocket-Book* of 1778 placed Lennox among the 'Nine Living Muses of Great Britain'. Of the compatibility of sexuality and morality Charlotte Lennox seems to have been persuaded: Harriot Stuart attracts one adoring suitor after another but describes her own conduct as 'irreproachable' (*HS* 197). Arabella's belief that everyone is an aristocrat in disguise actually has a leveling effect, making her, and potentially the reader, sympathetic to those who would otherwise be social and sexual outcasts, like Miss Groves or the prostitute at Vauxhall.

The fact that *The Female Quixote* appeared in print at all owed much to the interventions of Samuel Johnson and Samuel Richardson. It is hardly surprising, then, that Charlotte Lennox canvassed their support and acquiesced in their suggestions. From their patronage of female writers, Johnson and Richardson, on the other hand, perhaps gained a position of importance to which their own social origins scarcely entitled them. The publication of Frances Sheridan's *Memoirs of Miss Sidney Bidulph* (1761) also owed much to Richardson's intervention. At the age of 15, Frances Sheridan (née Chamberlaine) had written two sermons (now lost) and a two-volume romance, *Eugenia and Adelaide*. This in itself was an act of some daring, in direct defiance of her father's beliefs. Her father, the Reverend Dr. Philip Chamberlaine, a Church of Ireland cleric, only reluctantly allowed his daughter to learn to read, and writing he considered to be 'perfectly superfluous in the education of a female' and tending to 'nothing but the multiplication of love-letters'.[44] Later, when she was married to the actor Thomas Sheridan and living in London, she met Richardson, who submitted *Eugenia and Adelaide* to Robert Dodsley in March 1758. Dodsley rejected the work, which was not in fact published until 1791, 25 years after Frances Sheridan's death. Nevertheless, on the basis of reading *Eugenia and Adelaide*, Richardson encouraged Frances Sheridan to try a longer work, and

---

[41]   Small, *Charlotte Ramsay Lennox*, Appendix II, 235.

[42]   Cited by Small, 9.

[43]   Small, 48.

[44]   Alicia Lefanu, *Memoirs of the Life and Writings of Mrs. Frances Sheridan* (London: 1824), 4.

The Memoirs of Miss Sidney Bidulph was the result. The Sheridan family's own situation of financial hardship was also an inducement to publication.

Frances Chamberlaine had met the actor Thomas Sheridan after publishing a dramatic fable, 'The Owls', and a pamphlet defending him for his part in a theatrical riot in Dublin. They married in 1747, by which time Thomas Sheridan was the manager of the Smock-Alley theatre. Thomas had a turbulent career as a theatre manager in Dublin, culminating in a riot that wrecked the Smock-Alley theatre in April 1754. He left to become the principal actor at Covent Garden but was more ambitious to be seen as a gentleman and scholar, ultimately publishing works on elocution, education, grammar and linguistics. In November 1756 the couple returned to Dublin, and Thomas Sheridan resumed management of the Smock-Alley theatre. However, the theatre did not prosper and the Sheridans returned to London in 1758 with a debt of £7,000. Thomas had hoped to support the family by giving lectures to audiences in Oxford, Cambridge, Edinburgh and London, but in early 1760 these were still not finished. His insistence that he act on shares rather than receiving a salary from David Garrick at Drury Lane meant that a contract was slow to negotiate. In 1758 Frances had given birth to their fourth surviving child, two children having died in infancy. In the winter of 1759–1760, Frances Sheridan began work on *Sidney Bidulph* in the hope of easing the family's situation. The work was an outstanding success.

Grateful to Richardson, Frances Sheridan duly dedicated *Memoirs of Miss Sidney Bidulph* (1761) to 'exemplary Goodness and distinguished Genius' as personified by 'THE AUTHOR OF CLARISSA AND SIR CHARLES GRANDISON'. In an obvious glance at *Clarissa*, the heroine tells her friend Cecilia at the end of the novel: 'I have been set up as a mark … let me fulfil the intention of my Maker, by shewing a perfect resignation to His will'.[45] Sidney Bidulph might be another exemplary woman, suffering acutely, but never protesting, or perceiving her fate as unjust. The 'editor's introduction' – Sheridan kept up the pretence of the 'discovered' manuscript – recounts a conversation with a woman 'pretty far advanced in years', who would also underwrite Richardson's commitment, in *Clarissa*, to rewards in the next life, rather than in this. It is with this lesson in view that the old woman offers Sidney's letters to the editor. Though a woman of exemplary virtue, Sidney Bidulph was

> persecuted by a variety of strange misfortunes. This lady … to all human appearance, *ought* at last to have been rewarded even here – but her portion was affliction. What then are we to conclude, but that God does not estimate things as we do? It is ignorant, as well as sinful, to arraign his providence. (*SB* 7)

Yet, despite her debt to Richardson, and despite the obedience and submission which this statement of Christian orthodoxy would enjoin, Frances Sheridan used her prose fiction, audaciously, to undermine and subvert both these authorities.

---

[45]   Frances Sheridan, *Memoirs of Miss Sidney Bidulph*, ed. Patricia Köster and Jean Coates Cleary (Oxford: Oxford University Press/World's Classics, 1995), 459.

At the beginning of the novel, Sidney Bidulph is one of two surviving children of Sir Robert Bidulph (now deceased), the other being her brother, Sir George. Her mother is a woman of exemplary piety and strict notions. Sir George introduces Sidney to Orlando Faulkland, an Irishman, and she is attracted to him. Faulkland proposes to Sidney and is accepted. With the marriage agreed, a letter comes to light which reveals that Faulkland has, apparently, debauched a young woman (Miss Burchell), who is now pregnant. Sir George receives a letter, written by Faulkland, which offers to redeem Faulkland's reputation, but Sidney's mother reads only far enough to learn that Faulkland paid a price for the girl to her aunt: at this point she refuses to read further.

With the marriage called off, Sidney goes to stay with Lady Grimston, in Essex. Here she is introduced to Mr. Arnold and soon marries him, though she is not in love with him. She accepts Arnold at the insistence of her mother and Lady Grimston. Now residing at Arnold-abbey, Sidney discovers that her husband is having an affair with a neighbour, Mrs. Gerrarde, who turns out to be Miss Burchell's aunt. Mrs. Gerrarde, who knows of Sidney's previous engagement to Faulkland (though her husband does not), engineers a meeting between Sidney and Faulkland. Arnold, a witness to this compromising meeting, subsequently exiles Sidney and keeps their two children. Though Faulkland could clear her name, Sidney refuses to involve him in the matter for fear of a duel. She could incriminate Mrs. Gerrarde by revealing Miss Burchell's story, but as she and her mother have taken up Miss Burchell's cause, she will not do this either. Her refusal, also, to involve her brother leaves her in straitened circumstances. Abruptly, though, news arrives that Mrs. Gerrarde has eloped with Faulkland. This, we find, is an elaborate (and ultimately successful) ploy by Faulkland to redeem Sidney's reputation and have her reunited with Arnold.

Sidney's mother feels Faulkland must, in justice, marry Miss Burchell, and she enlists a somewhat reluctant Sidney (who is obviously still deeply attracted to him herself) to petition Faulkland on Miss Burchell's behalf. This she does, even though she is by this point in the novel a widow, and Faulkland still wants to marry her. Eventually Faulkland is indeed persuaded to marry Miss Burchell, and he goes back with her to his estate in Ireland. When her mother dies, Sidney discovers among her papers the original letter from Faulkland which her mother refused to read in its entirety. Here she discovers that a liaison between Faulkland and Miss Burchell was contrived by Mrs. Gerrarde to pay off her gambling debts. Later, Sir George reveals that he too had sex with Miss Burchell and that she told him that she neither hoped nor wished to marry Faulkland, who was supporting her financially: nevertheless, she had sworn Sir George to secrecy about their brief affair, lest the information injure her reputation in Faulkland's eyes and lead to the loss of an income.

Towards the end of the novel, Faulkland makes a dramatic appearance at Sidney's home in London, having, it seems, murdered his wife, whom he discovered in bed with a Major Smyth. Sidney is directed to marry Faulkland by her cousin, Mr. Warner, and this she does, only to discover, in the closing pages of *Sidney Bidulph*, that Mrs. Faulkland is still alive. The novel closes with Faulkland dead, either by natural causes or by his own hand, and with the narrative taking up the story of Sidney's daughters' misfortunes. The story was in fact continued in *Conclusion of Memoirs of Miss Sidney Bidulph*, published in 1767.

We can read Sidney's suffering not as a representation of the ineffability of Providence, nor as offering an exemplar of feminine stoicism, but rather as the darkest of satires on the duty of obedience. It was with the paternal injunction against letter-reading, surely, in mind that Frances Sheridan made Sidney's mother's failure to read Orlando Faulkland's letter in its entirety so decisive a cause of misery. Because her mother will not consider the possibility of mitigating circumstances, in Faulkland's case, Sidney marries Arnold instead: and Arnold is discovered to have a mistress. Not only that, she is disgraced, driven from her home and cut off from her children. Sidney's mother persuades her to marry Arnold because she fears people will talk about the broken engagement to Faulkland, and her daughter's reputation will be endangered. Yet the man she persuades her to marry is an adulterer, who was involved with Mrs. Gerrarde both before and after his marriage to Sidney, and his break with her would ultimately have had much worse consequences in terms of his wife's reputation if Faulkland's deception of Mrs. Gerrarde had not succeeded. Sidney discovers that her husband is having an affair and, like an exemplary wife following *The Whole Duty of Man*, does not reproach him for his infidelity. Yet as Sidney's mother later tells Arnold, if Sidney had reproached him for his infidelity when she discovered it, Arnold would not then have believed that Mrs. Gerrarde was Sidney's confidant. He would not then have believed that she was privy to the supposed secret of a relationship between Sidney and Faulkland, or that she arranged a meeting for them in her own house, and the sequence of events which culminated in Sidney's enforced exile could have been avoided. Sidney does not tell Arnold about her previous engagement to Faulkland because 'it might give a delicate mind pain' (*SB* 100) and cause him to be jealous, but because Arnold later finds out this information from others, he is all the more ready to believe she is still in love with Faulkland. Sidney and her mother forgive Arnold for his adultery, but as Sidney's brother points out, they were completely unforgiving of Faulkland's transgressions. As Mrs. Bidulph explains, the difference is duty: '[W]hat duty obliges us to pass by in a husband, it is hardly moral not to discountenance in another man' (*SB* 257). From considerations of duty, Sidney persuades Faulkland to marry Miss Burchell, but Miss Burchell is unfaithful to him and provokes him to murder. Sidney's brother George was well aware of Miss Burchell's character from the beginning, having had sex with her himself, but he had given his word never to reveal this so as not to injure her reputation. If he had broken this promise, the tragedies of the novel could have been avoided. Strict adherence to the dictates of duty and delicacy does not only result in misery; it also correlates with wider and deeper deviations from the moral law that affect everyone. Society is not well served by dutiful behaviour. Sidney's cousin Mr. Warner tells her to marry Faulkland in spite of the fact that he is a murderer – and it turns out that Faulkland's first wife is still alive.

The Memoirs of Miss Sidney Bidulph follows the trajectory of *Clarissa* only to undermine its moral implications. Sidney, like Clarissa, is so selfless that she wills almost nothing. As Anna Howe, in *Clarissa*, tells the heroine that she is attracted to Lovelace, so Sidney's friend Cecilia tells her that she is in love with Faulkland. She outdoes Clarissa as an exemplar of dutiful behaviour. When Faulkland proposes marriage, Sidney refers him to her mother. She will only accept him, or indeed love him, with parental approval. Sidney herself declares that 'I think we women should not love at such a rate, till duty makes the passion a virtue' (*SB* 27). Clarissa refuses to marry Solmes, the man her father and mother want her to marry, and continues to correspond with Lovelace. Sidney, on the other hand, suppresses her own feelings and breaks off her engagement to Faulkland as her mother wishes. In effect she marries Solmes, in the shape of Arnold. However, where Clarissa's misfortunes follow her flight from her father's house with Lovelace, Sidney's follow her marriage to the man her mother and Lady Grimston choose. Faulkland himself is a version of Lovelace. The reader who remembers how Anna Howe and Clarissa are swayed in Lovelace's favour by hearing of his generosity to his tenants may well be alarmed rather than reassured when Faulkland is discovered caring for his coachman's children after their mother has died. Sidney's rejection of him may well seem like the lucky escape that Clarissa did not have. Lovelace abducts Clarissa and keeps her captive by virtue of his own elaborate deceptions and machinations: Orlando Faulkland does the same with Mrs. Gerrarde. Faulkland even expresses himself in Lovelacean tones. In Richardson's novel, Lovelace triumphantly recounts to John Belford how he has contrived to entrap Clarissa and exclaims:

> What a matchless plotter thy friend! Stand by and let me swell!—I am already as big as an elephant; and ten times wiser! mightier too by far! Have I not reason to snuff the moon with my proboscis? (*C* 473)

Orlando Faulkland congratulates himself for tricking Mrs. Gerrarde in not dissimilar terms:

> Let no hero of romance compare himself to me, for first making difficulties, and then extricating myself out of them; let no giant pretend to equal me in the management of captive beauties in inchanted castles; let no necromancer presume to vie with me in skill for metamorphosising tigresses into doves, and changing imperious princesses into plain country nymphs! (*SB* 214–15)

The neat distinction Richardson would make between desirable and undesirable men proves unstable.

Despite Lovelace's villainy, and despite the fact that *Clarissa* was supposed to convince women that reformed rakes do not make the best husbands, female readers persisted in finding him attractive. When the first volumes of *Clarissa* were published, Lady Bradshaigh wrote to Richardson that 'you must know, (though I shall blush again) that if I was to die for it, I cannot help being fond of Lovelace'.[46] In Sarah

---

[46]   Cited by T.C. Duncan Eaves and Ben D. Kimpel, *Samuel Richardson. A Biography* (Oxford: Clarendon Press, 1971), 221.

Fielding's *Remarks on Clarissa* (1749), Miss Gibson, one of the conversationalists, is accused of preferring a Lovelace to a Hickman. The attractiveness of Lovelace caused Richardson difficulties even during the composition of *Clarissa*. Having read the description of Lovelace's death to a young woman 17 years old, Richardson was so disturbed by her tears for the villain that he resolved to make Lovelace even more overtly odious.[47] For the second edition of *Clarissa* in 1749, Richardson provided a Table of Contents which pointed readers to the appropriate interpretation. One entry reads: 'Gives a Character of Lovelace; [*Which is necessary to be attended to; especially by those who have thought favourably of him for some of his liberal actions, and hardly of her for the distance she at first kept him at*].[48] In *Letters and Passages Restored from the Original Manuscripts of the History of Clarissa* (1751), Richardson 'restored' an extended version of Lovelace's projected abduction and rape of Anna Howe, her mother and a maid-servant, which only appeared in summarized form in the first edition. The issue still received his attention in 1755. In *A Collection of the Moral and Instructive Sentiments, Maxims, Cautions, and Reflections, Contained in the Histories of Pamela, Clarissa, and Sir Charles Grandison*, Richardson listed under the heading 'Libertine. Rake', the following quotations from *Clarissa*:

> Libertines [*as well as women love them*] have not the ardors, *Miss Howe says*, that honest men have ...
> Libertines are generally more severe exacters of implicit obedience, and rigorous virtue, than other men ...[49]

Yet, as *Sidney Bidulph* illustrates, the man who abducts a woman, and who is not perfectly chaste, may actually be a more worthy character. Faulkland's account of his abduction of Mrs. Gerrarde, placed at the centre of the novel, subjects a version of Lovelace, and his plots in relation to Clarissa, to the classic casuistical test: do circumstances alter cases? The answer is, plainly, that they do. Faulkland's actions are vindicated as disinterested and morally admirable. Richardson might try to dictate what kinds of men women should or should not find attractive: *Sidney Bidulph* resists those coercions.

It could be argued that the novel recapitulates Richardsonian ideas of feminine virtue by positioning Sidney's passivity and unacknowledged sexuality at the novel's moral centre. Mrs. Gerrarde and Miss Burchell, as the sexually active women, are demonized. However, Anna M. Fitzer has argued that the transformation of Miss Burchell, over the course of the novel, from seduced innocent to designing 'rake in petticoats' also works to destabilize moral categories, specifically the moral

---

[47]   Eaves and Kimpel, *Samuel Richardson*, 209.

[48]   Samuel Richardson, 'Table of Contents', *Samuel Richardson's Published Commentary on* Clarissa *1747–65*, Vol. I, 96.

[49]   Samuel Richardson, *A Collection of the Moral and Instructive Sentiments, Maxims, Cautions, and Reflections, Contained in the Histories of Pamela, Clarissa, and Sir Charles Grandison*, in *Samuel Richardson's Published Commentary on* Clarissa *1747–65*, Vol. III, 149.

categories of virtuous and immoral femininity.[50] Though the heroine has some suspicions of Miss Burchell, she construes her demeanour in terms of a narrative of wounded and passive innocence: 'She loves Mr Faulkland, and had not herself the power to resist him' (*SB* 154). Sidney believes she has 'a heart naturally tender to an uncommon degree', as Miss Burchell is unwavering in her pursuit of marriage to Faulkland. She has a 'timorous accent' and 'melancholy eyes'. She is 'all made up of languishments and softness' (*SB* 298–9). Reading the novel with knowledge of the outcome, one is more inclined to read Miss Burchell as motivated by revenge against Sidney for being Faulkland's real love. When Lady Bidulph gives Miss Burchell the opportunity to tell the story of her 'seduction', she easily picks up the cues from a woman ready to believe that she has been wronged and further profits from Faulkland's own 'delicacy'. Miss Burchell asks:

> Did Mr. Faulkland ever tell you, madam, how the unhappy affair happened? My mother told her, she knew not particulars; that she had been referred to her for a full explanation; that Mr. Faulkland had always endeavoured to excuse himself, and went as far as to say, He was sure the lady herself would acquit him in a great measure. Ah, madam! Miss B. cried and shook her head. 'Tis as I expected, said my mother; Mr. Faulkland is an ungenerous man. A young lady of your modest appearance, I am sure, he must have taken more pains to seduce, than he will acknowledge. (*SB* 101–2)

Yet, as Fitzer points out, Sidney Bidulph is also guilty of some dissimulation. When her mother asks her how she feels about Faulkland after the disclosure of the incriminating letter from Miss Burchell, Sidney also responds to her mother's cues but really, as her journal reveals, spurns him more out of wounded pride than a duty to moral absolutes. She petitions Faulkland on Miss Burchell's behalf, but her letter can be read as an account of her own feelings:

> Need I name the amiable possessor of this heart? I need not; there is but one woman in the world who owns this description: for her let me be an advocate ... she, and she only, deserves your love. (*SB* 301)

She raves of Faulkland while in a fever and clearly denies her own real feelings.

The novel also intimates that the past cannot legislate for the present. Margaret Anne Doody has argued, indeed, that the connection between the past and the present is the real subject not only of *Memoirs of Miss Sidney Bidulph* (1761) but also of the *Conclusion* which appeared in 1767.[51] Sidney thinks that 'we ought always to form some laws to ourselves for the regulation of our conduct' (*SB* 27), yet the 'laws' which could be derived either from Richardson's novels, from a

---

[50]   Anna M. Fitzer, 'Mrs. Sheridan's Active Demon: *Memoirs of Miss Sidney Bidulph* and the Sly Rake in Petticoats', *Eighteenth-Century Ireland*, 18 (2003), 39–62.

[51]   Margaret Anne Doody, 'Frances Sheridan. Morality and Annihilated Time', *Fetter'd or Free? British Women Novelists, 1670–1815*, eds Mary Anne Schofield and Cecilia Macheski, Athens (Ohio: Ohio University Press, 1986), 345–6.

rigid understanding of religion, or even from the experiences of older women, prove to have little or no authority. The Richardsonian model was perhaps becoming, in Frances Sheridan's eyes at least, something of an antique. Richardson himself died in 1761, the year *Sidney Bidulph* was published. We are constantly reminded that the woman whom the editor visits, in the introduction, is 'pretty far advanced in years', or old, or venerable. Three weeks after the visit described in the introduction, she is dead. The code to which she adheres might, by analogy, be moribund: it is significant that the narrative itself begins at an earlier time, with the first entry dated 2 April 1703. Nor can the lesson of submission, or an uncomplicated adherence to vows, necessarily be derived from the experience of Sidney's mother, who was involved in a situation almost exactly replicating that of her daughter. A day had been arranged for Lady Bidulph's marriage, when a letter arrived informing her that the groom-to-be was already engaged to another young woman, whom he had seduced. He feels bound to honour his original vows, the marriage does not take place, and soon after he succumbs to madness and is confined for the rest of his life. From the parallel between her first engagement and her daughter's, Lady Bidulph derives 'a sort of horror' at the thought of a union between Sidney and Faulkland. Yet the rule for conduct she creates on the basis of this experience is not the only one which suggests itself. The fact that her suitor goes insane when returning to his first engagement might suggest that this was not a healthy course of action. Better, perhaps, for Sidney's mother to have married him, even though, or perhaps especially *because*, he was willing to break through 'every obligation divine and human to obtain me' (*SB* 31).

Lady Grimston is 'nearly of an age' with Sidney's mother, and 'extravagantly rigid' in her ideas. The description Sidney gives of the lady and her household makes it clear that she, and by extension her conceptions of duty and obedience, are an anachronism:

> Her servants are all antediluvians; I believe her coach-horses are fifty years of age, and the very house-dog is as grey as a badger. She herself, who in her youth never *could* have been handsome, renders herself a still more unpleasing figure, by the oddity of her dress; you would take her for a lady of Charles the First's court at least. (*SB* 61–2)

Lady Grimston's insistence on duty and obedience has been responsible for the misery of her two daughters. The first she forced into a marriage with a man she did not love, and the result was not happy. She had the same plans for her second daughter (now Mrs. Vere), who tells Sidney her story. Lady Grimston wanted her daughter to marry an elderly gentleman with a great estate, but Mrs. Vere refuses, having met, and fallen in love with, Mr. Vere. As a punishment for this defiance, her mother will not see her and threatens to disown her. With her father's encouragement, Mrs. Vere secretly marries, and Lady Grimston is so incensed that she threatens to separate from her husband unless he cuts his daughter out of his will. Her husband acquiesces, promising Mrs. Vere to draw up another will before he dies. However, he is seized with a 'paralytic disorder' which deprives him of the use of speech and limbs, and the new will is never written. When Mrs. Vere's father dies, Lady Grimston finds that the conditions she has insisted upon have also damaged her own financial interests, and most of the estate goes to Mrs. Vere's eldest sister. Mr. Vere's father now begins a suit against Lady Grimston for the settlement that should have been made upon her daughter – money that, even if she were willing to pay it, she does not now have. Meanwhile, Mr. Vere dies, and Mrs. Vere is delivered of a dead child.

Banished from her mother's house, Mrs. Vere is living with an old dean and his wife. Her father-in-law is still pursuing the lawsuit against Lady Grimston, but Mrs. Vere offers to give up half her jointure (the income she derives from marriage) if he will drop it. This he agrees to do, and Lady Grimston is partially reconciled with her daughter. Nevertheless, Mrs. Vere only visits her infrequently and lives alone near the home of one of her sisters-in-law. Sidney reflects: 'And yet [Lady Grimston] passes for a wonderful good woman, and a pattern of all those virtues of a religion which meekness and forgiveness characterize' (*SB* 77).

Running throughout the novel, too, as the summary above might indicate, is an acknowledgement that marriage is necessary primarily as a means of ensuring the legitimate inheritance of property. Women, and women's sexuality, are linked to sums of money, or are equated with money. Mrs. Vere's clandestine marriage results in a lawsuit between Lady Grimston and her husband's father fought over what, in purely financial terms, Mrs. Vere is worth. An estate depends on the precise dating of the conception of a child by Arnold's sister-in-law. Miss Burchell's sexual liaison with Faulkland is to pay off Mrs. Gerrarde's gambling debts. Sexual intercourse with the significantly named 'Miss Price' (whose story is told in an interpolated tale towards the end of the novel) would be taken by Mr. Ware as payment for her father's debts. A curious incident interpolated into the narrative proper seems to enact, and adapt to women's situation, Locke's dictum, in the *Two Treatises of Government*, that every man had an inalienable right of property in his own person. A young woman who is forbidden to marry the man of her choice is to undergo surgery to remove her breast. The operation is to take place on her 21st birthday. As she awaits the operation, she gives her brother a will in which she disposes of her own fortune to Mr. Main, the man she wishes to marry. As he also is a surgeon, she asks for him to be present while the breast is cut off. As she sits exposed, Main offers to examine the breast more closely and declares that it can be saved – even though he himself, obviously, would be the financial gainer in the event of her death. The episode could be read as a kind of sexual fantasy in which the necessarily passive woman can, by virtue of the 'medical' scenario, be allowed a seemingly unconscious sexuality – exposing her breasts. It can also be read as a declaration that women had the same rights and controls over their bodies and their sexuality that the individual, in the Lockean state, had over their property. The young woman can give her property, and her sexuality, to whomever she chooses.[52]

---

52   Ruth Perry offers an alternative reading. She sees the events of this scene as constituting a 'subtext that simultaneously critiques the masochistically passive protagonist

The novel reasserts the patterns of the older tradition of women's romances in that it exacts certain behaviour from men. Both Faulkland and Arnold undergo a period of trial, probation and reformation before becoming worthy of Sidney. Sidney's response to Faulkland is initially measured: he has not yet achieved the status of romance hero, despite his promisingly romantic name. As she writes to Cecilia: '[H]e is neither like an Adonis nor an Apollo ... he has no hyacinthine curls flowing down his back; no eyes like suns ... no rays of divinity about him' (*SB* 19). Only at the end of the novel, after Faulkland has seen her married to Arnold, waited for her, abducted Mrs. Gerrarde to save her reputation, married Miss Burchell at her insistence, apparently killed his wife and her lover, and been forced into exile, does Sidney say: 'I think I never loved him as I did in that moment' (*SB* 451). Orlando Faulkland, both in name and temperament, looks to Ariosto's Orlando Furioso, who pursued Angelica – though with the significant difference that Frances Sheridan's Orlando is not cured of his love for Sidney. In the meantime, Sidney's marriage to Arnold represents the more mundane realities of compromise. Arnold's musical aptitude seems to indicate that he, too, is at least a partially feminized man. Richard Leppert notes that conduct book writers of the period generally agreed that music was improper for a gentleman because it was unmanly.[53] However, for Sidney, Arnold's musical ability seems actually to connote sexuality. She writes: 'Lady Grimston, who is passionately fond of musick, has a very pretty organ in one of her chambers; Mr. Arnold was requested to give us a lesson on it ... He plays ravishingly; the creature made me envious, he touched it so admirably' (*SB* 64). A year after their marriage, Sidney's journal is interrupted by a quiet indication of an at least adequate sexual relationship: 'Here follows an interval ... in which time, though the Journal was regularly continued, nothing material to her story occurred but the birth of a daughter' (*SB* 116). And some 15 months later: 'another interval ... in which nothing particular is related, but that Mrs. Arnold became mother to a second child' (*SB* 119). Arnold, after he sins, suffers and reforms, becomes something like the kind of lover Sidney seems to want. She says of him: 'Mr. Arnold's *recovered* heart I prize infinitely more than I did when he first made me an offer of it ... Every look, every word, every action of his life, is expressive of a love next to adoration' (*SB* 266–9).

The earliest readers of *Sidney Bidulph* seem to have been uneasily aware of the force of the novel's critique. Samuel Johnson said to its author: 'I know not,

---

while it reinforces the message that women's bodies are vulnerable to male control and their health dependent on male knowledge'. See 'Colonizing the Breast: Sexuality and Maternity in Eighteenth-Century England', *Forbidden History: the State, Society and the Regulation of Sexuality in Modern Europe*, ed. John C. Fout (Chicago: University of Chicago Press, 1990), 135–6.

[53]   Richard Leppert, *Music and Image. Domesticity, Ideology and Socio-cultural Formation in Eighteenth-Century England* (Cambridge: Cambridge University Press, 1988), 24. Leppert also observes that there are very few portraits of upper-class males playing keyboard instruments such as the harpsichord, spinet or piano, as these were deemed to be particularly effeminate.

Madam, that you have a right, upon moral principles, to make your readers suffer so much'.[54] A writer in the *Monthly Review* for April 1761 had similar doubts about the moral tendencies of *Sidney Bidulph*:

> in the Romance now before us, the Author seems to have had no other design than to draw tears from the reader by distressing innocence and virtue, as much as possible. Now, tho' we are not ignorant that this may be a true opinion of human life, in some instances, yet, we are of opinion, that such representations are by no means calculated to encourage and promote Virtue.[55]

As we have seen, though, Sheridan's novel works to destabilize received conceptions of virtue, female and male. If constancy should be deemed a virtue, none of the characters in *Memoirs of Miss Sidney Bidulph* can lay claim to it. Everyone has two relationships. Lady Bidulph broke off an engagement and later married Sidney's father. Sir George Bidulph had a brief sexual liaison with Miss Burchell and later married another woman. Sidney was in love with Faulkland but married Arnold. Faulkland was in love with Sidney but married Miss Burchell. If Sidney's sudden change from poverty to wealth thanks to the generosity of her cousin Warner should seem to be a fairytale ending, a due reward for all her sufferings, we find, as the novel comes to a close, that this too has proved to be the 'source of new and dreadful calamities' (*SB* 467). It is entirely appropriate that the novel itself should be inconclusive. There is no marriage for the heroine, and no death either; so there is no reward, either on earth or in heaven. Fixed rules for behaviour, and didactic fiction, are becoming increasingly untenable: there can be no closure. To find inconclusiveness carried to even more radical lengths, in terms of both religion and narrative form, we must turn to a work contemporaneous with *Memoirs of Miss Sidney Bidulph*, namely, *The Life and Opinions of Tristram Shandy, Gentleman* (1759–1767).

---

[54]   James Boswell, *Life of Johnson*, ed. R.W. Chapman, corr. J.D. Fleeman (Oxford: Oxford University Press, 1970), 260.

[55]   *Monthly Review*, 24, 1761, 260.

Chapter 4
Tristram Shandy: Latitudinarianism and Liberty

As it developed over the course of the seventeenth century, Anglicanism came to locate itself in opposition to a still strong Roman Catholicism and an increasingly vocal Dissent. In order to maintain unity within a national Church threatened by divisive parties, the Latitudinarians, who developed what would prove to be the dominant school of thought, placed less emphasis on points of doctrine and dogma and more on the moral life. From the 1640s onwards, moderate Anglicans increasingly urged toleration and an attitude of charity to religious difference.[1] So, argued Benjamin Whichcote, 'Universal Charity is a thing final in religion'.[2] In *The Religion of Protestants, A Safe Way to Salvation* (1638), a highly influential work in terms of the Latitudinarian tradition, William Chillingworth allowed for the possibility of error in matters of faith: 'we [Protestants] pretend not at all to any assurance that we cannot erre'.[3] Anglicans of the seventeenth century were prepared to accept that in religion, no absolute certainty was to be found and, crucially, that unwitting error need not mean eternal damnation. Latitudinarianism, as we have seen, also allowed for involvement in commercial life and the pursuit of gain. It did not ask Anglicans to give up worldly pursuits or pleasures. Rational Anglicanism also offered its adherents the reassurance of an orderly universe operating according to predictable physical laws, as discovered by Isaac Newton. All these orthodox positions and attitudes – anti-Catholicism and suspicion of Dissent, the relative toleration of difference, a willingness to live without certainty, faith that was compatible with self-interest, the argument from design – may be found in the Rev. Laurence Sterne's controversial and highly successful novel, *The Life and Opinions of Tristram Shandy, Gentleman* (1759–1767).

The case for continuity between Sterne's religious values as a priest in the Church of England and the values implied in *Tristram Shandy* has been made before, preeminently by Melvyn New. In *Laurence Sterne as Satirist* (1969), New argued that the conservative ethic of Sterne's sermons finds its continuance in *Tristram Shandy* and that normative values in the novel are provided by orthodox Anglicanism.[4]

---

[1]   See John Coffey, *Persecution and Toleration in Protestant England, 1558–1689* (Harlow: Longman, 2000), 50.

[2]   *Cambridge Platonists*, 333.

[3]   William Chillingworth, *The Religion of Protestants, A Safe Way to Salvation* (1638), 157.

[4]   Melvyn New, *Laurence Sterne as Satirist. A Reading of Tristram Shandy* (Gainesville: University Press of Florida, 1969).

In his role as editor of the Florida edition of Sterne's works, and most particularly as editor of the *Sermons*, New has reinforced this view of Sterne and his first novel by encyclopaedic reference to Sterne's sources in Anglican sermons and other pious works. While the New of the *Sermons* found it difficult to support a reading of *Tristram Shandy* as theologically orthodox – conceding in his preface to the Notes that Sterne might have written the novel without thinking much about his religious beliefs – he nevertheless made many points of connection between sermons and novel, thus making a case for the continuity of attitudes in both.[5]

Any student of Sterne is indebted to New's work as an editor, but his understanding of Sterne's Sermons as continuous with an 'orthodox' tradition has minimized what was unconventional or even, from the point of view of contemporaries, improper about them.[6] New also omitted from his edition the original and provocative title, *The Sermons of Mr. Yorick*, under which Sterne first published them in London in 1760, having abandoned (or been persuaded to abandon) the still more provocative title, *The Dramatic Sermons of Mr. Yorick. By Tristram Shandy, Gentleman.*[7] More importantly, there is little recognition in the Florida edition of the *Works* that Anglicanism itself is capable of different inflections, both conservative and radical, or that the expression of Latitudinarian ideas in a work of fiction, rather than from the pulpit, might lead to a different emphasis. The changing historical context – the difference, say, between the political situation in which Bishop Joseph Hall (1574–1656), one of Sterne's favourite authors, delivered his sermons, and Sterne preached his – also receives little attention. What we find in *Tristram Shandy*, I argue, are the potentially liberal elements of the Latitudinarian tradition – tolerance, moderate scepticism, distrust of totalizing theories – serving a new reformist agenda at a time when the situation that led to the formulation of Latitudinarianism was itself beginning to change.

Laurence Sterne's earliest writing was political journalism in the service of the Whig cause, undertaken at the behest of his uncle, Archdeacon Jaques Sterne. From 1741–1742, he was involved in the often vicious business of anti-Tory propaganda. During the election campaign for the parliamentary seat of York city, Sterne wrote to support the Whig candidate, Cholmley Turner, trading slurs and insults with supporters of the Tory candidate, George Fox. Weary of the business, he repudiated party politics in a letter to the *York Gazetteer* in November 1742.[8] However, Sterne's rejection of party politics evidently did not prevent him from writing in support of what he might have understood as national, rather than party, interest. In his contributions to anti-Jacobite propaganda at the time of the '45 Rebellion, and in his sermons in general, Sterne was no friendlier to

---

[5]   *The Sermons of Laurence Sterne*, ed. Melvyn New, in *The Florida Edition of the Works of Laurence Sterne*, 5 vols (Gainesville: University Press of Florida, 1996), Vol. V, xx.

[6]   See Paul Goring, 'Thomas Weales's *The Christian Orator Delineated* (1778) and the Early Reception of Sterne's Sermons', *The Shandean*, 13 (2002), 87–97.

[7]   See Judith Hawley, Review article, *Essays in Criticism* 48 (1998), 80–88.

[8]   Ross, *Laurence Sterne*, 89.

Roman Catholicism than his Anglican predecessors. There are attacks on Roman Catholicism in such sermons as 'Pharisees and Publican in the Temple' or 'Job's Account of the Shortness and Troubles of Life', and on Dissent too in 'Penances' and 'Self-Examination'. He wrote an additional stanza for his friend John Hall-Stevenson's anti-Jacobite ballad, 'The Royal Hunters' March', published in the *Newcastle Journal* in November 1745.[9] Writing in the persona of 'A Commoner', in a piece published in the *York Journal: or, Protestant Courant* in July 1746, Sterne gloated over the massacre of the rebels at Culloden and argued that the city of York was too tolerant of Roman Catholics. Two items mentioned in the *York Courant* in November 1745 also suggest Sterne's authorship: one, a 'Loyal Song', with the chorus to be sung to the tune of Lillabullero (an anti-Catholic ballad dating back to the time of the Williamite wars in Ireland between 1689 and 1691), the other 'The Pope's dreadful Curse', being a transcription of Bishop Ernulph's excommunication. Both Lillabullero and Ernulph's ex-communication found their way into Sterne's novel. In Volume III of *Tristram Shandy*, Walter Shandy persuades the unsuspecting Dr. Slop to read the latter aloud. As Dr. Slop reads, Toby Shandy whistles Lillabullero.

Tellingly, the anti-Catholicism which is to be found in *Tristram Shandy* is most prominent in the early volumes of the novel and, most obviously, in the sermon on 'The Abuses of Conscience', included in fragmented form in Volume II, and delivered not by a clergyman but by Uncle Toby's servant Corporal Trim. 'The Abuses of Conscience' was originally delivered as an assize sermon at York Minster in 1750 and was subsequently published as a sixpenny pamphlet. In the sermon, Sterne reflects on the corrupting effects of what he sees as Roman Catholicism's reliance on the rituals of Mass, rosaries and confession:

> O Popery! What hast thou to answer for?—when, not content with the too many natural and fatal ways, through which the heart of man is every day […] treacherous to itself above all things;—thou hast willingly set open the wide gate of deceit before the face of [an] unwary traveller.[10]

The sentiments in the sermon are very much in keeping with Sterne's earlier writing.

In similar vein is Tristram's contrast, in Volume I of the novel, between the propensity of any man of the 'least spirit' to deviate from the straight line of narrative with the dullness, or mental straitjacket, of the muleteer driving his mule from Rome to Loretto 'without ever once turning his head aside either to the right hand or the left'.[11] Also included for satirical effect is the judgement of the Roman

---

[9]   Ross, Laurence Sterne, 127. I am indebted to Ross's biography of Sterne throughout this chapter.

[10]   Laurence Sterne, *The Sermons of Laurence Sterne*, ed. Melvyn New, in *The Florida Edition of the Works of Laurence* Sterne, 5v. (Gainesville: University Press of Florida, 1996), Vol. IV, 260.

[11]   Laurence Sterne, *The Life and Opinions of Tristram Shandy, Gentleman*, ed. Ian Campbell Ross (Oxford: Oxford University Press, 1983), 32.

Catholic Doctors of the Sorbonne on the matter of baptism before birth. The man–midwife Dr. Slop, who delivers the baby Tristram, would have been recognisable to York readers as Dr. John Burton, physician, Tory and suspected supporter of the '45 Rebellion. After the defeat of the uprising, Burton himself was arrested at the instigation of Jacques Sterne and was held in custody awaiting trial for almost a year. The depiction of Dr. Slop as a papist (which Burton was not) is a reflection of that suspicion and a conventional Whig tactic.

Some of Sterne's anti-Catholicism was probably genuinely felt and was in no way uncommon at the time. Some of it, though, may have been prompted by his desire to gain Jaques Sterne's favour. Like most of the writers considered in this study, Laurence Sterne needed patronage, if not so much in his later career as a successful novelist, then certainly in terms of his ambitions within the Church. Though he could count among his relations the founder of the Irish College of Physicians, a Dean of St. Patrick's Cathedral, Dublin, and even an Archbishop of York, his social origins were against him. Sterne's own father was an impecunious officer, a younger son of a younger son, who married the daughter of a military provisioner. The young Laurence Sterne moved from one barracks to another in England and Ireland, and the family was usually short of money. At the age of 10, Sterne was left in England in the care of his father's brother, Richard Sterne, on the understanding that he would redeem the entire cost of his upkeep and education as soon as he was able to do so. He was only able to gain a university education (and therefore entry to the Church) thanks to the generosity of his cousin, also called Richard Sterne. Laurence Sterne's success in obtaining a living within a week of being ordained in August 1738 was the result of the influence of his uncle. Jaques Sterne's patronage came at a price, however, and Laurence Sterne was called upon to write for the Whig cause. After Laurence's rejection of party politics in 1742, Jaques Sterne did not interest himself further in his nephew's progress and, indeed, did what he could to hinder it.

Nevertheless, given Sterne's reliance on ecclesiastical patronage in the 1740s and 1750s, before he became a celebrated author, one wonders how much of his anti-Catholic and anti-Methodist sentiment was designed to curry favour with either Jaques Sterne, who from 1746 to 1750 attempted to hound the nuns of Micklegate Bar Convent out of York, or with Archdeacon Frances Blackburne, who saw Methodists as cryptopapists (this was not an uncommon view). Sterne had preached for the absent Blackburne, and Blackburne had at one time tried to promote a reconciliation between Laurence and Jaques Sterne, though without result. It may be that the satirical portrait of Burton represents an attempt on Sterne's part to regain his uncle's favour.

The title 'The Abuses of Conscience' suggests a concern with the threat from Dissent, and Sterne had in fact taken the subject of the sermon, and some of its content, from Jonathan Swift's sermon 'On the Testimony of Conscience', one of only three sermons by Swift which had so far found their way into print. We do not know when 'On the Testimony of Conscience' was delivered, but it clearly speaks from a time when the nonconformity of Dissenters and recusancy were perceived as a threat to Church and State. Swift writes:

> Men often say, a Thing is against their Conscience, when really it is not. For Instance: Ask any of those who differ from the Worship established, why they do not come to Church? They will say, they dislike the Ceremonies, the Prayers, the Habits and the like, and therefore it goeth against their conscience: But they are mistaken.[12]

Just how closely Sterne's sermon follows Swift's in terms of argument and phraseology is made clear in Lansing Hammond's comparison of the two pieces in his study of Sterne's sources.[13] Swift writes: 'The word *Conscience* properly signifies that Knowledge which a Man hath within himself of his own Thoughts and Actions'. In Sterne's sermon we find: 'Conscience is nothing else but the knowledge which the mind has within itself'. In Swift: 'Whenever our Conscience accuseth us, we are certainly guilty', and in Sterne: '[W]henever a man's Conscience does accuse him he is guilty'. Swift: 'For very often, through the Hardness of our Hearts we do not suffer our Conscience to take any Cognisance of several Sins we commit' – and thus Sterne: 'did no such thing ever happen, as that the conscience of a man, by long habits of sin insensibly become hard'. There are many other such parallels.

Unlike Swift, however, Sterne does not concern himself directly with Dissent. Swift had delivered his sermon in a very different context, at a time when the Anglican Church of Ireland was under threat both from the majority Roman Catholic population and a strong Presbyterian community. When Sterne delivered 'The Abuses of Conscience' in York Minster in 1750, neither he nor the congregation would have perceived Dissent – however unwelcome – as a serious threat to national stability. In fact, by the time Sterne included 'The Abuses of Conscience' in Volume II of *Tristram Shandy* in 1759, alarm or even mere uneasiness about differences of opinion in the nation was receding. As previously noted, the sermon is delivered by a servant, Trim, and in that sense its delivery alone would most certainly have been seen as unorthodox. We find, though, that Trim 'officiated to whole campaigns in *Flanders*, as Clerk to the Chaplain of the Regiment' (*TS* 96). Sterne may have insisted on Trim's qualification to ensure that the sermon remained within the ambit of the Church of England. Methodists, after all, had raised considerable alarm by preaching outside church. The sermon ends, in orthodox style, by telling the congregation that the individual conscience is only to be trusted when it accords with 'that law already written'. However, when Sterne transferred his sermon to *Tristram Shandy* he deliberately problematized its authority. The sermon is placed, by Walter Shandy, on the same level with any other curiosities that come his way, among them Ernulphus's excommunication. As Carol Kay puts it: 'Words that

---

[12]   Jonathan Swift, *Sermons*, ed. Louis Landa, bound with *Irish Tracts 1720–23*, ed. Herbert Davis (Oxford: Basil Blackwell, 1968), 151.

[13]   Lansing Van Der Heyden Hammond, *Laurence Sterne's* Sermons of Mr. Yorick (New Haven: Yale University Press, 1948), 151–2.

once dealt eternal death, words that save souls, now yield entertainment and satisfy whimsy and curiosity'.[14] Walter Shandy suggests that the company listen to the sermon only to pass the time. It will only be read with the consent of those present. Dr. Slop is one of the company accepted in the parlour, even if he does fall asleep during that part of the sermon which would be most likely to effect his conversion. The sermon on the Abuses of Conscience is fragmented and interrupted by the interventions and responses of the company in the parlour, with each party bringing to the sermon his own preconceptions or private associations. Conscience 'fortified with Cases and Reports' reminds Trim and Toby of trenches and fortifications. The allegory of mercy and justice chained down under the feet of religion Trim takes to be an account of his brother Tom, imprisoned by the Inquisition. When Trim reaches that part of the sermon which identifies the situation where conscience *may* be relied upon, Dr. Slop falls asleep, only waking when a reference to 'the physician' reminds him of his own prerogatives. By 1759 Sterne could afford, in a sense, to embed the sermon in a much more relativistic discourse, and in 1768 *A Sentimental Journey*, which was based on Sterne's own travels through France and Italy between 1762 and 1767, saw a further softening of Sterne's attitudes towards Catholicism. Shamed by his own initial lack of generosity towards the mendicant monk he meets at Calais, Yorick later exchanges snuffboxes with him. Yorick guards the box given him by Father Lorenzo, he says, as he would 'the instrumental parts of my religion, to help my mind on to something better'. Here is an acknowledgement that the 'instrumental' parts of religion are not ends in themselves, and therefore that the rituals and practices of another confessional tradition are not necessarily as corrupting and deceptive as Sterne had once argued. *A Sentimental Journey* as a whole promotes tolerance of difference in custom, manners and religion.

Sterne brought toleration of difference to *Tristram Shandy* by way of Lockean psychology. In the chapter of *An Essay Concerning Human Understanding* entitled '*Of the Association of* Ideas', Locke reflects on the root cause of what he terms madness. It flows, he thinks, from a 'strong Combination of *Ideas*, not ally'd by Nature'. This combination, it seems,

> the Mind makes in it self either voluntarily, or by chance, and hence it comes in different Men to be very different, according to their different Inclinations, Educations, Interests, *etc*. Custom settles habits of Thinking in the Understanding, as well as of determining in the Will, and of Motions in the Body; all which seems to be but Trains of Motion in the Animal Spirits, which once set a going continue on in the same steps they have been used to, which by often treading are worn into a smooth path, and the Motion in it becomes easy and as it were Natural.[15]

---

[14]   Carol Kay, *Political Constructions. Defoe, Richardson and Sterne in Relation to Hobbes, Hume and Burke* (Ithaca: Cornell, 1988), 212.

[15]   John Locke, *An Essay Concerning Human Understanding*, ed. Peter Nidditch (Oxford: Clarendon Press, 1984), 396.

Madness, by this definition, is Sterne's starting point. The passage from Locke is loosely rendered on the first page of the *Tristram Shandy*:

> you have all, I dare say, heard of the animal spirits, as how they are transfused from father to son, &c &c.—and a great deal to that purpose:—Well, you may take my word, that nine parts in ten of a man's sense or nonsense, his successes and miscarriages in this world depend upon their motions and activity, and the different tracks and trains you put them into; so that when they are once set a-going, whether right or wrong, 'tis not a halfpenny matter,—away they go cluttering like hey-go-mad; and by treading the same steps over and over again, they presently make a road of it, as plain and smooth as a garden-walk, which, when they are once used to, the Devil himself sometimes shall not be able to drive them off it. (*TS* 5)

Tristram's father winds the clock on the first Sunday of every month, the same night on which he undertakes his 'little family concernments'. So the act of coition reminds Mrs. Shandy of clock-winding, and she interrupts Walter with a question connected by association with what they are doing: '*Pray, my dear*, quoth my mother, *have you not forgot to wind up the clock?*' Toby Shandy, injured at the Siege of Namur in 1695, enacts the military campaigns of the War of the Spanish Succession on his bowling green, and so he interprets most things in terms of his preoccupation. The 'zig-zaggery' of Walter's action as he pulls a handkerchief out of his right coat pocket with his left hand suggests to Toby the Siege of Namur. When Trim tells him that Dr. Slop is constructing a bridge in the kitchen, Toby Shandy takes it to be a model of the Marquis d'Hôpital's bridge. To explain his father's reaction to the crushing of his nose by Dr. Slop's forceps, Tristram has to trace back the family preference for long noses to the (apparently) excessive jointure his great-grandfather had to pay his great-grandmother, on account of his inadequate nose. Despite arguing, in *An Essay Concerning Human Understanding*, that all knowledge came from experience, Locke could still believe that reason, rightly used, would guide men to moral and religious truth. For him, an irrational or unnatural association of ideas is 'a Taint' that potentially 'infects Mankind'.[16] Although there is comedy and pathos in the eccentricities of *Tristram Shandy*'s characters, Sterne, unlike Locke, is not perturbed by the highly idiosyncratic paths taken by the individual mind. What bothers him is compulsion: 'so long as a man rides his HOBBY-HORSE peaceably and quietly along the King's highway, and neither compels you or me to get up behind him pray, Sir, what have either you or I to do with it?' (*TS* 12). The arbitrary association of ideas drives the narrative. Locke's qualms are Sterne's characters.

Latitudinarianism, as it developed in the late seventeenth century, was opposed to dogma. Insistence on points of theology fomented dissension and was therefore to be avoided. As a satire on dogmatism and rigidity, *Tristram Shandy* shows the influence of Latitudinarian thinking. Walter Shandy's regularity in the matter

---

[16]   Locke, *Essay*, 395.

of clocks and conjugal duties leads to Mrs. Shandy's unfortunate interruption. Tradition, and the country politics to which Walter Shandy subscribes, have convinced him that movement towards London is productive of corruption in the state. So convinced is he of the malign influence of an overimportant metropolis that he would have constables appointed to interrogate anyone travelling there and have them turned back to their lawful abodes if their journey were judged unnecessary. Thanks to a clause inserted by his father in his mother's marriage settlement, Tristram is bound to be born in the country rather than, as his mother would wish, in London. This ridiculous legalism ultimately leads to the presence of the man–midwife Dr. Slop at Tristram's delivery and the crushing of Tristram's nose. Walter Shandy is a slave to habit. His opinions are often idiosyncrasies which, over time, become rigid dogma. His father's conviction of the importance of Christian names might, Tristram speculates, have begun as a mere whim, or even a jest, but it becomes a matter in which he is 'all uniformity; – he was systematical, and like all systematic reasoners, he would move both heaven and earth, and twist and torture every thing in nature to support his hypothesis' (*TS* 45). The novel implicitly sympathizes more with Tristram and Elisabeth Shandy, as the victims of Walter's absurd schemes and reliance on often arcane authorities, than it does with any idea of the supposed national good.

Like his Anglican predecessors, Sterne was willing to live with uncertainty. In *The Religion of Protestants*, William Chillingworth had addressed the central intellectual problem of the reformation: what was to be the criterion of truth, or the 'rule of faith' in religion.[17] It was a dilemma he had experienced on a very personal level. Troubled by the lack of continuity between Protestantism and the early Church and feeling that there must be an infallible judge in matters of faith, Chillingworth converted to Catholicism around 1630. Reexamining the issues while at the English Jesuit college in Douai, however, Chillingworth came to the conclusion that he had erred and declared himself a Protestant again in 1634. He struggled with his return to the Church of England, refusing to subscribe to the Thirty-Nine Articles in September 1635. To know what it was possible to impose, it was necessary to know what God required of man for his salvation. What Chillingworth constructs in the pages of *The Religion of Protestants* is a Church in which there may be degrees of faith or certainty. In *The History of Scepticism from Savanarola to Bayle* (2003), Richard Popkin has called this approach 'mitigated scepticism'.[18] 'All which God reveales for Truth is true' is a thesis, as Chillingworth terms it, that will admit of absolute certainty. For the hypothesis (Chillingworth's term) 'That all the articles of our Faith were reveal'd by God', we can only achieve 'moral certainty' or a certainty reliant on probability and the general consent of mankind. No such certainty was available – or from

---

[17]   For an account of Chillingworth's life and ideas, see Robert Orr, *Reason and Authority. The Thought of William Chillingworth* (Oxford: Clarendon Press, 1967).

[18]   Richard Popkin, *The History of Scepticism from Savanarola to Bayle*, rev. edn. (Oxford: Oxford University Press, 2003).

the Anglican point of view, advisable – and so Anglican clerics of the seventeenth century argued against the pursuit of absolute certainty in matters of religion. John Tillotson used Chillingworth's conception of 'moral certainty' in his work *The Rule of Faith* (1676) to meet the challenge to religion from scepticism. Tillotson acknowledged that it was possible to doubt whether there was such a country as America. Reports of it could be fabricated: all men might be liars. But even without direct experience of the existence of America, we might nevertheless be assured, with a sufficient degree of certainty, that there was such a place. 'The case', he writes, 'is the very same as to the certainty of an ancient Book and of the sense of plain expressions: we have no demonstration for these things, and we expect none; because we know the things are not capable of it'.[19] Even as he acknowledged the force of the sceptical argument, though, Tillotson could still believe that reason allowed man limited access to the truth of revelation.

Where Sterne differs is in making scepticism the grounding principle of his novel and embracing its liberating possibilities, whilst still maintaining Anglican values. Nothing reaches a conclusion in *Tristram Shandy*: not Tristram's autobiography, not the 'Trista-paedia' that Walter writes to educate his own son, not the question about the extent of the wound to Toby Shandy's groin. The need to establish certainty is associated, very literally, with a loss of freedom in *Tristram Shandy*. The citizens of Strasburg, in Slawkenbergius's tale, want to establish whether the stranger's nose is real or not and follow him out of their town. Meantime, the French march in and take it over. Toby Shandy's enactment of the War of the Spanish Succession also begins in an attempt to establish certain knowledge, this time of the exact geographic location where he was wounded. However sympathetically Toby is presented, and despite the (paradoxically) unaggressive nature of his pursuit, there is an element of oppression in his obsession. It rules out other possibilities. Just as Walter Shandy gathers materials from unlikely sources to support his idiosyncratic hypotheses, Toby Shandy, too, incorporates everything into his fixation. The unexpected arrival of Dr. Slop instantly brings to his mind the writings of the engineer Stevinus, and the conversation is dominated, for a time, by the language of fortification. He turns Walter's hypothesis about 'radical heat' and 'radical moisture' into an account of the Siege of Limerick. He incorporates everything in the most literal sense, too, in that Trim takes the spouts and lead gutters from Toby's house and melts down his pewter shaving basin to make new cannons for the bowling green. Walter Shandy seeks to impose his ideas on Toby. We often see him, in relation to Toby, in the role of teacher: advising him of the analogical relationship between men and women, or about to give him a dissertation on duration and its simple modes, or giving him a lecture on systems of noses. As Tristram writes:

---

[19]   John Tillotson, *The Rule of Faith: or an Answer to the Treatise of Mr. I.S. entituled Sure Footing etc* (London: 1676), 118.

his aim in all the pains he was at in these philosophic lectures,—was to enable my uncle *Toby* not to *discuss*,—but *comprehend*—to *hold* the grains and scruples of learning,—not to *weigh* them. (*TS* 189–90)

Toby Shandy, it need hardly be said, does not discuss: still less does he comprehend. In the same way, though, Toby's hobbyhorse begins to encroach on his brother's house. Trim converts Walter's jackboots into a pair of mortars, and the lead weights from the nursery window contribute to more new field pieces. Both, in however muted a sense, are concerned with conquest.

Against the search for certainty, and dominion, Sterne opposes incompletion and fluidity. Fluids are remarkably pervasive in *Tristram Shandy*. Tristram speaks, for instance, of the 'millions of [propositions] … every day swiming quietly in the middle of the thin juice of a man's understanding' (*TS* 132). Obadiah approaches Dr. Slop in a 'vortex of mud and water' (*TS* 85). Susannah is a 'leaky vessel' (*TS* 229). When Obadiah is to ride out to buy yeast, the surrounding countryside is flooded. The sinovia, or lubricating fluid, round the abbess of Andoüillets's knee is hardened by kneeling for long matins (*TS* 404) – Catholicism, once again, is associated with a loss of freedom. Fluids work against certainty. While attempting to pinpoint the exact location where he was wounded, Toby finds his attempts at explanation baffled by water:

> What rendered the account of this affair the more intricate to my uncle *Toby*, was this,—that in the attack of the counterscarp before the gate of *St. Nicolas*, extending itself from the bank of the *Maes*, quite up to the great water-stop;— the ground was cut and cross-cut with such a multitude of dykes, drains, rivulets, and sluices, on all sides,—and he would get so sadly bewilder'd and set fast amongst them, that frequently he could neither get backwards or forwards to save his life; and was oft times obliged to give up the attack upon that very account only. (*TS* 68)

Toby's search for certainty in the matter of the parabola would, it seems, lead to the drying up of a whole list of fluids (*TS* 73), and Walter Shandy, concerned to find the precise location of the soul, refuses to countenance the notion that it resides in a 'certain very thin, subtle, and very fragrant juice or in a liquid of any kind' (*TS* 118). Tristram more than once describes the purpose of his work in terms of moving fluids. 'True *Shandeism*', he writes at the end of Volume IV, 'think what you will against it, opens the heart and lungs, and like all those affections which partake of its nature, it forces the blood and other vital fluids of the body to run freely thro' its channels, and makes the wheel of life run long and chearfully round' (*TS* 270). When Walter Shandy seeks consolation in the matter of his son's name, he goes to the fishpond.

Sterne's representation of the body also valorizes incompletion. Mikhail Bakhtin argued that the grotesque body, in Rabelais, subverted hierarchies and immutable truths in that such a body was not a closed or completed unit. The grotesque body is 'unfinished, outgrows itself, trangresses its own limits'.[20] Bakhtin continues:

> The stress is laid on those parts of the body that are open to the outside world, that is, the parts through which the world enters the body or emerges from it, or through which the body itself goes out to meet the world. This means that the emphasis is on the apertures or the convexities, or on various ramifications and offshoots: the open mouth, the genital organs, the breasts, the phallus, the potbelly, the nose.[21]

How far Bakhtin's reading of Rabelais is justified is a matter that need not concern us here: the principle he identified is relevant to Sterne. The grotesque body, as described above, tends to make its appearance in *Tristram Shandy* by way of pun and inference: pipes, pens, hornworks, cannons, breastworks, crevices, hobbyhorses, 'Slawkenbergius' for a mountain of excrement, and so on, not to mention noses and asterisks. *Tristram Shandy* also offers us bodies *prevented* from achieving incompletion, as it were, in that they are not completely open: Walter Shandy's weak ejaculation, Toby's wounded groin, Tristram's crushed nose, or the circumcision that will result, according to Dr. Slop, in a 'phimosis'. On the other hand, Toby's open mouth, as he whistles *Lillabullero*, undermines whatever he finds absurdly rigid. To Locke's assertion that wit and judgement are fundamentally different from each other, as 'wide as east is from west', Sterne opposes the products of open orifices: 'so are farting and hickuping, say I' (*TS* 153). An important location of incompletion in *Tristram Shandy* is the womb. Mrs. Shandy's labour lasts, we might remember, over four volumes, and, given the publication of the novel in installments, an actual time span of two years. Bakhtin also argued that one of the fundamental tendencies of the grotesque image of the body was to show 'two bodies in one: the one giving birth and dying, the other conceived, generated, and born'.[22] Again, this appears in muted form in *Tristram Shandy*. As Tristram is conceived, the clock is ticking: conception and the intimation of mortality coincide. Tristram is born in his father's 'declining years'.

Sterne also refuses closure by definition. Why it is that fish ponds have consoling properties he leaves 'to system builders and fish-pond diggers betwixt 'em to find out' (*TS* 233). On what is meant by 'love', Tristram asserts that:

> I am not *obliged* to set out with a definition of what love is; and so long as I can go on with my story intelligibly, with the help of the word itself, without any other idea to it, than what I have in common with the rest of the world, why should I differ from it a moment before the time? (*TS* 375)

---

[20]   Mikhail Bakhtin, *Rabelais and his World*, trans. Helene Iswolsky (Bloomington: University of Indiana Press, 1984), 26.

[21]   Ibid.

[22]   Ibid.

and he leaves the reader a blank page to draw his own picture of the Widow Wadman. Many matters are left unresolved: whether or not, for example, 'dear, dear *Jenny*' is wife, mistress, child, or friend. Tristram promises to provide a map as a guide to passages of doubtful meaning – it is never provided. The avoidance of closure means relinquishing authority. As narrator of a novel, Tristram is not concerned to persuade the reader of any proposition, argument, or point of view. In this respect, Tristram the writer differs from Sterne the preacher, even though Sterne, as author of *Tristram Shandy*, would still promote the Latitudinarian virtues of tolerance and charity in his novel. Tristram, unlike the preacher, is in no hurry to push towards any kind of conclusion, even when he discovers that in writing his autobiography he will always be defeated by time. He actually welcomes what might otherwise be construed as a defeat:

> I am this month one whole year older than I was this time twelve month; and having got, as you perceive, almost into the middle of my fourth volume—and no farther than to my first day's life—'tis demonstrative that I have three hundred and sixty-four days more life to write just now, than when I first set out ... It must follow, an' please your worships, that the more I write, the more I shall have to write—and consequently, the more your worships read, the more your worships will have to read.
>
> Will this be good for your worships eyes?
> It will do well for mine. (*TS* 228)

For Tillotson, the tolerance of uncertainty and incompletion was an irenical necessity: for Tristram, as for Sterne, it becomes an enabling condition.

Tristram is, in every sense, the child of uncertainty. His identity remains unfixed even at the end of Sterne's novel. The narrative concerning Tristram peters out just as he is being put into breeches: precisely the moment at which his gendered identity would be established.[23] After the visitation dinner, Toby Shandy asks Yorick how the matter of Tristram's name has been resolved. Yorick answers:

> Very satisfactorily ... no mortal, Sir, has any concern with it—for Mrs. *Shandy* the mother is nothing at all akin to him—and as the mother's is the surest side— Mr. *Shandy*, in course, is still less than nothing—In short, he is not as much akin to him, Sir as I am—
> —That may well be, said my father, shaking his head. (*TS* 265)

As his father sees it, Tristram's misfortunes began with his mother's interruption at the moment of conception, a moment which can apparently be identified with some certainty. Tristram declares: 'I was begot in the night, betwixt the first *Sunday* and the first *Monday* in the month of *March*, in the year of our Lord one thousand seven hundred and eighteen. I am positive I was' (*TS* 8). However, Tristram's certainty

---

[23]   'Boyhood proper began with the ceremony of the first pair of breeches, usually in the seventeenth century at around six years old'. Anthony Fletcher, *Gender*, 297.

is undermined by the fact that only eight months elapse between the first Sunday in March, and the fifth of November, the date on which Tristram is born.[24] It was popularly believed that a child could be born seven or nine months after conception, but not eight. Dr. Slop's punning on 'horn-works' serves to point up the suggestion of illegitimacy. Walter Shandy's conviction that his son's misfortunes began '*nine months before he ever came into the world*' may be correct, but perhaps not in the sense that he believes. Tristram might be of no family at all, as the novel intimates, or as an eight months child, he might be a freak of nature.

Sterne, unlike Locke, accepts that language is an unreliable medium for the communication of ideas. In *An Essay Concerning Human Understanding* (1690), John Locke saw language as an unreliable instrument for the transmission of ideas, grudgingly admitting the use of metaphors in 'Discourses, where we seek rather Pleasure and Delight, than Information and Improvement'.[25] He added, though:

> if we would speak of Things as they are, we must allow, that all the Art of Rhetorick, besides Order and Clearness, all the artifical and figurative application of Words Eloquence hath invented, are for nothing else but to insinuate wrong *Ideas*, move the Passions, and thereby mislead the Judgment; and so indeed are perfect cheat.[26]

Sterne, on the other hand, often points up the metaphorical nature of common expression, and therefore, by Locke's standards, its capacity to mislead. Where Locke's goal might be the communication of clear and distinct ideas, unimpeded, if possible, by the indeterminacy and relativity of language, determinate ideas (Locke's term) are scarcely available in *Tristram Shandy*. As John Traugott remarks, whole sections of the novel pass without a single determinate idea being expressed.[27] When we learn about the characters of Walter and Toby Shandy we do so from a context of situations. Meaning *is* contextual in *Tristram Shandy*: the experience of reading the novel is of waiting for meaning to be supplied. The significance of the interruption of Walter Shandy by his wife's question in the opening chapter – '*Pray, my dear have you not forgot to wind up the clock?*' – only becomes clear as Tristram begins to supply a context for it. As Sterne's imagined reader interjects: '[T]here is nothing in the question, that I can see, either good or bad' (*TS* 6). Sterne revels in precisely those conditions which Locke viewed with unease. When the Widow Wadman pronounces the word *fiddlestick*, it could have

---

[24]   J. Paul Hunter, 'Clocks, Calendars and Names. The Troubles of Tristram and the Aesthetics of Uncertainty', *Rhetorics of Order/Ordering Rhetorics in English Neoclassical Literature*, ed. J. Douglas Canfield and J. Paul Hunter (Newark: University of Delaware Press, 1989), 183. The 'mistake' was first noted over a century ago by H.R.P.C., 'A Mistake in *Tristram Shandy*', *Notes and Queries*, 8th series, 7, 12 January 1895, 28–9.

[25]   Locke, *Essay*, 508.

[26]   Ibid.

[27]   John Traugott, Tristram Shandy'*s World: Sterne's Philosophical Rhetoric* (Berkeley: University of California Press, 1954), 27.

14,000 different meanings (*TS* 527). Noses and whiskers may acquire a bawdy significance if Sterne wishes it. A bridge means one thing for Dr. Slop and another for Toby Shandy. All meaning is relative.

Tristram Shandy advances the potential liberalism of the Latitudinarian position, but when Sterne began writing *Tristram Shandy*, he was not entirely motivated by a disinterested concern for the public good. His mind was very much on self-promotion. In November 1759, with *Tristram Shandy* ready for the printers, he wrote to a Mrs. F.:

> Now you desire of knowing the reason of my turning author? why truly I am tired of employing my brains for other people's advantage.—'Tis a foolish sacrifice I made for some years to a foolish person.—I depend much upon the candour of the publick.[28]

By 1747 Sterne had acquired the livings of two Yorkshire parishes, Sutton and Stillington, and two prebendal stalls – a prebend being the share of cathedral revenues allotted to a resident cleric. He had also had two sermons published. Other eighteenth-century clergymen with family connections similar to Sterne's own might have been contented with such preferment and circumstances, as he enjoyed, but Sterne evidently hoped for more.[29] Sterne, as we have seen, needed patrons, and in 1749 he allied himself with the Rev. John Fountayne, whom he had known at Cambridge, and who was now Dean of York Minster. He supported Fountayne in the matter of a disputed ecclesiastical appointment and for his pains earned the commissaryship of the Peculiar Court of Pickering and Pocklington. Sterne also wrote a Latin sermon for Fountayne to enable the dean to gain his doctorate in divinity. His most significant intervention on Fountayne's behalf, however, was his participation in the brief paper war between Fountayne and Dr. Francis Topham. The dispute between them revolved, again, around the power of ecclesiastical patronage. In *A Political Romance* (1759), Sterne represented the dispute about the right to confer the commissaryship of the Peculiar Court of Pickering and Pocklington as a quarrel over an 'old-case-Pair-of-black-Plush-Breeches', with an earlier quarrel over registrarship of the Exchequer and Prerogative Court appearing as the attempt by the sexton Trim (Topham) to obtain an 'old Watch-Coat' belonging to the Parson (Fountayne). With the antagonism between the parties in danger of becoming a matter of public ridicule, Archbishop Gilbert intervened, and all copies of *A Political Romance* were ordered to be burnt. Sterne's literary efforts had made his clerical preferment less, rather than more likely.

Perhaps the suppression of *A Political Romance*, early in 1759, finally convinced Sterne of the futility of relying on patronage for advancement. In the summer of that year, with the first volume of *Tristram Shandy* in the hands of Robert Dodsley, the London bookseller, he reflected on the counsel of friends who advised him not to publish his witty, bawdy novel:

---

[28]   *Letters of Laurence Sterne*, ed. Lewis Perry Curtis (Oxford: Clarendon Press, 1935), 84.
[29]   Ross, *Laurence Sterne*, 183.

> Mr. Fothergil, whom I regard in the Class I do you, as My best of Criticks and
> well wishers—preaches daily to Me Upon Your Text—"get Your Preferment
> first Lory! he says—& then Write and Welcome" But suppose preferment is long
> acoming (& for aught I know I may not be preferr'd till the Resurrection of the
> Just). (*Letters* 76)

Sterne was writing again very soon after the suppression of *A Political Romance*,
approaching the bookseller Robert Dodsley with a proposal for a new book as
early as May 1759. Sterne suggested to Dodsley that he publish immediately
the material he had sent, and if the work sold, he, Sterne, would have another
volume ready by Christmas. Exactly what form this original draft took we do
not know. Sterne wrote to Dodsley that the plan, as he might see, was 'a most
extensive one, – taking in, not only, the Weak part of the Sciences, in which the
true point of Ridicule lies – but every Thing else, which I find Laugh-at-able in
my way' (*Letters* 74). It may be that 'A Fragment in the Manner of Rabelais',
which was published in bowdlerized form by Sterne's daughter Lydia in 1775,
represents part of the original draft. In this fragment, only 1,500 words long,
we find one Longinus Rabelaicus proposing to put together a 'Kerukopaedia',
a guide to the art of writing sermons. In the second chapter, Homenas, another
Rabelaisian character, is discovered stealing his sermon for the next Sunday
from a volume of Samuel Clarke's sermons. In any event, Dodsley was not
happy with the bargain Sterne proposed, evidently considering the £50 Sterne
demanded for one volume too great a risk (*Letters* 80). Sterne countered with a
proposal to publish two octavo volumes at his own expense in York, so that the
market for the book could be tested. (This proposal also kept the copyright in his
own hands.) Dodsley would then sell the work from his shop in Pall Mall: this
Dodsley ultimately agreed to do. In a postscript to his letter, Sterne also indicated
that he had followed Dodsley's advice in revising the original draft to make it
more attractive to a metropolitan audience. To promote the book further, Sterne
wrote a letter puffing his own work one month after its publication in December
1759, which his mistress Catherine Fourmantel was to transcribe, sign with her
own name, and send to David Garrick. 'If you have not seen it, pray get it &
read it, because it has a great character as a witty smart Book', writes 'Catherine'
(*Letters* 85). Its author, apparently, has a 'great Character in these Parts as a man
of Learning & wit'.

If the first two volumes of *Tristram Shandy* had been made less provincial,
thanks to Dodsley's advice, there was still in them much of the frustration Sterne
felt about his own circumstances. In the fictional world of *Tristram Shandy*
Sterne could at least rehearse his sense of grievance. It is difficult not to identify
Tristram's protest with what one imagines Sterne might have felt about the course
of his own life, up until 1759:

> On the fifth day of *November*, 1718 … was I *Tristram Shandy*, Gentleman,
> brought forth into this scurvy and disasterous world of ours … not but the
> planet is well enough, provided a man could be born in it to a great title or to a

great estate; or could anyhow contrive to be called up to publick charges, and employments of dignity and power;—but that is not my case … I have been the continual sport of what the world calls Fortune … in every stage of my life, and at every turn and corner where she could fairly get at me, the ungracious Duchess has pelted me with a set of as pitiful misadventures and cross accidents as ever small HERO sustained. (*TS* 9, 10)

However, while the novel is very much occupied by the issue of misfortune, Sterne could also use it to correct those same misfortunes, partly by rewriting his own genealogy.

Sterne seems to have been acutely conscious of what he perceived as the disparity in rank between his father and mother. In a note appended to his own account of his father's marriage, he implied that his father's only reason for marrying Agnes Hobert was that he was in debt to her father.[30] The idea that his mother interrupted what might otherwise be a straightforward line of masculine 'gentlemanly' descent may well inform the opening of *Tristram Shandy*, in which Tristram's mother interrupts Walter Shandy at the moment of insemination and causes Tristram's 'animal spirits' to disperse. However, the terms in which Tristram (or Sterne) imagines conception give priority to the male, thus minimising his mother's influence on his social standing. The animalculists believed that the homunculus – a miniature but fully formed human being – could be found in each spermatozoon. The role of the mother, by the animalculists' account, was merely to act as a receptacle for its growth. Tristram Shandy makes his first appearance as an homunculus *en route* to the womb. The existence of the homunculus was not universally accepted as an account of how the embryonic human being was formed – if anything, it was the minority view.[31] The majority of preformationists were ovists rather than animalculists – the ovists being those who maintained the primacy of the female in generation. Tristram Shandy, though, makes his first appearance as the fully formed homunculus who is, significantly, a 'little gentleman'. The title page also tells us that what follows is the life and opinions of Tristram Shandy, 'gentleman'.

In *Tristram Shandy*, he could also promote a version of himself in the shape of Yorick. Though not a success in worldly terms – indeed, this is a kind of success for which Yorick seems to care little – the fictional parson is an appealing figure of comedy and pathos who attracts the sympathy of passersby even as they gaze on his tombstone and repeat the inscription, 'Alas poor *Yorick*!' Sterne could represent the events leading to the suppression of *A Political Romance* in such a way as to reflect credit on Yorick. The parson, it seems, is not a supplicant seeking to gain credit with patrons, but rather the honest and innocent victim of a humourless and malicious world, careless of his friend Eugenius's lectures on discretion. Yorick, we

---

[30]   Ross, *Laurence Sterne*, 24

[31]   See Laqueur, 173. See also Louis A. Landa, 'The Shandean Homunculus: The Background of Sterne's "Little Gentleman"', *Restoration and Eighteenth-Century Literature: Essays in Honor of Alan Dugald McKillop*, ed. Carroll Camden (Chicago: University of Chicago Press, 1963), 49–68.

find, always fails to get the credit he deserves, either for paying for the midwife's licence or for lending his horses. In the book, though, his reputation might be saved. Yorick, we find, had damaged his reputation by riding a 'lean, sorry jack-ass of a horse' (*TS* 16). The poor horse he rides does not denote poverty, though, but identifies the parson rather as a Quixotic idealist, too generous for his own good. The rather convoluted explanation for his choice of mount devolves, finally, on the parson's excessive generosity in lending every good horse he had to any needy person in the parish, with the result that he had a bad horse to get rid of every 10 months. The ability to perform acts of charity was an indicator of social status, and Sterne was nettled by the story of his generosity to a widow, told by John Hill in *The Royal Female Magazine* of April 1760, both because it was untrue and because it was beyond his means to accomplish.[32] Given that Tristram insists that Yorick's horse 'was a horse of chaste deportment', one wonders if this too was an attempt, by Sterne, to vindicate his reputation by answering rumours of his sexual infidelities.[33]

Most striking, from the point of view of self-promotion, was the inclusion of 'The Abuses of Conscience', now read by Corporal Trim. A whole chapter on the attitude Trim adopts before speaking implicitly satirizes the idea that rhetoric is an exact science, but gratifyingly, the audience in the book largely reacts to Sterne's rhetorical ploys just as he might have hoped. Walter Shandy's curiosity is aroused by the seeming challenge to Scripture with which the sermon begins:

> HEBREWS xiii. 18.
> ——*For we* trust *we have a good Conscience.*——
> "TRUST!—Trust we have a good conscience!"
> [Certainly, *Trim*, quoth my father, interrupting him, you give that sentence a very improper accent; for you curl up your nose, man, and read it with such a sneering tone, as if the Parson was going to abuse the Apostle … I have a great desire to know what kind of provocation the Apostle has given.] (*TS* 98–9)

Favourable comment on the sermon's language, reasoning and dramatic qualities – the latter being one of Sterne's specialities in the pulpit – is interjected by Walter Shandy. For Toby Shandy, the sermon is deficient only in being too short. Sterne expressed his own hopes that the potential success of his fictional work might promote him as a cleric in Tristram's final remark on the sermon, while at the same time sounding a slightly sour note of disillusion:

> in case the character of parson *Yorick*, and this sample of his sermons is liked, —that there are now in the possession of the *Shandy* Family, as many as will make a handsome volume, at the world's service,—and much good may they do it. (*TS* 114)

---

[32]   Alan B. Howes, *Sterne. The Critical Heritage* (London: Routledge and Kegan Paul, 1974), 73.

[33]   See Ross, *Laurence Sterne*, 117–20, *et passim*.

The death of Yorick halfway through the first volume of *Tristram Shandy* can be read as a symbolic renunciation of his clerical identity on Sterne's part, although, as the inclusion of the sermon might itself suggest, it is a renunciation which was far from complete. The idiosyncratic time scheme of the novel actually allows Yorick to return, and Yorick returned again as the author of *A Sentimental Journey* in 1768.

If the ethical point of view in the novel is essentially the same as that of the *Sermons*, it is safe to say that Sterne found writing the former more pleasurable than the latter. In a letter of 1761 he wrote: 'I shall write as long as I live, 'tis, in fact, my hobby-horse: and so much am I delighted with my uncle Toby's imaginary character, that I am become an enthusiast' (*Letters* 143). *Tristram Shandy* itself may well have begun as a somewhat uneasy satire on sermon-writing and sermon-stealing. Cancelled readings in 'A Fragment in the Manner of Rabelais' suggest that Sterne's first intention was to have Homenas borrow his sermon from Dr. John Rogers, whose name would allow a bawdy play on 'rogering it'. After cancelling Rogers, Sterne substituted 'Norris', for Dr. John Norris and then finally inserted 'Clark'.[34] Lansing Hammond's study of Sterne's sermons and Melvyn New's edition of the *Sermons* have shown that Clarke, Rogers and Norris were all sources from which Sterne himself borrowed for his own homiletic work. Originality was not prized in the Anglican sermon: the 35th of the Thirty-Nine Articles of the Church of England listed only 21 approved topics for preaching. Morality was not, after all, an area in which the Anglican preacher would be expected to make new discoveries. Yet Sterne was self-conscious enough about his own plagiarism to make it the starting point for this, possibly the earliest draft of *Tristram Shandy*. It was a matter he alluded to in the preface to *The Sermons of Mr. Yorick* (1760), and the issue surfaces again in Volume VI, Chapter xi of *Tristram Shandy*. Inscribed on the first page of one of Yorick's sermons is the reflection: '– *For this sermon I shall be hanged, – for I have stolen the greatest part of it*' (*TS* 343). Although the *Sermons* were actually more successful with the public than *Tristram Shandy*, Sterne himself does not seem to have been happy with didacticism. In a letter to David Garrick in 1762, he gave his opinion of a play written by a lady:

> Tis from the plan of Diderot, and possibly half a translation of it—The Natural Son, or, the Triumph of Virtue, in five acts—It has too much sentiment in it, (at least for me) the speeches too long, and savour too much of *Preaching*—this may be a second reason, it is not to my taste. (*Letters* 162)

Nevertheless, Sterne carried over to *Tristram Shandy* many of his techniques as a preacher, and the work is itself much occupied with the subject of rhetoric.

Sterne was practised in methods of engaging, and holding, his congregation's attention, and some of those techniques are replicated in *Tristram Shandy*. The opening sentence of the novel (like the opening sentence of the sermon on

---

[34]   Melvyn New, 'Sterne's Rabelaisian Fragment: A Text from the Holograph Manuscript', *PMLA* 87 (1972), 1092n.

the abuses of conscience) is moderately shocking, insofar as it offers an affront
to ideas of filial piety:

> I wish either my father or my mother, or indeed both of them, as they were in
> duty both equally bound to it, had minded what they were about when they begot
> me. (*TS* 5)

The cryptic opening paragraph engages the curiosity of Sterne's imagined reader:

> Pray, what was your father saying?—Nothing.—Then positively, there is nothing
> in the question, that I can see, either good or bad. (*TS* 5–6)

Tristram Shandy presents the reader with imagined characters, dramatic situations
and appeals to feeling, but all these were very characteristic of Sterne in the pulpit.
As Melvyn New's edition of the *Sermons* also makes abundantly clear, these were
techniques which were not unique to Sterne as an Anglican preacher. The sermons of
Bishop Hall and Archbishop Herring, among others, offered drama and sentiment.
Sterne's imagining of the departure of the Prodigal Son in his sermon on Luke xv.
13 – '*And not many days after, the younger son gathered all he had together, and
took his journey into a far country*' – might serve as a typical example:

> —I see the picture of his departure:—the camels and asses loaden with his
> substance, detached on one side of the piece, and already on their way:—the
> prodigal son standing on the fore ground, with a forced sedateness, struggling
> against the fluttering movement of joy, upon his deliverance from restraint:—the
> elder brother holding his hand, as if unwilling to let it go:—the father,—sad
> moment! with a firm look, covering a prophetic sentiment, "that all would not
> go well with his child,"—approaching to embrace him, and bid him adieu.
> (*Sermons* 187)

Sterne supplies, at length, the 'interesting and pathetic passages' (*Sermons* 186)
which the Scriptures leave out.

Where Sterne's status as a figure of authority in the pulpit might have been
clear, his status as an author was far from evident, as he himself was well aware.
Volumes I and II of *Tristram Shandy* suggest a certain deference on Sterne's
part towards his potential audience, although there is an intermittent confidence,
as well, about his own abilities and prospects. '[M]y life and opinions are
likely to make some noise in the world, and, if I conjecture right, will take in
all ranks, professions, and denominations of men whatever, – be no less read
than the *Pilgrim's Progress* itself', writes Tristram (*TS* 7). Still, Walter Shandy's
peculiarities are tentatively introduced:

> I would sooner undertake to explain the hardest problem in Geometry, than
> pretend to account for it, that a gentleman of my father's great good sense …
> could be capable of entertaining a notion in his head so out of the common
> track,—that I fear the reader, when I come to mention it to him, if he is the least
> of a cholerick temper, will immediately thow the book by; if mercurial, he will

> laugh most heartily at it; and if he is of a grave or saturnine cast, he will, at first sight, absolutely condemn as fanciful and extravagant. (*TS* 43)

Tristram (or Sterne) also anticipates objections to Toby Shandy's hobbyhorse (*TS* 69), and there is a note of ingratiation in Sterne's self-conscious flattery of the reader's intelligence: 'As the reader (for I hate your *ifs*) has a thorough knowledge of human nature' (*TS* 24). We find him cultivating a relationship of equality with readers who would be in a position to exclude him from their company:

> As you proceed further with me, the slight acquaintance which is now beginning betwixt us, will grow into familiarity; and that, unless one of us is in fault, will terminate in friendship ... Therefore, my dear friend and companion, if you should think me somewhat sparing of my narrative on my first setting out,—bear with me. (*TS* 10)

We might read the guying of the whole business of dedications in Volume I, Chapter ix, as an oblique revelation of Sterne's willingness to sell himself:

> If therefore there is any one Duke, Marquis, Earl, Viscount, or Baron, in these his Majesty's dominions, who stands in need of a tight, genteel dedication, and whom the above will suit ... it is much at his service for fifty guineas. (*TS* 14)

His facetious reference to his bookseller as the person to whom the money should be paid – 'Be pleased, my good Lord, to order the sum to be paid into the hands of Mr. *Dodsley*, for the benefit of the author' – perhaps indicates a sense that in relation to Dodsley, he was indeed in the position of supplicant.

If Smollett had reservations about involvement in the market, Sterne had no such qualms. Where Sterne differs from Smollett is in his acceptance of the fact that his success was dependent on opinion. The tolerance of subjectivity in the novel itself is of a piece with Sterne's own participation in the market. Sterne, we know, revised early drafts of *Tristram Shandy* guided by the comments of the London bookseller, Robert Dodsley, and the aim of those revisions seems to have been to make the novel more appealing to a metropolitan audience. He had Catherine Fourmantel send his letter recommending the book to David Garrick, who would in turn, presumably, act as a former of opinion about the book. Ultimately *Tristram Shandy* did indeed promote Sterne, to an extent which must have astonished and delighted him. Just as Sterne had hoped, the success of *Tristram Shandy* did allow him to publish a collection of sermons. Two volumes were published in May 1760 on the basis of the success of Volumes I and II of *Tristram Shandy*. Going through six editions in Sterne's lifetime, the *Sermons* actually out-did *Tristram Shandy* as a commercial success.[35]

It says much for Sterne's sense of himself, still, as cleric, that his address to 'You Messrs. the monthly Reviewers' in Chapter iv of Volume III (January 1761), reflected not on the astonishing success that *Tristram Shandy* had so far

---

[35]   Ross, *Laurence Sterne*, 245.

enjoyed, but on the criticism which *The Sermons of Mr. Yorick*, Volumes I and II, had attracted. The content of the sermons had, in fact, been praised.[36] It was the manner of publication which had caused offence. Sterne had explicitly traded on the success of *Tristram Shandy* by publishing the sermons under the name of Mr. Yorick. This Owen Ruffhead, writing in the *Monthly Review* of May 1760, characterized as no less than 'the greatest outrage against Sense and Decency, that has been offered since the first establishment of Christianity'.[37] Even at so late a date as 1765 Sterne still conceived of his sermons as in some sense redeeming him. He characterizes further volumes of sermons as 'stand[ing] penance' for his '7 & 8 graceless Children' (*Letters* 252) – in other words, Volumes VII and VIII of *Tristram Shandy*.

By the time Volume III was published in 1761, Sterne's identity had undergone a process of change. The role of successful author offered him a new position of privilege. From this lofty position, he could forgive his critics: 'Heartily and from my soul, to the protection of that Being who will injure none of us, do I recommend you and your affairs' (*TS* 128). Even in the space of the few months which elapsed between the publication of the first and second editions of Volumes I and II, Sterne's social horizons had risen. In April 1760, he took the bold step of dedicating the second edition – mockery of dedications notwithstanding – to no less a figure than Prime Minister William Pitt, then at the height of his popularity thanks to English successes in the Seven Years War. The humility of the dedication, allegedly written in 'a bye corner of the kingdom, and in a retired thatch'd house' was somewhat bogus, as Sterne most probably wrote it in London, and in any case, he had recently moved from the country parsonage to York itself.[38] The appearance of the Author's Preface in Volume III may be a typically Shandean joke, but it is also suggestive of a growing sense, on Sterne's part, of his own identity as that public figure, the author. In Volumes III and IV he could invoke the name of Garrick (twice) as someone who was now a friend. In the guise of Tristram the writer, he could imagine himself overcoming the social handicap of being a younger son, as his father had been. Only after the death of his brother Bobby does Tristram declare, exactly halfway through the book, that 'it is from this point properly, that the story of my life and my OPINIONS sets out' (*TS* 269).

The preface addresses the difficulties posed by the range of reactions to the novel. By January 1761, when Volumes III and IV appeared, the response to *Tristram Shandy* had gone from initial appreciation to an adverse reaction once Sterne's profession was known. Numerous bawdy pamphlets had appeared, at once imitating and attacking *Tristram Shandy*. Among them were *Explanatory Remarks on the Life and Opinions of Tristram Shandy by Jeremiah Kunastrokius* (April 1760), *The Clockmakers Outcry Against the Author of The Life and Opinions of Tristram Shandy* (May 1760) and *Tristram Shandy's Bon Mots, Repartees, odd*

---

[36]   Howes, 77.

[37]   Ibid.

[38]   Ross, *Laurence Sterne*, 9.

Adventures, and Humorous Stories ... and a New Dialogue of the Dead, between Dean Swift, and Henry Fielding, Esq. (June 1760). The first biography of Sterne had appeared, in the shape of an article by John Hill in the *Royal Female Magazine* of April 1760. Bishop Warburton had written to Sterne, advising him against 'violations of decency and good manners'.[39] Oliver Goldsmith had attacked Sterne (though not by name) in *The Citizen of the World*: 'a bawdy blockhead often passes for a fellow of smart parts and pretensions' – with much more to the same effect.[40] An anonymous author (perhaps Ralph Griffith, founder and editor of the *Monthly Review*) intervened to justify the re-evaluation of Sterne (rather than the novel itself) in the *Grand Magazine* of June 1760. Sterne still had his appreciative readers, though. A fellow cleric, the Rev. John Brown, wrote to Sterne from Geneva that '– Tristram Shandy has at last made his way here. Never did I read any thing with more delectation'.[41] An unidentified critic in the *Imperial Magazine* (1760) wrote, 'No man is equal to [Sterne] in the "ridentem dicere verum" [speaking the truth while laughing], and I think, he and his work may both justly be styled originals'.[42] Edmund Burke, reviewing *Tristram Shandy* in the *Annual Register* of 1760, judged that 'the life of *Tristram Shandy* has uncommon merit'.[43]

One possible response to popularity, and notoriety, appears in the opening sentence of the Preface:

> No, I'll not say a word about it,—here it is;—in publishing it,—I have appealed
> to the world,—and to the world I leave it;—it must speak for itself. (*TS* 153)

However, Sterne also takes on the diversity of comment on the novel. He addresses 'my dear Anti-Shandeans, and thrice able critics, and fellow-labourers' – the latter a reference, presumably, to the 'swarm of imitators' – as well as, in the same sentence, 'you, most subtle statesmen and discreet doctors renowned for gravity and wisdom' (*TS* 153). All the diverse responses to the novel could potentially be brought together into some sort of unanimity and coherence under the terms of Locke's antithesis of wit and judgement: Tristram begins by wishing that everyone, including him, would be given both of these gifts (*TS* 154). He then imagines all of them, writer and readers alike, vacillating between extremes of agreement and disagreement as they would be swayed in one direction by judgement, and then in the other by wit – but still with a unanimity of movement. Halfway through the preface, however, Tristram concedes that 'the fervent wish in your behalf with which I set out, was no more than the first insinuating *How d'ye* of a caressing prefacer stiflng [sic] his reader, as a lover sometimes a coy mistress into silence' (*TS* 157). In place of this 'stifling', the preface draws to a conclusion with the breaking of a pattern:

---

[39]   Howes, 87.
[40]   Ibid., 92.
[41]   Ibid., 102.
[42]   Ibid., 105.
[43]   Ibid., 106.

—Here stands *wit*,—and there stands *judgment*, close beside it, just like the two knobbs I'm speaking of, upon the back of this self same chair on which I am sitting. …

Now for the sake of an experiment, and for the clearer illustrating this matter,— let us for a moment, take of one of these two curious ornaments (I care not which) from the point or pinnacle of the chair it now stands on. (*TS* 159)

The Preface ends by ceasing to aim for coherence: 'I have no abhorrence whatever, nor do I detest and abjure either great wigs or long beards … mark only, – I write not for them' (*TS* 160).[44]

By the end of Volume IV, Sterne could see himself as a monarch choosing his kingdom and issued a challenge: '[T]he thing I *hope* is, that your worships and reverences are not offended – if you are, depend upon't, I'll give you something, my good gentry, next year, to be offended at' (*TS* 270). This could be read as a threat or a promise: the bawdiness of the novel evidently did not detract from its appeal, even if, as John Mullan has commented, some readers read Sterne selectively, then and later, for the sentiment.[45] Sterne was well aware that the controversy surrounding his work contributed to sales. In a letter to Stephen Croft in May 1760 he noted: 'There is a shilling pamphlet wrote against Tristram', and added, '– I wish they would write a hundred such' (*Letters* 107). Writing to Croft again in February 1761, after the publication of Volumes III and IV, Sterne reported 'One half of the town abuse my book as bitterly, as the other half cry it up to the skies – the best is, they abuse and buy it, and at such a rate, that we are going on with a second edition, as fast as possible' (*Letters* 129–30). Frank Donoghue has argued that Sterne actually increased the bawdiness of his work in order to reclaim it, in effect, from his imitators, but the evidence is far from clear.[46] Volumes V and VI (1762) contained material no less (but also no more) salacious than previous volumes. What does emerge is an unwillingness to tone down the content, at the same time that Sterne still courted respectability. Sterne offered another dedication, this time to his aristocratic friend Viscount Spencer, with a request to dedicate the story of Le Fever to his wife. The acceptance of the dedication by Lady Spencer might have offered an assurance that the work was suitable for female readers.[47] *The Clockmaker's Outcry*, for example, had claimed, in mock-serious vein, that *Tristram Shandy* had made it impossible for any respectable woman to speak of clocks without embarrassment. In his flirtatious dialogue with the female reader of the novel, however, Sterne

---

[44]   For a fuller discussion of the breaking of patterns in *Tristram Shandy*, see Mark Loveridge, *Laurence Sterne and the Argument about Design* (London: Macmilllan, 1982).

[45]   John Mullan, *Sentiment and Sociability. The Language of Feeling in the Eighteenth Century* (Oxford; Clarendon Press, 1990), 148–57.

[46]   Donoghue, 77.

[47]   Ross, *Laurence Sterne*, 269.

spoke from an attitude to women that predated – and bypassed – 'politeness'. His assumed woman reader is not innocent, or passive, in sexual matters.

On the whole, though, by 1762 Sterne seems less occupied by the question of criticism. There are some waspish or dismissive references to the reviewers, and at the beginning of Volume V, he could talk to his male reader on equal terms, very literally over the heads of the jackass critics:

> Did you think the world itself, Sir, had contained such a number of Jack Asses?—
> How they view'd and review'd us as we passed over the rivulet at the bottom of
> that little valley. (*TS* 329)

Volumes V and VI attracted a mix of praise and censure, as before, but also a measure of indifference. Thomas Becket (of Becket and Dehondt, Sterne's publishers from 1762 onwards) told Sterne that copies were selling slowly, and although Sterne wrote that he had 'no doubt about the edition selling off' (*Letters,* 191–2), some anxiety surfaces in Tristram's reference to 'ten cart-loads of thy fifth and sixth volumes still – still unsold' (*TS* 439). It was at this time that Sterne began to consider the publication of further volumes of sermons.

Nevertheless, in the dedication of Volume IX (1767) to William Pitt, now Lord Chatham, Sterne styled himself, simply, 'The Author', rather than 'Your well wisher, and most humble Fellow-Subject', as he had done in 1760. (Pitt, too, had undergone changes in status since 1760: he had been out of office since 1761, but was ennobled in 1766.) Whatever the fluctuations of opinion about his work, Sterne's identity as author, by 1767, was very much established. In Volume VII (1765) Tristram seemed to retract the note of protest voiced some six years earlier:

> I think myself inexcusable, for blaming Fortune so often as I have done, for
> pelting me all my life long, like an ungracious dutchess, as I call'd her, with so
> many small evils. (*TS* 415)

However, Chapter xiii of Volume IX (1767) suggests how writing, in Sterne's mind, equated with the attainment of gentility. It also communicates something of the effortfulness of maintaining that identity:

> Now in ordinary cases, that is, when I am only stupid, and the thoughts rise
> heavily and pass gummous though my pen …

> —I never stand confering with pen and ink one moment … I change my shirt—put
> on a better coat—send for my last wig—put my topaz ring upon my finger; and in
> a word, dress myself from one end to the other of me, after my best fashion.

> Now the devil in hell must be in it, if this does not do … A man cannot dress, but
> his ideas get cloath'd at the same time; and if he dresses like a gentleman, every
> one of them stands presented to his imagination, genteelized along with him—so
> that he has nothing to do, but take his pen, and write like himself. (*TS* 506)

Writing in a certain style conferred gentility: and gentility could be put on and off like a coat.

The contrast with Tobias Smollett is striking. Smollett's novels, at least up until *Sir Launcelot Greaves*, enact the tension that existed in their author's mind between an older idea of the gentleman and one who, in order to earn the money to support his gentlemanly status, had to sacrifice his independence. Sterne, too, is attached to an older ideal of the gentleman, but he seems to have accepted rather more readily the idea that it was becoming obsolete. While Walter and Toby Shandy are depicted with much affection, they represent the old order in *Tristram Shandy*, and it is on the verge of petering out. The landed gentleman Walter Shandy is between 50 and 60 years of age at the time of Tristram's conception. Toby Shandy will never father children. Even the Shandy bull is incapable of reproduction. *Tristram Shandy* might read both as an elegy for older ideals of the gentleman and as a record of their mutation into an understanding of the situation of the writer. Toby Shandy is an embodiment of Steele's ideal of the gentleman in *The Christian Hero* (1701), a work which itself aimed to redefine the heroic in terms of the new 'polite' ethic. Steele, writing to reform soldierly manners, would have a military man perform his role with temperance and moderation. Toby Shandy is a model of precisely those qualities Steele had recommended – 'that Sublime and Heroick Virtue, Meekness, a Virtue which seems the very Characteristick of a Christian, and arises from a great, not a groveling Idea of things' – whilst also retaining his military character.[48] Tristram insists, on many occasions, on Toby's courage. However, the political occasion for this conception of the gentleman was of course now long distant, and Toby's courage never has to be put to the test because he has already been removed, permanently, from the battlefield. His theatre of activity, as he replicates the Williamite wars in miniature on his bowling green, is small, private and essentially self-delighting. He is a version of the writer. Like Sterne, he is reconciled to disagreement and dissent: 'A great matter, if they had differed, replied my uncle *Toby*, – the best friends in the world may differ sometimes' (*TS* 106).

Tristram Shandy began as a novel of protest against the forces, and the hierarchical system, that kept Laurence Sterne in a subordinate position. As it developed over an eight-year period, though, it also recorded the fluctuations in Sterne's fortunes in a different and commercial world. Perhaps Sterne's success as an author compensated in his own eyes for his relative failure in his other, more traditional profession. Although the novel contains Tristram's memorable complaint, and although it reflects what we can see as Sterne's dissatisfaction with his own situation, there is no need to see it as evidence of religious unbelief – revealing, perhaps, the 'real' Sterne, the Sterne who found it difficult to write sermons. To be sure, there are no tangible rewards and incitements to virtue in *Tristram Shandy*, after the manner of Richardson and Fielding, no emphatic endorsements of Providence, but *Tristram Shandy* still invokes the idea of balance and providential compensations. Walter Shandy proposes to counter the misfortune

---

[48]   Steele, *Christian Hero*, 51.

of Tristam's crushed nose by naming his child Trismegistus, and he has recourse to 'that great and elastic power within us of counterbalancing evil, which like a secret spring in a well-ordered machine, though it can't prevent the shock – at least it imposes on our sense of it' (*TS* 223). When Toby strikes Walter's shins with his crutch, Walter's delight with his own wit about chances makes him forget about the pain in his leg. Tristram writes of the relief gained by throwing his wig up to the ceiling, when he discovers that he has burnt a sheet of good writing:

> nor do I think anything else in *Nature*, would have given such immediate ease. this, like a thousand other things, falls out for us in a way, which tho' we cannot reason upon it,—yet we find the good of it, may it please your reverences and worships—and that's enough for us. (*TS* 233)

The pain of Toby's wound is offset by the pleasure he gains from enacting sieges on the bowling green. In Book IV, Chapter iv, the undeserved misfortunes of the grenadier who was unjustly whipped, or of Trim's brother Tom, imprisoned by the Inquisition, might be seen as 'balanced' by Toby's gift of his bowling green, and a pension, to Trim. Walter Shandy's grief over the death of Bobby is mitigated by the fragments of philosophy he is able to utter, and Tristram, once again, describes this in terms of proportion:

> A blessing which tied up my father's tongue, and a misfortune which set it loose with a good grace, were pretty equal: sometimes, indeed, the misfortune was the better of the two; for instance, where the pleasure of the harangue was as *ten*, and the pain of the misfortune but as *five*—my father gained half in half, and consequently was as well again off, as it had never befallen him. (*TS* 282)

One might say that *loss* of balance, in the form of the weights in the sash-window, leads to the misfortune of Tristram's accidental circumcision. Tristram also makes a facetious claim for balance as an aesthetic principle in his work. He maintains that he purposefully leaves places open to objections from critics so as to sustain it:

> You see as plain as can be, that I write as a man of erudition;—that even my similes, my allusions, my illustrations, my metaphors are erudite,—and that I must sustain my character properly, and contrast it properly too,—else what would become of me? (*TS* 70)

We might think, here, of Fielding's comic justification of dull prefatory chapters by way of an appeal to the principle of contrast in *Tom Jones*:

> Contrast, which runs through all the Works of Creation, and may, probably, have a large Share of constituting in us the Idea of all Beauty, as well natural as artificial: for what demonstrates the Beauty and Excellence of anything but its Reverse? … To say the Truth, these soporific Parts are so many Scenes of *Serious* artfully interwoven, in order to contrast and set off the rest … (*TJ*, I, 212–15)

Tristram tears out the chapter describing the journey to the visitation dinner because including it would destroy 'that necessary equipoise and balance (whether of good or bad) betwixt chapter and chapter, from whence the just proportions and harmony of the whole work results' (*TS* 252). '[A] good quantity of heterogeneous matter', writes Tristram, must be inserted, in order to 'keep up that just balance betwixt wisdom and folly' (*TS* 504). When Toby Shandy perplexes Dr. Slop by wishing that he had seen '*what prodigious armies we had in Flanders*', Tristram writes that the safest way to take off the force of an unexpected wish is to 'wish the *wisher* something in return of pretty near the same value, – so balancing the account on the spot' (*TS* 125).

One could go on. Toby's whistling of *Lillabullero* while Dr. Slop reads the ex-communication forms a kind of harmony-in-disharmony. Describing his father rising from the bed, Tristram speaks of 'the transition from one attitude to another – like the preparation and resolution of the discord into harmony, which is all in all' (*TS* 221). Walter and Toby Shandy shaking their heads over women and childbirth, with entirely different thoughts in mind, might be regarded as concord in discord: 'never did two heads shake together, in concert, from two such different springs' (*TS* 227). As various commentators have pointed out, the disorder and incoherence of the work are only apparent. The action of the last book is anticipated in the first. There is a definite and closely observed chronology. This is not to try to make *Tristram Shandy* into *Tom Jones* – it is too idiosyncratic, too driven by the associative powers of the individual mind to conform to any overarching structure. But it is still very much informed by the kinds of Christian consolation the eighteenth-century mind favoured.

It is also very much informed by secular conceptions of forces making for harmony or coherence in society – as are the sermons. As John Traugott puts it: '[T]he phenomenon of sentimentalism in Sterne's age may well be an intuitive development of a new principle of cultural coherence at a time when the mystique of Church and State were being rapidly attenuated'.[49] One finds the same language of harmony and concord in Adam Smith's *Theory of Moral Sentiments* (1759) as in Sterne's *Tristram Shandy* and the same realisation that total unanimity might not be possible. Smith describes the situation of a sufferer who finds that spectators are not as moved by his distress as he himself is:

> The person concerned is sensible of this, and ... passionately desires a more complete sympathy. He longs for the relief which nothing can afford him but the entire concord of the affections of the spectators with his own. To see the emotions of their hearts, in every respect, beat time to his own, in the violent and disagreeable passions, constitutes his sole consolation. ... What they feel, will, indeed, always be, in some respects, different from what he feels, and compassion can never be exactly the same with original sorrow ... These two sentiments, however, may, it is evident, have such a correspondence with one

---

[49]   Traugott, 4, 5.

another, as is sufficient for the harmony of society. Though they will never be unisons, they may be concords, and that is all that is wanted or required.[50]

In Sterne's sermon 'Vindication of Human Nature', he argues, against the proposition that the individual lives entirely for himself, that: 'Compassion has so great a share in our nature, and the miseries of this world are so constant an exercise of it, as to leave it in no one's power *to live to himself*' (*Sermons* 71). In *Tristram Shandy*, sympathy transcends isolation, as when Toby Shandy sits in silent sympathy while his brother lies prostrate on the bed, stricken with grief over his son's crushed nose. It quells anger, as when Walter Shandy, after berating Toby about his obsession with sieges, is moved to ask Toby's forgiveness by the sight of his brother's good-natured upturned face. The cult of sentiment or, more generally, the shift towards feeling as the basis of moral judgement may also be seen as rooted in the idea of a code of manners suitable to man in a commercial society. Nicholas Phillipson has argued that Adam Smith's *Theory of Moral Sentiments* should be seen 'not as a general theory of morals, but as an account of the process by which men living in a commercial society acquire moral ideas and may be taught to improve them'.[51] As with David Hume, no divine hand of regulation, nor ideas of natural law, are required to maintain the society Smith invokes. Custom and the prevailing sentiments of mankind suffice. One feels, though, that an all-embracing sympathy, in Smith's scheme, serves the same totalizing and ultimately coercive purpose as a shared religion in the thinking of an earlier period. Sterne in *Tristram Shandy* does not try to coerce. In fact, he was far too ironic about feeling for the taste of his contemporaries, too inclined to end the tender moment with bathos, and too aware of how sexual desire might inform compassion – as in the case of the Widow Wadman's concern about the extent of the injury to Toby's groin.[52] In *A Sentimental Journey*, the rush of sentiment is almost invariably undermined by a reminder of baser origins and motives, as when Yorick reflects that his new-found feelings of charity towards the French are 'more warm and friendly to man, than what Burgundy (at least of two livres a bottle, which was such as I had been drinking) could have produced'.[53] Even his gift of a snuffbox to the monk is designed to make a favourable impression on the woman he has just met at the remise door.

By neither preaching nor instructing, Sterne partially surrendered what had long been regarded in humanist thought as one of the chief functions, and justifications, of secular literature. The writers that Sterne draws on, though, suggest that he still

---

    [50]   Adam Smith, *The Theory of Moral Sentiments*, in *British Moralists 1650–1800*, ed. D.D. Raphael (Indianapolis: Hackett, 1991), Vol. II, 212.

    [51]   Nicholas Phillipson, 'Adam Smith as Civic Moralist', *Wealth and Virtue. The Shaping of Political Economy in the Scottish Enlightenment*, eds Istvan Hont and Michael Ignatieff (Cambridge: Cambridge University Press, 1983), 182.

    [52]   For a fuller discussion of this topic, see Mullan, 147–200.

    [53]   Laurence Sterne, *A Sentimental Journey Through France and Italy by Mr. Yorick*, ed. Gardner D. Stout, Jr. (Berkeley: University of California Press, 1967), 68.

saw himself as writing in a humanist tradition: *Tristram Shandy* owes much to Rabelais, Robert Burton and Montaigne. However, Sterne takes his cue from that side of humanism which did not emphasize reform or reverence for authority. I have already suggested that Sterne took from Rabelais a way of subverting hierarchies. In Burton he might find a precedent for his own relativism. It is possible that Sterne read Burton as a fellow sceptic. As J.M. Bamborough points out, some readers of Burton found in him a moral or spiritual relativist.[54] The rehearsal of the disagreements of obscure authors in the *Anatomy* might be read as a satire on humane learning itself, with Burton inventing some of his authorities as part of the joke – precisely Sterne's practice in *Tristram Shandy*. Walter Shandy reveres authority, and he can find one to support almost any of his eccentric notions. Some of these are real, some of Sterne's own invention. In *The Anatomy of Melancholy*, Burton, in the persona of Democritus Junior, defends himself against the charge of plagiarism by pointing out that he usually acknowledges his sources and that he has used his borrowings in his own way.[55] Sterne borrows from Burton, Montaigne, Locke and others but often dislocates quotation from its original context and reconstitutes it in his own work so as to give it a different emphasis.

In the closing chapter of the novel, Walter Shandy uses the fact that noble language may be found to speak of war, but not of the sexual act, as proof of the honour of the former and the bestiality of the latter. This is, in fact, either a reversal of Montaigne's argument when he writes on this subject in the essay 'On Some Verses of Virgil' or an extreme and selective reading of some of Pierre Charron's observations in 'Of Wisdom' – and Charron was himself heavily indebted to Montaigne.[56] In Uncle Toby's 'Apologetical Oration', which defends his participation in war, Sterne reverses the sense of some passages from 'Democritus to the Reader' in *The Anatomy of Melancholy* which form part of a diatribe *against* war.

In Montaigne's scepticism, and in his awareness of custom as a determinant of human behaviour, Sterne might have found a precedent for his own liberalism. In the *Essays* Sterne could find a precedent, too, for the form and style of *Tristram Shandy*: informal, digressive, apparently spontaneous, personal, immediate. Montaigne wrote of his own life – an 'ordinary life, without distinction' as he once described it – and his style, still in keeping with classical standards of decorum, would therefore be 'low'. By giving his work the then unusual title of 'essais', Montaigne signified that these were attempts, or trials: attempts to catch the *progress* of his thoughts, rather than the conclusions. In Montaigne, Sterne could find a humanist who reneged on what might have been seen as his duty of public service, just as Sterne turned from his clerical life to the life of an author.

---

[54]   J.B. Bamborough, Introduction to *The Anatomy of Melancholy*, eds Thomas C. Faulkner, Nicolas K. Kiessling and Rhonda L. Blair (Oxford: Clarendon Press, 1989), Vol. I, xxxiii.

[55]   Robert Burton, *The Anatomy of Melancholy*, Vol. I, 11.

[56]   Melvyn New (ed.), Notes to *Tristram Shandy*, in *The Florida Edition of the Works of Laurence Sterne*, Vol. III, 549–50.

Montaigne sold his post as magistrate and retired to his library, solemnizing his retirement with a Latin inscription on the wall which referred to the 'freedom, tranquillity and leisure' of his retreat.[57] Sterne, though, who declared that he wrote 'not to be fed, but to be famous', could hardly have concurred with Montaigne's more stoic address to the reader: 'I have had no thought of serving either you or my own glory'.[58] Sterne, as one might expect, probably read Montaigne as more 'modern' than he actually was.

With an emphasis on simplicity of doctrine and rationality, and with its relative dismissal of tradition and authority, Latitudinarianism could lend itself to reformist thought. In 1766 the Anglican cleric, Rev. Francis Blackburne, friend and biographer of the republican Thomas Hollis, and the same Blackburne from whom Sterne had once had hopes of patronage, published *The Confessional, or a Full and Free Enquiry into the Right, Utility, Edification, and Success, of Establishing Systematical Confessions of Faith and Doctrine in Protestant Churches*. Blackburne argued that belief in the Scriptures as the word of God was sufficient for intending Anglican clergy and that the requirement for subscription to the Thirty-Nine Articles should be abolished.[59] Blackburne himself had struggled with the issue of subscription. The controversy surrounding *The Confessional* led to the Feathers Tavern petition of 1771, and though the petition was defeated, it prompted some examination of an unreformed British constitution.

John Gascoigne traces a line from Bishop Benjamin Hoadly's notorious sermon of 1716 on 'The Nature or Kingdom of Christ', in which he offered the view that Christ left behind him no judges over the consciences of the people, through Blackburne's *Confessional*, to Anglican clergy such as John Disney and John Jebb, who became Unitarians, and Christopher Wyvill, who remained within the Church and founded the reformist Yorkshire Association, which itself provided a model for subsequent reform movements.[60] Blackburne and Sterne moved in the same circles in Yorkshire, with Sterne having at one time preached a sermon for the absent Blackburne. One cannot imagine Sterne struggling, like Blackburne, over the matter of subscription or willingly engrossing himself in matters of theological controversy. For much of his life he aimed for preferment within the Church. What he did struggle with, though, was the writing of sermons. Didacticism did not come easily to him, perhaps for personal reasons, but also, one feels, because the political and religious climate had changed since Richardson and Fielding engaged with the threat from Methodism and Jacobitism in the 1740s. In their own distinct

---

[57]   Montaigne, Michel de, *The Complete Works of Montaigne. Essays, Travel Journal, Letters*, trans. Donald M. Frame (London: Hamish Hamilton, 1957), ix–x.

[58]   Ibid., 2.

[59]   Francis Blackburne, *The Confessional, or a Full and Free Enquiry into the Right, Utility, Edification, and Success, of Establishing Systematical Confessions of Faith and Doctrine in Protestant Churches* (n.p., 1767), xlvi *et passim*.

[60]   John Gascoigne, 'Anglican Latitudinarianism and Political Radicalism in the Late Eighteenth Century' *History* 71 (1986), 22–38.

and separate ways, we can see Blackburne and Sterne both questioning authority and working out the liberal possibilities of Latitudinarianism.

The context for *Tristram Shandy* is war: the War of the League of Augsburg (1689–1697) in which Toby Shandy fights but which ends, for him, with his wound at the Siege of Namur in 1695; the War of the Spanish Succession (1702–1713), which Toby and Trim enact on the bowling green; and the Seven Years War (1756–1763), during which Volumes I to VI of the novel were published. From the English point of view, the first of these wars was primarily about ensuring a Protestant succession and putting down James II's attempt to invade Ireland and use it as a springboard to recover his former kingdom. More broadly, though, it was a war fought to contest French ambitions in Europe and the threat of French dominance. The War of the Spanish Succession was once more fought over the threat of French hegemony after a Bourbon prince, Philip d'Anjou, grandson of Louis XIV, became Philip of Spain in 1700. The breadth of the conflict was unprecedented. The War of the Spanish Succession involved military action across continental Europe, in Quebec and the West Indies, and naval operations in the Mediterranean, the North Atlantic and the Caribbean, along the North American seaboard and off the coast of West Africa. This wider sphere of conflict reflected the importance of colonies and trade to the powers involved. One of the provisions of the Treaty of Utrecht (1713), and a sign of Britain's increasing importance as an imperial power, was the ceding to Britain, by Spain, of the *assiento*: that is, the right to supply slaves to the colonies.

By the time of the Seven Years War, the European territory and interests of a Hanoverian monarch still had to be defended but dynastic issues mattered rather less than trade; and the interests of trade were served by the retention and acquisition of colonies. British military and naval successes in the war were formidable. In India in 1757, Robert Clive retook Calcutta from the Nawab of the rich province of Bengal, seized Chandernagore from the French, and ultimately took control of Bengal itself. Senegal, the sugar island of Guadeloupe, and Quebec were taken from France in 1759. There was a decisive victory over the French at Wandewash, in South India, in 1760, and Britain took the *Compagnie des Indes'* main trading base at Pondicherry. Martinique, Grenada, St. Lucia and St. Vincent in the Caribbean, and in Canada, Montreal fell to the British in 1762. By the time of the Treaty of Paris in 1763, Britain was confirmed in its possession of Canada and had won the right to expand westwards in North America to the Mississippi. In 1688, Britain was a second-class nation, unable or unwilling to influence European relations; by 1763 it was the foremost imperial power.[61]

Sterne's choice of the Siege of Namur for the wounding of Toby, and as the cause of his retirement from military service, was not accidental. There were in fact two sieges, one in 1692, when the French took Namur from the Allies, and a second siege in 1695. Though England and its allies ultimately took the garrison,

---

[61]   See Geoffrey Holmes, *The Making of a Great Power. Late Stuart and Early Georgian Britain 1660–1722* (London: Longman, 1993), 229 *et passim*.

the second Siege of Namur was, at that date, one of the bloodiest battles ever fought and very much a pyrrhic victory, with some 12,000 deaths on the allied side. The French lost around 8,000 men. Laurence Sterne might have learned of the battle from his relation Brigadier-General Robert Stearne, who had served with the Royal Regiment of Foot in Ireland and was present at the siege. The young Sterne stayed at the Brigadier-General's castle in Westmeath for a year.[62] He might also have gathered additional details from Rapin's *History of England* (1732–1745), a work that he consulted during the writing of *Tristram Shandy*.[63] Toby Shandy's retirement from the theatre of war to the harmless diversions of his bowling green immediately after the Siege of Namur, his subsequent inability to father children, and Walter and Toby Shandy's distortions of Montaigne and Burton point to Sterne's own anti-war sentiments. Opposition to war is not in itself an especially liberal attitude, and protests against the bloodiness and futility of war may also be found in the writings of Swift and Fielding. Historians have spoken of popular revulsion against the War of the Spanish Succession and the Seven Years War on account of the scale of the conflict, the loss of life and the financial cost.[64] Uneasiness with the martial version of the hero in the seventeenth and eighteenth centuries might be traced back through such works as Fielding's *Amelia* (1752), Steele's *The Christian Hero* (1701) or Milton's *Paradise Lost* (1667).

However, Sterne's opposition to compulsion *is* radical, and libertarian, and speaks from the new European order of the 1760s. '[T]he fortune of war' says Toby, 'has put the whip into our hands *now*' (*TS* 493), and for him, it should be used to protect the defenceless and persecuted, like the Moorish girl whom Trim's brother Tom finds sweeping the floor of a shop in Lisbon. Linda Colley has argued that the realisation that the nation was now a great imperial power not by virtue of trade, but by force of arms, raised deeply troubling questions about Britons' conception of themselves as a uniquely liberty-loving people.[65] How could Britain's massively extended dominion over, say, French Catholics in Quebec or over non-Christian Asians be justified? Sterne's response, in *Tristram Shandy*, is implicitly to oppose conquest, in whatever form it might take: whether it be Walter Shandy's dogmatic notions or Toby Shandy's appropriation of Walter's jackboots.

Few literary careers better illustrate the increasing legitimacy of fiction in the eighteenth century than that of Laurence Sterne. Before the publication of the first two volumes of *Tristram Shandy* in 1759–1760, he was an obscure cleric living in Yorkshire, whose attempts to climb the ladder of preferment within the Church had not been as successful as he had hoped. As an author, he had a European reputation. Few novels better illustrate the reversal of priorities in terms of sermons

[62]   Ross, *Laurence Sterne*, 28.

[63]   See Theodore Baird, 'The Time-Sceme of Tristram Shandy and a Source', *PMLA* 51 (1936): 803–20.

[64]   See Holmes, 239; Holmes and Szechi, 282–4; Paul Langford, *A Polite and Commercial People. England 1727–1783* (Oxford: Clarendon, 1989), 346.

[65]   Linda Colley, *Britons. Forging the Nation 1707–1837* (1992) (New Haven and London: Yale University Press/Yale Nota Bene, 2008), 101–5.

and fiction in the eighteenth century than *Tristram Shandy*. Sterne included his sermon 'The Abuses of Conscience' in his novel, hoping that a successful novel would promote sales of a collection of sermons – as it did. The *Monthly Review* for December 1759 praised Sterne's ingenuity and supposed didactic intent: 'The address with which he has introduced an excellent moral sermon, into a work of this nature (by which expedient, it will probably be read by many who would peruse a sermon in no other form) is masterly'. However, the extent to which Sterne's sermon does not cohere with the novel points to the conditions which made for the growing legitimacy of fiction. Mikhail Bakhtin argued that the novel, as a form of discourse, is opposed to any monologic system:

> images of official-authoritative truth, images of virtue (of any sort: monastic, spiritual, bureaucratic, moral, etc.) have never been successful in the novel … For this reason the authoritative text always remains, in the novel, a dead quotation, something that falls out of the artistic context.[66]

Yorick's sermon falls out of Stevinus's writings on fortification: it is connected with embattlement and restriction. Once relocated in the novel, it is fragmented and challenged. After Trim's reading, it is lost again through a hole in Yorick's pocket, trodden in the dirt by his horse's foot, buried 10 days in the mire, and sold by a beggar for a half-penny. After the sermon ends, *Tristram Shandy* resumes its own characteristic discourse, which is a discourse without absolutes or rules. The sermon falls: the novel rises.

---

[66] Mikhail Bakhtin, *The Dialogic Imagination*, ed. Michael Holquist, trans. Caryl Emerson and Michael Holquist (Austin: University of Texas Press, 1981), 344.

Chapter 5
'Hurtful Insignificance'?:
The Novel in the Later Eighteenth Century

By 1770 the novels of Richardson, Fielding, Sterne and Smollett, along with those of approved women writers such as Sarah Fielding, Charlotte Lennox and Frances Sheridan, had given the novel as a genre a degree of respectability, or at least currency. Nevertheless, the later eighteenth century was also the period when hostility to the novel was expressed in the sharpest terms.[1] A letter from T. Row in the *Gentleman's Magazine* of December 1767 voiced a common complaint:

> Mr. URBAN,
> It must be a matter of real concern to all considerate minds, to see the youth of both sexes passing so large a part of their time in reading that deluge of familiar romances, which, in this age, our island overflows with. 'Tis not only a most unprofitable way of spending time, but extremely prejudicial to their morals, many a young person being entirely corrupted by the giddy and fantastical notions of love and gallantry, imbibed from thence. There is scarce a month passes, but some worthless book of this kind, in order to catch curiosity by its novelty, appears in the form of two volumes 12mo. price five or six shillings, and they are chiefly the offspring, as I take it, of the managers of the circulating libraries, or their venal authors. Some few of them, indeed, have come from better pens, but the whole together are an horrible mass of hurtful [i.e. harmful] insignificance, and, I suppose, may amount now to above an hundred volumes; I speak at the lowest.[2]

In similar vein, the Rev. Vicesimus Knox, headmaster of Tunbridge school, felt that the multiplication of novels had contributed to the degeneracy of the age. Romances, he thought, had been favourable to virtue since they exhibited patterns of perfection. Richardson's novels, on the other hand, morally worthy as they were, included 'the lively description of love, and its effects', which it would have been better to omit.[3] Fielding, though entertaining, also included scenes which might

---

[1]   This reaction has been well documented. See W.F. Galloway, 'The Conservative Attitude toward Fiction, 1770–1830', *PMLA* 55 (1940), 1041–59; John Tinnon Taylor, *Early Opposition to the English Novel* (New York: King's Crown Press, 1943); and Joseph F. Bartolomeo, *A New Species of Criticism. Eighteenth-Century Discourse on the Novel* (Newark: University of Delaware Press, 1994), esp. 112–32.

[2]   Ioan Williams (ed.), *Novel and Romance 1700–1800. A Documentary Record* (London: Routledge and Kegan Paul, 1970), 272.

[3]   Vicesimus Knox, Essays, Moral and Literary (1779), 2v. (New York: Garland, 1972), Vol. II, 187.

corrupt the young mind. Smollett was too coarse. The multitude of works imported from France had nothing to recommend them. The sentimental manner of current novels had, he thought, 'given an amiable name to vice', and they weakened the mind.[4] Once addicted to novels, the reader was unlikely to submit to serious study – serious study being the reading of Livy, Sallust, Homer and Virgil. Since entertainment would always be sought, though, the boy's library might contain stories of voyages and travels, true histories and such narratives as *Telemachus* and *Robinson Crusoe*, along with Plutarch's *Lives* and the *Spectator*. No wonder that in her preface to *Evelina*, published anonymously in 1778, Fanny Burney could write that in the republic of letters, there was no one less respectable than a novelist.

Vicesimus Knox was an extreme critic of the novel and its potential to corrupt. More temperate critics were still suspicious, however. James Beattie, professor of Moral Philosophy at Marischal College, Aberdeen, includes a lengthy discussion of prose fiction in his *Dissertations Moral and Critical* (1783). The majority of his essay is taken up with tracing the relationship between the development of civilisation and the development of prose fiction.[5] After the fall of the Roman Empire, there was little learning, or commerce, and men believed in superstitious and extravagant tales – an argument by now long familiar, and articulated, for instance, in Smollett's preface to *Roderick Random* (1748). As late as the fourteenth century, Sir John Mandeville was presenting as fact ridiculous stories about a race of men 50 feet tall, or beings who had eyes in their shoulders. Feudal government promoted chivalry, and in fictional terms this produced the romance. The romance was appropriate for an ignorant and credulous age, which could believe in giants, dwarves, enchanted castles and necromancy. No sooner had *Don Quixote* appeared, though, than chivalry vanished, and the old romance was replaced by serious romances (such as *Robinson Crusoe*, *Clarissa*, or *Sir Charles Grandison*) or comic romances, such as the works of Marivaux, Le Sage, Smollett and Fielding.

For Beattie, the use of fiction or fable to convey moral or political instruction was justified, particularly in the case of the common people, who were not qualified to understand argument. Yet he is still uneasy about the blurring of boundaries between truth and fiction, for adherence to truth is man's 'indispensable duty'.[6] In Xenophon's *Cyropedia*, a history of Cyrus the Great, for example, the outlines of the story are true, but the author also inserts many invented incidents. The fondness for fabulous narrative in the Orient is indicative of the Asian's indolence and credulity. The *Arabian Nights* is a work with which most young people in Britain will be acquainted, and it is a work characterized by 'great luxury of description … and variety of invention', but 'nothing that elevates the mind, or touches the heart'.[7] The *Spectator*, *Rambler* and *Adventurer* offer fables in

---

[4]   Ibid., 189.

[5]   James Beattie, *Dissertations Moral and Critical*, (1783) (New York: Garland, 1971).

[6]   Beattie, 505. One might compare Beattie's position here with that articulated a full century earlier by John Bunyan in his introductory verses to *A Pilgrim's Progress* (1678).

[7]   Beattie, 510.

the Eastern manner but with a moral tendency. Johnson's *Rasselas* (1759) and Hawkesworth's *Almoran and Hamet* (1761) are also worthy examples, though the latter might induce some perplexity about divine Providence.

Pilgrim's Progress (1678) shows that the author possessed powers of invention, which, 'if they had been refined by learning, might have produced something very noble'.[8] However, Bunyan's fiction offends against probability, and the work conveys theological errors. *Gulliver's Travels* (1726) is a worthy and useful work insofar as it attacks human pride and folly, and the style of the narrative gives it an air of truth. Nevertheless, the last of the four voyages is 'an absurd, and an abominable fiction'.[9] It contains filthy and indecent images, and attributing reason and happiness to a race of beings who have no religion undermines belief. The misanthropy of the last book will make the reader dissatisfied with human nature, and therefore with Providence, which made man as he is. The allegory by means of which Swift represents the Reformation in *A Tale of a Tub* (1704) is too mean for its subject and links 'solemn truths' with 'ludicrous ideas'.[10] *Robinson Crusoe*, on the other hand, is one of the few works which may safely be put in the hands of children. Richardson is moral, but too tedious, and his exemplars are so perfect as to discourage imitation. The character of Lovelace is liable to be too attractive to the young male reader. Smollett goes beyond the realms of probability, and Beattie can find nothing of moral value in his works. Fielding is wise and well-read in the classics, but too particular in describing the errors of his hero in *Tom Jones*. After this lengthy discussion, Beattie ends rather defensively:

> Let not the usefulness of Romance-writing be estimated by the length of my discourse upon it. Romances are a dangerous recreation ... I would therefore caution my young reader against them: or, if he must, for the sake of amusement, and that he may have something to say on the subject, indulge himself in this way now and then, let it be sparingly, and seldom.[11]

By the 1770s and 1780s, the habit of novel-reading had evidently become common enough to obtrude itself upon the attention of those charged with the education of the young throughout Great Britain, from the master of Tunbridge School to the professor of moral philosophy at Marischal College. Apart from criticisms of particular novels, Row, Knox and Beattie revive a number of old objections to fiction, such as the charge of deception and the view that time spent reading works of entertainment was time spent unprofitably. Knox and Beattie also represent the beginnings of a change in taste in the direction of more refined standards which lasted well into the nineteenth century. However, a concern about the pernicious effects of novel-reading seems to have been generated, primarily, by the sheer increase in the numbers of novels published. An emphasis on overwhelming

---

[8]   Ibid., 514.
[9]   Ibid., 515.
[10] Ibid., 516.
[11] Ibid., 573–4.

quantity, as well as metaphors of consumption, can also be found in the comments of writers more favourably disposed towards fiction. The authors here are John and Anna Laetitia Aikin (later Barbauld), writing in their *Miscellaneous Pieces in Prose and Verse*, of 1773:

> Of all the multifarious productions which the efforts of superior genius, or the labours of scholastic industry, have crowded upon the world, none are perused with more insatiable avidity, or disseminated with more universal applause, than the narrations of feigned events, descriptions of imaginary scenes, and delineations of ideal characters.[12]

This sense of overwhelming quantity was not unfounded, by the standards of the time. James Raven calculates that new novel titles were three times more numerous in 1790 than in 1750 and that in 1788, the number of new novels being published was more than 10 times the annual total of any year between 1700 and 1720.[13] The concept of perpetual copyright was finally overturned in 1774, and thereafter the way was opened for the reprinting of any book whose copyright had expired. Although there was a dip in new novel production between 1775 and 1783, total novel production, including reprints, increased fourfold between 1750 and 1790.[14] From 1777 onwards, the bookseller George Kearsley published his popular series *The Beauties of ...*, with selections from Sterne, Fielding, Richardson, Goldsmith and others. In November 1779 James Harrison launched his weekly *Novelists Magazine*, publishing older fiction in extract form. This was followed by the *New Novelists Magazine* in 1781. Cooke's editions of 'classic' fiction were issued in the 1790s in 6d weekly numbers.[15] Raven's *Bibliographical Survey* lists 1,421 new titles published between 1770 and 1800, and by 1800 some 90 new novels were being published annually; the total, including reprints, was more than 150. These figures should be taken in the context of a growth in the production of printed material generally: Raven estimates a threefold increase in publication between 1740 and 1800.[16]

The explosion in novel production should be seen in the context of the more general boom in consumerism which characterized the last third of the eighteenth century, to which reference has already been made. Once a market for fiction existed, a successful work would inspire less worthy imitations, as Clara Reeve observes in her history of the novel, *The Progress of Romance* (1785).[17] Thereafter

---

[12]   Williams, *Novel and Romance*, 280.

[13]   James Raven, *Judging New Wealth, Popular Publishing and Responses to Commerce in England, 1750–1800* (Oxford: Clarendon, 1992), 38.

[14]   See James Raven and Antonia Forster (eds), *The English Novel 1770–1829: A Bibliographical Survey of Prose Fiction Published in the British Isles*, Vol. I, 1770–1829 (Oxford: Oxford University Press, 2000), 27.

[15]   Raven and Forster, 89.

[16]   However numerous the new titles, though, it should be noted that the size of editions was small, most being produced in editions of no more than 500.

[17]   Clara Reeve, *The Progress of Romance*, 7.

the circulating libraries would make such works available to everybody in the cheapest manner, making them a 'public evil'. More than 20 circulating libraries were operating in London by 1770, some of them owned by the same firms who published fiction. The later eighteenth century saw the development of these specialist booksellers. By the 1770s, the major novel-publishing firms were John and Francis Noble, Thomas Becket and Peter de Hondt (the publishers of Volumes V and VI of *Tristram Shandy*), John Bew, John Roson and Thomas Lownds (the publisher of Horace Walpole's *The Castle of Otranto* and Fanny Burney's *Evelina*). Between 1770 and 1800 publication of fiction by the firms of Thomas Hookham, the Robinsons, the Nobles, and William Lane expanded, with the last becoming the most prolific publisher of new novel titles. Lane published 80 new titles in the 1780s, 217 in the 1790s, generally of the potboiler variety. As Raven notes, six of the nine 'horrid' novels which enthral Isabella Thorpe in *Northanger Abbey* were published by Lane.[18]

As we have already seen, novels themselves responded to the growth of consumerism. In *Humphry Clinker* (1771), Matthew Bramble finds that England is a place where luxury, and the acquisition of commodities, results in the breakdown of social distinction. Every 'upstart of fortune' could acquire the trappings of a gentleman. As McKendrick argues, acquisition served important social and political functions.[19] Possessions could underline the exclusive status of the nobility or the professional status of the educated élite. Conversely, though, consumer goods signalling status could simply be acquired by those who had the money to do so. Luxury also signified dependency and effeminacy. The spread of luxury could be connected with other social evils. In Richard Graves's *The Spiritual Quixote* (1773), Geoffry Wildgoose takes issue with the pursuits of a virtuoso, who later turns out to be the tyrannical father of Wildgoose's inamorata, Julia Townsend: as in *Clarissa*, the spirit of acquisition equates with arbitrary authority. In Oliver Goldsmith's *The Vicar of Wakefield* (1766), contact with the market, and aspirations to gentility, always lead to misfortune. A merchant in town decamps with nearly all of Primrose's fortune of £14,000. In order to raise money to make a better appearance in the world as his daughters, it seems, are to be taken on as companions to two ladies in town, Primrose's son Moses is sent to market to sell a horse but returns with only a gross of green spectacles. Primrose himself goes to the market but is also cheated of his money. Mackenzie's *The Man of Feeling* (1771) repeats the pattern. Harley, a modest and rather passive young man of slender means, reluctantly agrees to go to London to court the favour of a baronet. Once in town, he is fleeced by card-sharpers and the baronet rejects his suit. He visits Bedlam, and among the inmates finds a stock-jobber ruined by fluctuations in the market and a young woman whose intended husband died of a fever whilst he strove to improve his prospects by going to the West Indies. Returning from London, Harley tells a fellow traveller that 'The immense riches

---

[18]   Raven and Forster, 80.
[19]   McKendrick, 2.

acquired by individuals have erected a standard of ambition, destructive of private morals and of public virtue'.[20] He subsequently meets an old man, Edwards, ruined by a squire whose first concern was profit. Edwards is forced to take on more expenses than he can afford, and a merchant who has money belonging to him goes bankrupt. He survives with his son, on a smaller farm, until the arrival of a press gang. Edwards takes his son's place as a recruit and goes to the East Indies. Here he sees an old Indian tied to a stake and given 50 lashes every day to induce him to reveal the whereabouts of treasure. Nearing his own village, Harley discovers that a schoolhouse has been pulled down because it stood in the way of a squire's prospect. In 'A Fragment', entitled 'The Man of Feeling Talks of what he does not Understand', he criticizes the desire for wealth driving the establishment of a British empire in India. The narrative concludes with Harley becoming ill as a result of nursing Edwards through a fever and welcoming death as a means of 'retiring from life' (*MF* 94).

The characteristic response to luxury in such novels is to turn to the margins in search of a place free from corruption. This in itself might be seen as part of the long programme, by the middle classes, to separate the idea of virtue from birth. David Morse argues that, by the reign of George III, virtue had been 'so extensively redefined in terms of the lowly, the feminine, the primitive and the culturally marginal that the aristocratic connotations of the term were virtually obliterated'.[21] The significant and more memorable figures in *The Man of Feeling* are the beggar, the penitent prostitute and the ruined farmer, rather than Harley himself. Contemporary readers certainly found this to be the case: the story of Old Edwards was extracted and published in four magazines between 1778 and 1810, as well as in gift books and anthologies.[22] Goldsmith's country idyll in *The Vicar of Wakefield* owes as much to his nostalgia for Ireland as it does to Horace, and Smollett's ideal, too, is a place on the margins which might restore personal and national health and moderation, as we find in the depictions of Scotland, and more briefly, Wales, in *Humphry Clinker*. As Smollett's sympathetic representation of a Methodist, Clinker himself might be said to represent the uncorrupted margins.

In *The Spiritual Quixote* Geoffry Wildgoose, a gentleman, undergoes a temporary conversion to Methodism and becomes an itinerant preacher. His conversion allows Graves to satirize the sect's excesses, but it also gives him a spokesman who could articulate an earnest version of Anglicanism which was going out of fashion – Graves himself was an Anglican cleric. When the virtuoso argues that the collecting of medals is as useful an activity as history and chronology, or even poetry, painting and sculpture, Wildgoose replies that the only branch of knowledge worthy of pursuit is 'the knowledge of our fallen state,

---

[20]   Henry Mackenzie, *The Man of Feeling*, ed. Brian Vickers, with an Introduction and Notes by Stephen Bending and Stephen Redgrave (Oxford: Oxford University Press, 2001), 62.

[21]   David Morse, *The Age of Virtue. British Culture from the Restoration to Romanticism* (London: Macmillan, 2000), 24.

[22]   Mackenzie, *The Man of Feeling*, 117n.

and of our redemption, as revealed in the Bible'.[23] Graves evidently approves of Methodistical preaching when it reaches, and reforms, an audience unmoved by the more conventional and rational Anglican sermon. Insofar as Methodism might promote social disorder, though, Graves was evidently opposed to it. The example of Wesley and others, argues Dr. Greville towards the end of the novel, might be followed by men who 'prefer the ease and Advantage of a Teacher to the drudgery of a mechanic trade' (*SQ* 451).

However, if novels could offer a critique of luxury, the novel itself, as contemporary commentators saw, was a commodity in the market; and the antipathy to consumption in these works was by no means total. It could hardly be. The defence of trade predated Whig apologetics after the Restoration, and there was really no opposition to capitalism as such, whatever the local anxieties about such matters as the East India Company.[24] *The Vicar of Wakefield*, despite its subject matter, is a light-hearted comedy, and there is no real misogyny in Goldsmith's depiction of the Primrose females' quest for gentility. One could say that they are, in fact, surrogates for his own uncertain search for gentility, a search which he might have perceived as comic, so long as it was distanced from him. Part of the value of Scotland for Smollett, as he represents the case in *Humphry Clinker*, is that here commerce and hierarchy can co-exist. Patriarchy survives in the shape of Campbell, the Highland laird, who appears at an open window to be greeted by the prostration of his vassals and dependents. Yet Edinburgh and Glasgow thrive, and commerce might also be introduced in such Highland communities as Argyll: 'a company of merchants might, with proper management, turn to good account a fishery established in this part of Scotland' (*HC* 256). For Graves, too, consumption and order are not incompatible. In some respects the new order merits his approval. In Worcester, for example, Wildgoose finds hardly any Methodists, for 'a considerable part of the town had their attention taken up by their China work, lately established there, under the auspices of the ingenious and excellent Dr. Wall' (*SQ* 324). When Jerry Tugwell, Wildgoose's rusticated companion, remarks on the condition of the workers sweating at an ironworks, Wildgoose undertakes to prove to him that the division of labour is inevitable – and beneficial to all. The presence on the periphery of the novel of miners, workers in the potteries, and many other trades testifies to the commercial realities of late eighteenth-century life.

Each of these works is conscious, too, in different ways, of its own place in the market. *Humphry Clinker*, for example, opens with an exchange of letters in which the Rev. Jonathan Dustwich bargains with a bookseller for the sale of the letters which form the subsequent narrative. Dustwich, for his part, is sure that the letters tend 'to the information and edification of mankind: so that it becometh a sort of

---

[23]   Richard Graves, *The Spiritual Quixote, or The Summer's Ramble of Mr. Geoffry Wildgoose. A Comic Romance*, ed. Clarence Tracy (London: Oxford University Press, 1967), 117.

[24]   Raven, *Judging New Wealth*, 89.

duty to promulgate them *in usum publicum*' (*HC* 1). The market, then, might serve the public interest insofar as it offered a means of conveying instruction. Goldsmith prefaced his work with a most defensive 'Advertisement', in which everything in the work could, apparently, be deemed a fault, depending on the vagaries of public taste. In fact, he judged the taste of his audience very well. Critics found *The Vicar of Wakefield* a welcome alternative to the dangerous tendencies of novels. For Lady Sarah Pennington, the work provided one exception to her general rule that very few romances and novels were worth reading.[25] An anonymous review in the *Critical Review* of June 1766 concurred: 'We find nothing in this performance to turn the attention upon the writer, or to inflame the passions of the reader; as we see daily practised by the common herd of novelists'.[26] Though a writer in the *Monthly Review* found the novel especially difficult to characterize, he thought it deserved praise for its 'moral tendency; particularly for the exemplary manner in which it recommends and enforces the great obligations of BENEVOLENCE'.[27]

Goldsmith's desire to take on the rank and influence of the gentleman is particularly clear in *The Vicar of Wakefield*, and despite the work's valorization of retirement and simplicity, this ambition could in fact only be made available by an involvement in the market. Much of *The Vicar of Wakefield* is based on the changes of status which Goldsmith himself either endured or hoped for. Primrose undergoes rapid downward changes of fortune, and a reduction in fortune and expectations was something Goldsmith himself had experienced. Thanks to the improvidence of his father, he had to enter Trinity College, Dublin not as a pensioner, as his father had been, but as a sizar, distinguished from wealthier students by his uniform and earning his tuition and board by waiting on them at table.[28] In 1747 Goldsmith's father died, leaving no money for his expenses at college. Family tradition dictated that Goldsmith should take orders, and he presented himself for ordination, only to be rejected by Bishop Synge. After returning from Europe in 1756, Goldsmith scraped a living as an apothecary's assistant, an usher and a corrector of the press in Richardson's printing shop.

Early in the novel, Primrose meets a stranger at an obscure inn. This is Burchell, whose inability to pay his bill seems to have been caused by his excessive charity – a familiar pattern. Burchell's description of himself, in the third person, draws on elements of Goldsmith's own life, but suitably embellished and uprated: 'He early began to aim at the qualifications of the soldier and the scholar; was soon distinguished in the army, and had some reputation among men of learning ... in his own whimsical manner he travelled through Europe on foot, and now, though he has scarce attained the age of thirty, his circumstances are more affluent than ever'

---

[25]   G.S. Rousseau (ed.), *Goldsmith: The Critical Heritage* (London: Routledge and Kegan Paul, 1974), 51.

[26]   Ibid., 46.

[27]   Ibid.

[28]   Ralph M. Wardle, *Oliver Goldsmith* (Lawrence: University of Kansas Press, 1957), 25 ff.

(*Goldsmith*, IV, 29–30). Burchell's mistake has been his excessive benevolence, another circumstance based on Goldsmith's own efforts to be more charitable than his resources warranted. Most of the work is concerned with retaining gentility without money: Mrs. Primrose tries to use the family's plough horse to ride to church, and the straps of her saddle break. The family decides to have their portrait painted and find that the finished article is too big to fit into any room in the house. Goldsmith could scarcely hope to support gentility without money in London, where he lived and worked as a writer, but he might sustain it in a place with, as he pictures it, simpler demands, and less refined manners: in other words, in Ireland. He would also have been less subject to the requirements of the same market which might offer to promote his interests. Primrose speaks of a distant neighbourhood where it will still be possible for him to 'enjoy [his] principles without molestation' (*Goldsmith* IV, 25).

Social position in the novel is fluid: hardly anybody's identity is stable. Primrose sends his eldest son, George, to town, and when he meets with him again three years later, his son is, briefly, an actor. He has also been usher at a school, unsuccessful author, prospective colonialist, teacher, musician, art connoisseur and thesis examiner. Burchell appears at first as a penniless stranger but proves to be a landed gentleman. The two ladies from town are actually prostitutes. George's account of his experiences and his humiliations, particularly as an author, is clearly based on Goldsmith's own life. Burchell/Thornhill, on the other hand, is a fantasy of the esteem and independence Goldsmith dreamt of enjoying. Almost the first thing that Primrose notices about Burchell is his inappropriate independence of view:

> But what surprised me most was, that though he was a money-borrower, he defended his opinions with as much obstinacy as if he had been my patron. (*Goldsmith* IV, 28)

In fact his poverty is only a disguise: he is actually a gentleman. His fame is such that Primrose has heard of him, and Primrose describes Sir William Thornhill in terms which place him as the Christian gentleman: 'a man of consummate benevolence' (*Goldsmith* IV, 29). Burchell is an authority on taste, and in the end, it is he who controls events, springs surprises and dispenses justice.

For Scottish writers like Smollett and Mackenzie, the conflict between involvement in the market and independence was particularly acute. 'In 1707', argues John Robertson, 'Scotland effectively faced a choice: either the nation preserved its existing political institutions at the cost of severely restricting its economic opportunities, or it yielded up its institutional independence and accepted union with England in return for free trade across the border and access to the English commercial empire'.[29] The Act of Union, then, gave the priority to commerce and wealth. So, in terms of the tradition which J.G.A. Pocock has

---

[29]   John Robertson, 'The Scottish Enlightenment at the limits of the civic tradition', *Wealth and Virtue. The Shaping of the Political Economy in the Scottish Enlightenment*, eds Istvan Hont and Michael Ignatieff (Cambridge: Cambridge University Press, 1983), 137.

termed 'civic humanist', but which is also known as classical republicanism, or as Robertson has it, simply the 'civic tradition', this meant that Scotland, by virtue of the Act of Union, had lost the basis for independent, and therefore uncorrupted, virtuous activity on the part of those citizens who would have formed the élite. Given the inescapability of the market in the eighteenth century, and particularly in the later eighteenth century, this predicament might not only present itself in Scotland, but writers in the Latitudinarian tradition, like Sterne and Graves, seem fairly untroubled by it. We might remember that one of the characteristics of Latitudinarianism was its capacity to reconcile morality with worldly gain: the commandments of God, as Tillotson reminded his congregation, were 'not grievous'. Smollett and Mackenzie, though, plainly are troubled by the potential conflict between independence and involvement in the market, and the lack of a truly independent and effectual protagonist anywhere in Mackenzie's fiction is telling. The device of the 'found' manuscript seems to have been particularly useful to Mackenzie: all of his fictional works begin with it. Perhaps it enabled him to distance himself from direct engagement with the market. The significant figures in *The Man of Feeling* are the sufferers at the hands of economic activity. Moreover, both Smollett and Mackenzie often demonstrate a surprising sympathy with outsiders whose virtue might seem to be severely compromised: the 'Lady of Quality' in *Peregrine Pickle*, Martin the highwayman in *Humphry Clinker*, the lying beggar and the prostitute in *The Man of Feeling*, Harriet in her 'fallen' condition in *The Man of the World* (1773) or Savillon in *Julia de Roubigné* (1777), who is obliged to assist in running a slave colony in Martinique. These figures might well be seen as versions of the Scottish predicament.

Given the implicit acceptance of the primacy of opinion, and the market, in these works, it is scarcely surprising that none of them can offer a return to the ideal of the independent country gentleman with any real conviction. *The Man of Feeling* begins with the narrator briefly describing Ben Silton, a baronet's brother, as a virtuous example now in a state of decline. More than that, he is now 'forgotten and gone'. In *The Vicar of Wakefield*, for most of the novel, the role of gentleman as moral ideal is actually vacant. The true gentleman, in the sense that he owns land and has power and influence, proves to be Burchill, but for most of the novel he is disguised as a poor man, or else he is simply absent. The ideal of the independent country gentleman might be said to remain, in *Humphry Clinker*, in the shape of Jery Melford and Matthew Bramble. Yet there is something a little unconvincing about this. Jery is thinly drawn as a character, and many of his letters function to describe his uncle or to convey Bramble's views through another channel. Though we see Bramble engaged in acts of charity, and helping to restore Baynard's estate, his inclination always seems to be to retreat from the world – although, as John Sekora notes, Smollett devotes more space to London, in the book, than he does to the whole of Scotland.[30] The matter of Lydia's possible

---

[30]   John Sekora, *Luxury. The Concept in Western Thought from Eden to Smollett* (Baltimore: The Johns Hopkins University Press, 1977), 277.

elopement with an actor, which forms the starting point for Bramble's travels in *Humphry Clinker*, seems scarcely to justify either the length of the journey or the length of time Bramble spends in places so offensive to his nervous system. The journey is more compelling than the place where it eventually ends, and the gentleman, in these works, is characteristically a traveller: which is to say, that the conception of gentility was itself undergoing change.

Most telling, in terms of secularization and the establishment of novelistic discourse, is the view of preaching as unacceptable, and the clergy as ineffectual, in these works. Graves's concern to court his audience rather than preaching to them is made apparent in the matter of the epigraphs to *The Spiritual Quixote*. As printed in the first edition, these were: 'Amusement reigns Man's great Demand' quoted from Edward Young, and 'Romances are almost the only Vehicles of Instruction that can be administered to a refined and Voluptuous People', from Jean-Jacques Rousseau. The public taste for romances, then, dictated the means available to the writer. The words 'and voluptuous' were in fact added by Graves's publisher in order to correct the author's own translation of Rousseau – a matter which caused him some irritation.[31] Clearly he was concerned, at the very least, not to antagonize his audience. Moreover, the opening pages, which feature a facetious prefatory anecdote, a postscript (at the beginning of a novel), an advertisement and a mock dedication to the king's pastry-cook, testify to the influence of Sterne. Graves's lightness of touch in the novel owes much to the example, in *Tristram Shandy*, of an unpatronising narrative voice. In any case, as we are shown at an early stage in *The Spiritual Quixote*, preaching to the gentry can be counterproductive. Powell the vicar preaches a sermon on hypocrisy, which Wildgoose takes as a personal reflection on his 'slight offences against the rules of chastity with his mother's maid' (*SQ* 17). (These are never specified.) This is enough to make him absent himself from church, and a little later he becomes a convert to Methodism. Almost the first character Geoffry Wildgoose encounters on his travels is the worldly parson Pottle, and Wildgoose reduces him to stuttering inarticulacy in an episode recalling Adams's visit to Parson Trulliber in *Joseph Andrews*. *The Man of Feeling* also eschews preaching. As we hear from the cleric who has been carrying the manuscript with him as wadding for his gun, the narrative defies categorisation: '"[Y]ou may call it what you please," said the curate; "for it is no more a history than it is a sermon"' (*MF* 4). The Introduction to *The Man of Feeling* also offers an oblique reflection on the inadequacy of the clergy. An unnamed narrator is out shooting with a curate, described as 'fatter than I': enough to place the cleric as worldly and indolent. The curate, we find, carries the remains of the manuscript, which make up *The Man of Feeling*, as wadding for his gun. He is impervious, then, to its potential to move or reform the reader. He is a thoroughly rationalist Anglican, we may assume, since the absence of syllogisms from the work causes him to discard it. In *The Vicar of Wakefield*, Primrose represents an ideal of Christian stoicism and charity, but he is penniless and almost powerless either against his

---

[31] See Graves, *Spiritual Quixote*, 476n.

wife and daughters, or against Thornhill. He is only effective as a reformer when in the prison: Primrose never preaches to the gentry.

Richardson, Fielding and Smollett promoted the legitimacy of their novels by claiming that they were true to experience – if not indeed based on a true story, as Richardson alleged of *Pamela*. In *Joseph Andrews*, Fielding is at pains to distance his fiction from the heroic romance, and in *Tom Jones* the hero, or Sophia, must be rescued from misfortune or distress without the aid of marvels; otherwise, Fielding could not use his fiction to support his case for a rational religion. In the opening sentence of the preface to *Roderick Random*, Smollett asserts that no satire is more entertaining and improving than that in which 'nature is appealed to in every particular' (*RR* xliii). Romance, on the other hand, 'owes its origin to ignorance, vanity and superstition'. If the later eighteenth century saw a degree of moral panic about the novel, it is also true to say that this view of romance, that implicitly connected it with Catholicism, began to change, and realism was no longer an imperative in terms of fictional respectability. The prejudice against fiction as a form of deception began to fade, Beattie's strictures notwithstanding. The beginnings of a rehabilitation of romance may be seen in Knox's brief remarks, and Clara Reeve's *The Progress of Romance* (1783) makes a similar argument at much greater length, and with much more detailed reference to individual works.

Euphrasia, one of Reeve's dialogists, ventures the opinion that romances 'have always been the favourite entertainment of the most savage, as well as the most civilized people'.[32] Civilisation is connected with probability in fiction, but romance is no more improbable than the epic, which is revered. The story of Sindbad [sic] the Sailor in the *Arabian Nights*, argues Euphrasia, is worthy of Homer, who in any case is himself guilty of some absurdities. Epic poetry, then, is the 'parent of Romance'.[33] The heroic romances might have taught young women to comport themselves like queens and princesses, but they also inculcated virtue, gallantry in men, and the avoidance of 'improper familiarities'.[34] Great men of the reign of Queen Elizabeth I read, and wrote, romances. In fact, though romances might have been productive of absurdities, and 'some real evils', they are, argues Euphrasia, less dangerous than some works of later times.[35] Also among the novels which combine respectability with improbability are the Oriental tales, which Euphrasia argues should not be despised. She lists Johnson's *Rasselas* (1759), Hawkesworth's *Almoran and Hamet* (1761) and Frances Sheridan's *Nourjahad* (1767) among the more worthy inheritors of the tradition begun by the *Arabian Nights*. Also of 'great merit' and 'moral tendency' are such original and uncommon novels as *A Tale of a Tub* (1704), *Gulliver's Travels* (1726), *Tristram Shandy* (1759–1767) (even though it is not a 'woman's book'), *The Life of John Buncle, Esq.* (1756, 1766) and *The Castle of Otranto* (1765).

---

[32]   Reeve, I, 14.
[33]   Ibid., I, 25.
[34]   Ibid., I, 67–8.
[35]   Ibid., I, 105–6.

The last-named of these was probably one of the most influential works of the latter half of the eighteenth century, and it produced many imitators. It also did much to promote the habit of novel reading. One edition of 500 copies was published by Thomas Lownds in December 1764. An abridgement of *Otranto* appeared in the *Universal Magazine* for 11 April 1765, followed by a second edition of 500 copies published by Bathoe and Lownds. Pirated editions of the first and second editions appeared in Dublin. In 1766 a third edition of *Otranto* was published by Bathoe. James Dodsley published a fourth edition in 1782, followed by a fifth in 1786. Two editions of *Otranto* were published in 1791, one by Dodsley and the other, an illustrated edition, printed in Parma; 1793 saw the publication of two more editions, one by Wenman and Hodgson in London, and the other by Himbourg in Berlin. The novel was reprinted with extensive omissions in the *New Wonderful Magazine, and Marvellous Chronicle* 4, in 1794. Jeffery's illustrated edition of *Otranto*, with headings in Italian, appeared in 1796. French translations appeared in 1767 and 1797, and an Italian translation in 1795.

The initial reception of *The Castle of Otranto* by reviewers was not particularly favourable. The *Critical Review* for January 1765 condemned the book's subject matter. Its contents were absurd and 'rotten'. The *Monthly* (February 1765) was kinder:

> Those who can digest the absurdities of Gothic fiction, and bear with the machinery of ghosts and goblins, may hope, at least, for considerable entertainment from the performance before us: for it is written with no common pen; the language is accurate and elegant; the characters are highly finished; and the disquisitions into human manners, passions, and pursuits, indicate the keenest penetration, and the most perfect knowledge of mankind.[36]

However, when Walpole revealed himself in the preface to the second edition as the work's author, the *Monthly* had to recant. While the reviewer believed the work to be a genuine antiquity, absurdities could be excused as 'sacrifices to a gross and unenlightened age'.[37] But it was incredible and incomprehensible that such a refined and polished author as Horace Walpole should advocate 'the barbarous superstitions of Gothic devilism'. His claim to have modelled *Otranto* on the works of Shakespeare, in the preface to the second edition, was no excuse. Supernaturalism and marvels in these plays were just necessary sacrifices to the '*caecum vulgus*' [the blind multitude].

Perhaps Walpole took a less serious view of the dangers posed by superstition, or Catholicism. By 1764, apparently, the errors of popery could be replayed for the purposes of entertainment, at least for consumption by the polite – or, to put it another way, popish errors might serve as a convenient screen for fantasies to which the middle-class Anglican reader did not violently object. Colin Haydon argues that after 1750, there was a broadening divide between 'increasingly enlightened

---

[36] *Monthly Review*, 32, 1765, Vol. I, 97.
[37] Ibid., 394.

patricians and intolerant opinion 'out of doors'.[38] The popular mentality looked back to the seventeenth century, and it had often been useful to the supporters of Hanover to point to the threat from Jacobitism and Catholicism. In due course, this tactic would come back to haunt them: opposition to the proposed Roman Catholic Relief Bill of 1778 culminated in the Gordon Riots of 1779. Horace Walpole, though, offered his readers a bogus translation of a manuscript allegedly found in the library of an 'ancient Catholic family', which told of 'Miracles, visions, necromancy, dreams and other preternatural events'. 'William Marshall, Gent.' speculated that the author of *The Castle of Otranto* might have been an 'artful priest', employing his abilities to 'enslave a hundred vulgar minds'. No such threat was posed, presumably, to the reader of his own time and class.

Walpole presents his novel as a translation by William Marshall of a work written in Italian by Onuphrio Muralto, Canon of the Church of St. Nicholas at Otranto. *The Castle of Otranto* tells of the ambition of Manfred, prince of Otranto, to keep succession to the title of Otranto in his own family, even if he must defy conventional morality and intimations of divine disapproval to do it. As the novel begins, an enforced marriage which would pass the title of Otranto to the heirs of Manfred is prevented when a gigantic helmet crushes Conrad, Manfred's sickly son, just as he is about to marry Isabella, daughter of the Marquis of Vicenza. Manfred, though already married to Hippolita, proposes to marry Isabella himself in order to father an heir and seal a family tie with the Marquis, who has the only other possible claim to Otranto. However, at the moment when his intentions become clear, the sable plumes round the helmet rise to the height of the castle windows and wave in a 'tempestuous manner'. The picture of Manfred's grandfather utters a sigh, and as Manfred follows the ghost of his ancestor, Isabella escapes.

The rightful heir appears in the shape of the seeming peasant, Theodore, whom Manfred imprisons for daring to recognize the similarity between the gigantic helmet and a helmet which usually rests on the statue of Alfonso the Good, a former prince of Otranto. At the point when Manfred is about to execute Theodore, Theodore kneels to pray, his shirt falls from his shoulder and the priest recognizes the peasant as his son – the priest being the erstwhile Count Falconara. The castle connects with the church – which are the only two locations in *The Castle of Otranto* – by way of Theodore. Manfred promises to spare Theodore's life, if the priest will return Isabella to him, but at this point portents appear again in the shape of the helmet, the plumes and the sounds of a trumpet and trampling horses. Theodore is the rightful heir and Manfred, as we discover halfway through the narrative, is actually a usurper. In the end, Manfred is brought to a sense of the sinfulness of his actions when he kills his own daughter, Matilda, in mistake for Isabella – though he remains signally unpunished for this act, except by his own guilt. Throughout the novel, Hippolita, Isabella and Matilda behave with exemplary piety, with Matilda even blessing her father, and begging *his* forgiveness, as she dies.

---

[38]   Colin Haydon, *Anti-Catholicism in Eighteenth-Century England, c.1714–1780. A Political and Social Study* (Manchester: Manchester University Press, 1993), 187.

It is clear in both the prefaces that Walpole wrote, either as William Marshall or in his own right, that his concern is not with truth, even supposing such a thing were available. Whatever the erroneous beliefs of the canon of St. Nicholas, or the characters, the important point seems to be that there is nothing in the work's language or the characters' conduct which 'savours of barbarism'.[39] Content, we might say, is almost nothing. Manners are everything: 'The style is the purest Italian'. *Otranto's* concern with counterfeiting – Manfred ultimately reveals that his claim to the title was based on a forged will – reflects the preoccupation with artificiality in almost all the novels considered in this study. In fact, despite its appearance of novelty, *Otranto* rehearses familiar themes. Identity in the novel is uncertain: neither Theodore, Manfred, nor the priest are what they appear to be. There is an abrupt disjunction between divinely ordained modes of inheritance and manmade arrangements. The many leaky compartments in *Otranto* (as in *Tristram Shandy*) are suggestive of a fundamental breakdown of hierarchies. Manfred is always locking the gates of the castle, or sending Isabella to her apartment, or confining Theodore to the giant helmet, only to find that these seemingly watertight spaces are not sealed.

Although his blending of what he considers as 'two kinds of romance' seems to offer release – 'the great resources of fancy have been dammed up' – Walpole himself seems to have been somewhat troubled by the question of mixed categories, stressing the purity and beauty of the language, in his 'translator' persona, and mounting a rather elaborate defence of his juxtaposition of servants with princes in the preface to the second edition. It is this practice which leads him to invoke the example of Shakespeare:

> I might have pleaded, that having created a new species of romance, I was at liberty to lay down what rules I thought fit for the conduct of it: but I should be more proud of having imitated, however faintly, weakly, and at a distance, so masterly a pattern, than to enjoy the entire merit of invention … . (*CO* 13)

We might see the work as a particularly apt exemplification of the idea advanced by Fred Botting, that the 'history in which Gothic circulates is a fabrication of the eighteenth century as it articulates the long passage from the feudal orders of chivalry and religiously sanctioned sovereignty to the increasingly secularized and commercial political economy of liberalism'.[40] *The Castle of Otranto* invokes the chivalric signifiers of gentility in order to sanction inheritance, but always in fragmented form. William Marshall is apologetic about the presence in the novel of no better moral than the Old Testament threat: '*the sins of the fathers are visited on their children to the third and fourth generations*' (*CO* 6, 7) – an apology which suggests scant respect for the Old Testament. From our own, twenty-first century, perspective, we might rather note that the influence of the past over the present in

---

[39]   Horace Walpole, *The Castle of Otranto*, ed. Michael Gamer (London: Penguin, 2001), 5.

[40]   Fred Botting, 'In Gothic Darkly: Heterotopia, History, Culture', *A Companion to the Gothic*, ed. David Punter (Oxford: Blackwell, 2000), 5.

The Castle of Otranto, as in, say, *Sidney Bidulph* and *Tristram Shandy*, points to a new, secular determinism.

The publication history of *Otranto* also suggests an ambivalent relationship with the market on the part of Walpole, though from a somewhat different position to other authors considered here. Horace Walpole, as third son of Sir Robert Walpole, Member of Parliament and a man of independent fortune, was no indigent gentleman writing either for a living, or to try to establish his gentility. Yet Walpole is quite as concerned with the reaction of his audience as other authors, as the two prefaces to the work might indicate. The pretence of history might allow Walpole to surprise his readers with the novelty of supernatural marvels – rather as the motley collection of antiquities at his mock-Gothic castle in Strawberry Hill might also provoke surprise. The reaction of spectators is a recurring concern in the work. The device of the gigantic helmet is introduced almost immediately, presumably to provoke wonder. When Conrad is crushed, there is a 'confused noise of shrieks, horror, and surprise' (*CO* 18). Later events provoke 'astonishment', 'surprise', 'fright and horror', 'wonder' and 'shock'. At one point, the narrator describes the domestics as 'urged by their own curiosity and love of novelty' to leave the castle and join in the search for Isabella (*CO* 64). Such are something like the reactions, one imagines, Walpole hoped to produce in an audience hungry for novelty themselves. The attention devoted to surprising marvels in *Otranto* is juxtaposed with an exaggerated account of piety and duty in the shape of Hippolita, Isabella and Matilda, that might be seen as compensating for the emphasis on mere entertainment. In his preface to the first edition, Walpole does seem conscious that the work he offers tells against the potential for reform inherent in the proliferation of print:

> Letters were then in their most flourishing state in Italy, and contributed to dispel the empire of superstition, at that time so forcibly attacked by the reformers. It is not unlikely that an artful priest might endeavour to turn their own arms on the innovators; and might avail himself of his abilities as an author to confirm the populace in their ancient errors and superstitions … Whatever his views were, or what ever effects the execution of them might have, his work can only be laid before the public at present as a matter of entertainment. Even as such, some apology for it is necessary. (*CO* 5, 6)

Until reaction to the novel had been tested, anonymous publication by Thomas Lownds shielded Walpole's identity, although he could, presumably, have had the work printed at his own press at Strawberry Hill.

In 1777 Clara Reeve published *The Champion of Virtue*, a work which by the second edition became *The Old English Baron*. In it, she offered to correct the excesses of *Otranto*:

> we can conceive, and allow of, the appearance of a ghost; we can even dispense with an enchanted sword and helmet; but then they must keep within certain limits of credibility: A sword so large as to require an hundred men to lift it;

a helmet that by its own weight forces a passage through a court-yard into an arched vault, big enough for a man to go through; a picture that walks out of its frame; a skeleton ghost in a hermit's cowl:—When your expectation is wound up to the highest pitch, these circumstances take it down with a witness, destroy the work of imagination, and, instead of attention, excite laughter ...

In the course of my observations upon this singular book, it seemed to me that it was possible to compose a work upon the same plan, wherein these defects might be avoided.[41]

It could be argued, though, that Reeve's decreased reliance on the supernatural is not only a matter of literary manners, but it also marks a further shift in the direction of secularization and democratization. Reeve's subject, too, is the restoration of the true heir, and, implicitly, the change from a feudal order to a different mode of succession. Where Manfred was a usurper, Lord Fitz-Owen, the baron of the title, more prosaically bought the estate from his kinsman Sir Walter Lovel, who has in turn built himself another house in Northumberland. The rightful heir is actually the peasant Edmund, who has been brought up in Fitz-Owen's family, as his (peasant) father hates and mistreats him: thus the true heir has received an appropriately gentlemanly education. The decay of the old aristocracy might be indicated by the neglected and decrepit wing of the castle, which is believed to haunted, and in which Edmund has to spend three nights. It is 'hung round with coats of arms, with genealogies and alliances of the house of Lovel' (*OEB* 42). Here Edmund finds, in pieces, the old armour of his father, and a ring. When Edmund is convinced, by certain supernatural appearances, of his gentle birth, Father Oswald advises him to 'make a friend of some great man, of consequence enough to espouse your cause, and to get this affair examined into by authority' (*OEB* 63). Sir Philip Harclay duly takes Edmund in on terms which allow him rank without birth, as it were. He characterizes Edmund as '[n]ot my natural son, but my relation; my son by adoption, my heir!' (*OEB* 88). Edmund takes on an assumed name, which is actually Sir Philip's mother's family name. Sir Philip (rather than Edmund) challenges Sir Walter Lovel to a joust, and when Sir Walter loses, he confesses to having given the order to kill the former Lord Lovel and to having let Edmund's mother die.

Identity, here, is something which can be legally established by proofs. Given only a door which will open to none but Edmund's hand, a suit of armour and some nocturnal groans, Edmund begins to establish his identity by questioning his foster-mother Margery Twyford, who duly reveals the circumstances of his discovery and produces a necklace with a locket, taken from his real mother, on which the Lovel insignia is engraved. After having told Margery to give her evidence when required, Father Oswald declares the proofs of Edmund's birth to be 'strong and indisputable' (*OEB* 63). Having heard testimonies and witnesses,

---

[41]   Clara Reeve, *The Old English Baron. A Gothic Story.* ed. James Trainer (London: Oxford University Press, 1967), 5.

Lord Graham agrees that there are 'strong presumptive proofs that this young man is the true heir of Lovel; but they ought to be confirmed and authenticated' (*OEB* 121). Accordingly, Edmund must take properly commissioned persons to the place where his dead parents were buried and have his story authenticated by his foster-parents. He could even, if required, produce the cloak in which his dying mother was wrapped. The narrative duly records the disinterment of the skeletons, with the recommendation by a priest that all the witnesses sign a written account of the discovery, an attested copy to be sent to Sir Philip and the Barons.

Problems are raised at the end of the novel, though, by the fact that Lord Fitz-Owen is the legal occupant of the Lovel estate, and he and Sir Philip bargain, at one point, over whether the cost of Edmund's maintenance and education offsets the arrears he might expect from the estate. Fitz-Owen voluntarily gives up the estate and returns to his old castle in Wales (*OEB* 138). Edmund then marries Fitz-Owen's daughter. As James Watt has rightly argued, the elements of the gothic are capable of different nuances and inflections.[42] In these cases, we might say that Walpole and Reeve represent different ends of the spectrum. *Otranto* is more concerned, as one might expect from the aristocratic Walpole, with keeping people out of the castle, while *The Old English Baron*, written by a clergyman's daughter, focuses on getting people in.[43] *The Old English Baron* also represents a feminization of Walpole, insofar as it eschews violence and horror. By qualifying Walpole's use of ghosts and marvels, it made possible Anne Radcliffe's use of the 'explained supernatural', in which, as William Enfield wrote later in a review of *The Mysteries of Udolpho* (1794), the reader could experience 'the strange luxury of artificial terror', without having to yield to 'the weakness of superstitious credulity'.[44]

After the dip in the production of new novels in the late 1770s, there was a revival in the late 1780s, which Raven and Forster attribute, in part, to a new emphasis on the female novelist and reader.[45] Out of the total number of novels first published in the 1770s, 10 percent of novels named men as the authors, compared to 6 percent naming women.[46] Only in 1775 were more novels published with the names of women authors than with the names of men. As the eighteenth century progressed, the percentage of novels whose title pages boasted a named author continued to increase, so while in the 1780s, 5 percent of all new novels named a male author, compared with 10 percent naming a female author, by the 1790s, 21 percent of new novels were acknowledged as the work of a woman author, compared with 17 percent naming men. Between 1788 and 1790, 33 women authors were named on title pages and in prefaces.

---

[42]   James Watt, *Contesting the Gothic. Fiction, Genre and Cultural Conflict, 1764–1832* (Cambridge: Cambridge University Press, 1999).

[43]   Walpole did not actually inherit the title Earl of Orford until 1791.

[44]   Williams, 393.

[45]   Raven and Forster, 27.

[46]   Ibid., 45.

Fanny Burney's *Evelina* (1778) is an early indicator of this renewed emphasis on the woman reader. If the growth of commerce necessitated a redefinition of gentility and independence, luxury and the metropolis provide Fanny Burney's heroine with opportunities for autonomy and self-definition, and once again, the cleric is either an irrelevance, or is re-imagined so as to confer legitimacy on potentially transgressive acts. Though Evelina writes to her guardian, the Rev. Mr. Villars, that she longs to return to the country retreat of Berry Hill, a series of contrived accidents places Evelina in town. From London, she writes apparently artless letters recounting the excitements of assemblies, plays, the opera, shopping and encounters with unconventional women, among them her own grandmother, Madame Duval. Madame Duval is 'uncontrolled mistress of her time, fortune, and actions' and travels with a male companion to whom she is not married.[47] The receipt of these letters by Villars, who only infrequently comments on them, effectively validates them. Villars even writes, at one point, that he cannot thank Evelina too much for 'the minuteness of your communications' (*E* 101). Villars functions as a permissive patriarch, pushed to the margins: the narrative is dominated by Evelina. Ignorant of 'proper' behaviour, she laughs at a fop and effectively chooses her own partner at a dance. Like Lennox's Arabella, she has to 'endure' the attentions of a number of suitors. For 'Berry' we might read 'bury', and sent back to the country, halfway through the novel, Evelina writes that she 'cannot journalize; cannot arrange my ideas into order' (*E* 294). The town equates with public life, and the possibility of self-expression, for Burney as much as her heroine.

Evelina's social position is fluid: her birth and situation are obscure. She is really the legitimate daughter of Sir John Belmont, but he refuses to acknowledge her, a situation which is represented as her misfortune, but which actually functions to free her from patriarchy. Halfway through the novel, Sir John writes a letter rejecting Evelina once more, and Evelina, with telling evasion, writes to Villars that 'I dare not, even to you, nor would I, could I help it, to myself, acknowledge all that I think; for, indeed, I have, sometimes, sentiments upon this rejection, which my strongest sense of duty can scarcely correct' (*E* 201). We are invited to read this as the reluctant impiety of an exemplary girl, extorted from her by the behaviour of an unnatural father: but we might equally read it as a relief at the idea of liberation which can scarcely be acknowledged.

Evelina's status as a lady is always up for negotiation: Madame Duval's intention is to have her return to France and restore her to her fortune by means of a lawsuit, a proposal which Evelina views with horror. Burney's own status as a 'proper lady' (to borrow Mary Poovey's term) is also up for negotiation, in the sense that she is always testing the limits of what a woman writer might do. She has her heroine mix with some 'vulgar' connections – the Branghtons and Captain Mirvan – from whom Burney derives some broad and more characteristically masculine comedy. Over and over again, she places Evelina in situations where she is 'forced' to behave unconventionally or improperly: she can therefore

---

47   Frances Burney, *Evelina*, ed. Kristina Straub (London: Macmillan, 1997), 118.

escape censure. Evelina cannot be blamed for laughing at the fop or choosing her own dance partner (and marriage partner) because she does not know the rules. The rules can in any case be rewritten by women. For almost all the novel, Evelina's mentors and companions are women: Lady Howard, Madame Duval and the satirical Mrs. Selwyn. This is not to say, of course, that the masking of challenges to convention, or the deflection of blame, is without risk. As critics have observed, Evelina's entrance into the world seems fraught with fear and alarm, a condition which might plausibly be said to mimic Burney's own feelings about publicity. Her journal, begun in March 1768, shows her to be much concerned with being 'proper', so as not to threaten the social aspirations of her father, the distinguished musical historian, Dr. Charles Burney.

For Charlotte Smith, the market for novels by and for women provided, above all, a way out of financial dependency. When she began *Emmeline* (1788), she had just separated from her husband after more than 20 years of marriage. She was left with little income and nine children to support. Anne Ehrenpreis points to a letter written by the author in 1793, in which she claimed to 'love Novels no more than a Grocer does figs', as proof of Charlotte Smith's own indifference to the form – though the comment might have been a reaction to the effort of producing one four-volume novel every year for more than a decade.[48] William Cowper described Charlotte Smith as a 'pitiable case … [c]hained to her desk like a slave to his oar, with no other means of subsistence for herself and her numerous children, with a broken constitution'.[49] The novel itself was partially autobiographical, with Smith's profligate husband appearing as Mr. Stafford and her own nomadic existence pictured in the heroine's ceaseless travel. Charlotte Smith, like Fanny Burney, places her female characters in unconventional situations, a feature of *Emmeline* which attracted adverse comment. In *The Spectre* (1789), Henry James Pye commented on Mrs. Smith's unfortunate tendency to have her female characters err, without incurring blame.[50] Adelina, for example, gives birth to an illegitimate child, and her brother William Godolphin is moved by her distress to declare that he can only feel compassion and tenderness towards her (*Emmeline* 280). Godolphin's forgiveness is the more telling as he eventually goes on to marry Emmeline. Emmeline herself breaks off her engagement, which lasts for almost the entire novel, to the impetuous Delamere – albeit with many mitigating circumstances. Nevertheless, Emmeline is effectively allowed to have a relationship with one man and then choose another.

Mary Wollstonecraft, writing for the *Analytical Review* in July 1788, considered that the story of Emmeline was of precisely the kind which would excite false expectations and encourage young female readers to long for adventures, and

---

[48]   Anne Henry Ehrenpreis (ed.), Introduction to *The Old Manor House*, by Charlotte Smith (London: Oxford University Press, 1969), ix–x.

[49]   Cited by Ehrenpreis (ed.), *The Old Manor House*, xii.

[50]   Cited by Anne Henry Ehrenpreis, in the Introduction to *Emmeline. The Orphan of the Castle*, by Charlotte Smith (London: Oxford University Press, 1971), ix–x.

Mary, her own novel of the same year, pictured the effect on Eliza, Mary's mother, of the popular novels of her own time:

> When [Eliza] could not any longer indulge the caprices of fancy one way, she tried another. The Platonic Marriage, Eliza Warwick, and some other interesting tales were perused with eagerness. … What delicate struggles! and uncommonly pretty turns of thought! The picture that was found on a bramble-bush, the new-sensitive plant, or tree, which caught the swain by the upper-garment, and presented to his ravished eyes a portrait.—Fatal image!—It planted a thorn in a till then insensible heart, and sent a new kind of knight-errant into the world. But even this was nothing to the catastrophe, and the circumstance on which it hung, the hornet settling on the sleeping lover's face. What a *heart-rending* accident! She planted, in imitation of those susceptible souls, a rose-bush; but there was not a lover to weep in concert with her, when she watered it with her tears.—Alas! Alas![51]

Despite the refined sensibility she learns from such works, Eliza is actually indifferent to her own daughter, and Mary's hopes for a close friendship with Ann, a clergyman's daughter, are disappointed when Ann proves to be preoccupied with thoughts of a lost love. Mary, a much more rigorously intellectual figure, receives an education thanks only to her own solitary reading of Thomson, Young and Milton, and *her* ideas of religion come to her from contact with the natural world. Mary's hopes for a useful, rather than a purely ornamental, life are able to be enacted only in terms of self-sacrifice. Marrying a man she does not love, in order to unite two estates, she is able to fulfil her dream of relieving the financial distresses of Anne and her family, and the work is punctuated with other acts of benevolence and charity. She cares for the less active and independent Anne and travels to Portugal with her, only to see her die. Still, the plot of *Mary*, unfinished as it is, is not entirely dissimilar to that of *Emmeline*, nor even *The Female Quixote*, and the work can even be seen as a late manifestation of sensibility. Mary herself writes a 'rhapsody on sensibility' (*Wollstonecraft* I, 59), and the account of her agonized wait for Henry would not be out of place in the novels Wollstonecraft satirized. Like the typical heroine of romance, Mary has a number of suitors: she is married to one man but falls in love with the more sensitive and feminized Henry. She has another male admirer, in the shape of a 'man of learning'. Brief as it is, though, *Mary* gestures towards a more intellectual romance, with fewer evasions of the repercussions of female dependency.

By the 1780s, the atmosphere of alarm about luxury and increased consumption, and the related perception of novels as acutely dangerous, seems to have diminished somewhat, although there were always those ready to point to the pernicious effects of the circulating library. In his work of compilation, *Elegant Extracts: or, useful and entertaining Passages in Prose, Selected for the Improvement of Young Persons*

---

[51]   Mary Wollstonecraft, *The Works of Mary Wollstonecraft*, eds. Janet Todd and Mailyn Butler, 8v. (London: William Pickering, 1989), Vol. I, 8.

(1784), Vicesimus Knox includes some fiction. It is a very selective choice, though: in 'Narratives, Dialogues etc.', which forms the final Book in *Elegant Extracts*, the story of Le Fevre, from *Tristram Shandy*, takes first place, with the death of Yorick, a portrait of Uncle Toby, and Trim on the fifth commandment also included. From *A Sentimental Journey*, Knox extracts Yorick's charity to the monk, The Starling and The Captive. 'The Business and Qualifications of a Poet Described' is taken from Johnson's *Rasselas*, and the volume closes with Books I and II of *Gulliver's Travels*. In *Winter Evenings* (1788), another volume of moral essays, Vicesimus Knox seems to have partially overcome his earlier antipathy to novels:

> There are ... many novels of real and substantial value, such as appear to have owed their origin to true genius and to classical taste. Wherever they exhibit genuine pictures of life and manners; and wherever they furnish matter for reflection, they certainly constitute some of the most useful books for the instruction of young persons. They are so pleasing that the mind is gradually allured by them to virtue and wisdom, which it would perhaps never have duly considered and fully adopted had they been recommended solely by dull argumentation.[52]

Nevertheless, the essay in which these remarks are contained was entitled 'Of Trifling Compositions', and Knox names no novels which exemplify his case for the instructive potential of fiction – in fact: 'among the great variety and multitude of novels with which the world abounds, very few are capable of teaching morality'. On the other hand, and no doubt thinking of his own compilations: 'The miscellanies of a writer really possessed of abilities, and published by himself, or with his approbation, and under his immediate inspection, may certainly be very valuable'.[53]

A more determined politicisation of the novel, and an enhanced sense of what it might achieve, also began to take shape in the 1780s. As early as 1780, the radical writer Thomas Holcroft gave a manifesto for the novel in his preface to *Alwyn*, distinguishing the novel from the digressive and aristocratic romance:

> MODERN writers use the word Romance, to signify a fictitious history of detached and independent adventures; and, under that idea, call the Telemaque of Fenelon, and the Cyrus of Ramsay, Romances. Le Sage's Gil Blas, and Smollett's Roderick Random, though of a different species, come under the same denomination. A Novel is another kind of work. Unity of design is its character. In a Romance, if the incidents be well marked and related with spirit, the intention is answered; and adventures pass before the view for no other purpose than to amuse by their peculiarity, without, perhaps, affecting the main story, if there should be one. But in a Novel, a combination of incidents, entertaining in themselves, are made to form a whole; and an unnecessary circumstance becomes a blemish.[54]

---

[52]   Vicesimus Knox, *Winter Evenings: or, Lucubrations on Life and Letters* (1788), 3v. (New York: Garland, 1971), Vol. III, 293.

[53]   Ibid., 296.

[54]   Cited by Gary Kelly, *The English Jacobin Novel, 1780–1805* (Oxford: Clarendon Press, 1976), 14–15.

He concluded that 'the legitimate Novel is a work much more difficult than the Romance, and justly deserves to be ranked with those dramatic pieces whose utility is generally allowed' and paid tribute to *Tom Jones*. Gary Kelly argues that Holcroft's first Jacobin novel, *Anna St. Ives* (1792), also owes much to Richardson's *Clarissa*, perhaps following William Godwin's *Italian Letters* of 1784, which was obviously modelled on Richardson's novel.[55] The 'legitimate' novel, then, as Holcroft himself termed it, had truly been taken up by anti-establishment writers. The case for fiction was subsequently made more forcefully in a number of Jacobin novels. In the preface to *The Adventures of Hugh Trevor* (1794–1797), Holcroft raised the question of the suitability of novels for the purpose of exploring weighty moral and political issues:

> Every man of determined inquiry, who will ask, without the dread of discovering more than he dares believe, what is divinity? what is law? what is physic? what is war? and what is trade? will have great reason to doubt at some times of the virtue, and at others of the utility, of each of these different employments. What profession should a man of principle, who is anxiously desirous to promote individual and general happiness, chuse for his son? The question has perplexed many parents, and certainly deserves a serious examination. Is a novel a good mode for discussing it, or a proper vehicle for moral truth? Of this some perhaps will be inclined to doubt.[56]

Holcroft, though, both in the preface and in the novel itself, once again made a case for the seriousness of the novel as a literary form:

> Others, whose intellectual powers were indubitably of the first order, have considered the art of novel writing as very essentially connected with moral instruction. Of this opinion was the famous Turgot, [Physiocrat and Controller-General of France, 1774–6], who we are told affirmed that more grand moral truths had been promulgated by novel writers than by any other class of men.

In *Caleb Williams* (1794) William Godwin acts, we might say, in the tradition of Addison and Steele in the *Spectator* by bringing philosophy to people who would never normally read it. For this purpose fiction, as he writes in the preface, is an appropriate vehicle:

> The following narrative is intended to answer a purpose more general and important than immediately appears upon the face of it. ... It is but of late that the inestimable importance of political principles has been adequately apprehended. It is now known to philosophers that the spirit and character of the government intrudes itself into every rank of society. But this is a truth highly worthy to be communicated to persons whom books of philosophy and science are never likely to reach. Accordingly it was proposed in the invention of the following

---

[55] Kelly, 17.

[56] Thomas Holcroft, *The Adventures of Hugh Trevor*, ed. Seamus Deane (Oxford: Oxford University Press, 1978), 3.

work, to comprehend, as far as the progressive nature of a single story would allow, a general review of the modes of domestic and unrecorded despotism, by which man becomes the destroyer of man.[57]

Since some of Godwin's friends – Thomas Holcroft among them – were being prosecuted for high treason just at the time *Caleb Williams* was about to appear, the preface was withdrawn from the first edition but was restored to the second edition of 1796. Nevertheless, the *Monthly Review* was persuaded of the case for a philosophical fiction. Reviewing *Caleb Williams* in October 1794, William Enfield writes:

> Between fiction and philosophy there seems to be no natural alliance:—yet philosophers in order to obtain for their dogmata a more ready reception, have often judged it expedient to introduce them to the world in the captivating dress of fable.[58]

Christopher Lake Murray, reviewing Godwin's *St. Leon* (1799) in the *Monthly Review* for September 1800, was less convinced. Commenting on Godwin's use of fiction as a vehicle, he rehearses some familiar objections:

> Is it a mode of instruction which such a philosopher ought to select? Is truth obliged to invoke the aid of the wildest of fictions; and will it be said that virtue and contentment are best taught in the school of romance?[59]

By this stage, though, as Paul Keen argues, the novel had become implicated in an anxiety about an unrestricted reading public.[60] While men of education and intelligence could be trusted to debate philosophical issues without necessarily wishing to act upon dreams of an unattainable social liberty, women and the labouring classes – who might form a large part of the readership for novels – could not be trusted to think or act rationally. The *British Critic* reflected, comfortably, that the style of Godwin's *An Enquiry Concerning Political Justice* (1793) would dissuade the most dangerous sectors of the reading public from reading it, and the length of Holcroft's *Hugh Trevor*, at three volumes, would probably prevent it from causing mischief.[61]

    Caleb Williams can be read as simply an exposition of Godwin's anarchist politics, as expressed in *Political Justice*. Like *Political Justice, Caleb Williams* makes the case against laws and institutions. It tells the story of an upright and honourable gentleman, Ferdinando Falkland, who secretly kills the tyrannical and boorish Squire Tyrrel after a series of extreme provocations. The crucial insult,

---

[57]   William Godwin, *Caleb Williams*, ed. David McCracken (Oxford: Oxford University Press, 1982), 1.

[58]   *Monthly Review*, n.s. 15, 1794, Vol. III, 145.

[59]   *Monthly Review*, 33, 1800, Vol. III, 24.

[60]   Paul Keen, *The Crisis of Literature in the 1790s. Print Culture and the Public Sphere* (Cambridge: Cambridge University Press, 1999), 137 *et passim*.

[61]   Keen, 56.

though, is to Falkland's sense of honour – here Godwin attacked the code of chivalry which had recently been rehabilitated by Edmund Burke in his *Reflections on the Revolution in France* (1790). Falkland allows a worthy tenant farmer and his son to be convicted of the crime and executed: as elsewhere in *Caleb Williams*, courts and the law always produce injustice. The narrative is related in the first person by the eponymous hero, who at an early stage in the novel becomes Falkland's secretary. Driven by insatiable curiosity, he speculates about Falkland's guilt and becomes convinced that Falkland is indeed the murderer. Motivated by loyalty and a sense of obligation, though, he is determined not to reveal the secret. Once Falkland realizes that Williams knows of his crime, he subjects his secretary to inexorable persecution, and the third volume of the novel – which Godwin actually wrote first – is concerned with Williams's flight, imprisonment, escape, recapture, further imprisonment and so on. In the manuscript, Godwin ended the novel with Williams confined in prison and losing his reason. In the conclusion to the novel as it first appeared in print, however, Williams confronts a now haggard Falkland with an accusation of murder in court, and Falkland confesses his guilt and forgives Williams. Three days later he dies, and Williams finds that he himself has become the murderer. The novel ends with a reflection on the 'poison of chivalry'.

Falkland, then, or perhaps Falkland and Tyrrel, represent the 'despotism' of which Godwin spoke in the preface, and Williams's own recourse to law in the end inevitably produces more misery. Overtly, the novel puts forward the necessitarian doctrine. Falkland could not have acted otherwise because he was enslaved by the principle of chivalry: he is not naturally evil. Caleb Williams's friend and mentor, Mr. Collins, tells a now destitute Williams:

> I regard you as vicious; but I do not consider the vicious as proper objects of indignation and scorn. I consider you as a machine: you are not constituted, I am afraid, to be greatly useful to your fellow men; but you did not make yourself; you are just what circumstances irresistibly compelled you to be. I am sorry for your ill properties; but I entertain no enmity against you, nothing but benevolence. (*CW* 310)

However, the novel succeeds *as* a novel – that is, a work which does not pronounce dogmatic truth – precisely because there is much in it which does not cohere either with Godwin's statement in the Preface, or with the principles of *Political Justice*.

Godwin's own thinking, both in *Political Justice* and *Caleb Williams*, owed much to his religious upbringing. He was the son of a strict Calvinist minister, and only religious texts were read in the house. At the age of 11, he was boarded out to a puritanical Sandemanian minister, Samuel Newton, who whipped him for the slightest deviation from religious practice or thought. The followers of Robert Sandeman were even more extreme than the Scottish Calvinists against whom they were reacting – two central tenets were that reason should not be sullied by emotion or faith and that wealth was inherently sinful. These two principles figure prominently in *Political Justice*. Between 1777 and 1783, Godwin was a clergyman in various Dissenting churches but was finally expelled in 1780 because of a theological dispute. He then earned a living as a hack writer in London.

In terms of plot and characterisation, *Caleb Williams* consistently speaks from a perception of man's nature as sinful. Guilt is omnipresent, not only in the shape of Falkland's relentless pursuit of Williams, but also in Williams's sense of the terrible burden of the secret he possesses. Falkland tells Williams that he might as well think of escaping from 'the power of the omnipresent God', as from his master. In a later account of writing the novel, which formed the preface to the 'Standard Novels' edition of 1832, Godwin revealed that he had consulted that vindication of the workings of Providence, 'God's Revenge against Murder' as he composed *Caleb Williams*. The narrator reflects, at one point, that man is not an individual but is rather like a 'twin-birth', with two heads and four hands, and there are many doubles and divided selves in the novel. The vengeful Falkland is like Williams's guilty self or, alternatively, the brutal Tyrrel is the once noble Falkland's other half. Characters who appear to be Williams's friends, like Forester or Collins, soon become his accusers. Escape from guilt ultimately proves to be impossible.

When Godwin rejected his Sandemanian upbringing, he also the rejected the idea of predestination, and a tyrannical God. It could be argued, though, that both found their way back into his fiction in the shape of the predetermined fate which is announced in the second sentence of *Caleb Williams*: 'I have been a mark for the vigilance of tyranny, and I could not escape' (*CW* 3). Falkland, to whom Williams remains so strangely loyal, stands for the God Godwin had overtly rejected, but to whom he is still tied by deep feelings of remorse and even love. In fact, sympathy finds its way back into *Caleb Williams* despite Godwin's expressed adherence to pure reason – a principle that he later qualified. Moreover, in the insatiable curiosity of Williams, which leads to exile and misery, might be figured Godwin's own anxieties or regrets either about his expulsion from his congregation or about the consequences of his own political speculations. The third book, which Godwin wrote first, is a dark imagining of the situation of an outcast.

Almost in spite of the political intentions of the author, then, *Caleb Williams* allows the reader precisely that room to speculate, that independence of judgement, which Godwin otherwise recommended as the basis of a free society. In Godwin's thinking, the independence which allowed for participation in the political process was now not a financial situation, but rather a state of mind. All the 'mind forg'd manacles' must be thrown off, and unlimited private judgement allowed. It was a principle with which the radical writers did not always conform in their novels, which could too easily become secular sermons.

In the late-eighteenth century, it is in fiction of Jane Austen, above all, that we find a secular version of the Anglican position on the matter of private judgement: the conscience could be trusted, so long as it conformed with the moral law as taught by a Church that allowed its adherents some room for manoeuvre. The reader of Austen's fiction has a moral guide in the shape of the author, but her plots admit of no reduction to simple dogma. Her characters are, indeed, usually bound to act on their own private judgement. In *Pride and Prejudice* (1813), Elizabeth

Bennet's assessment of Darcy takes place in the privacy of her own mind, without the intervention of parents. Conversely, Anne Eliot, in *Persuasion* (1818), relies on the judgement of Lady Russell in the matter of a proposed marriage to Captain Wentworth, and the decision leads to much misery and confusion. There are few, if any, reliable figures of authority, least of all the clergy, despite the fact that Austen herself was the daughter of a cleric. In *Pride and Prejudice* the Reverend Mr. Collins is an obsequious and self-important fool, whose readings from Fordyce's sermons only serve to render him the more ridiculous in the eyes of the Bennet daughters. Edmund, in *Mansfield Park* (1814), is destined for orders and is a worthy figure, but his moral judgement is deeply flawed in the matter of Mary Crawford. It is the heroine Fanny Price, rather, who represents moral clarity. The relative positions of cleric and heroine as represented in Lennox's *The Female Quixote* have here been quite reversed. Indeed, despite Austen's support for the institutions of law and marriage and the existing social order, *Northanger Abbey*, written around 1798 though not published until 1818, demonstrates the deeper decline of patriarchy and piety. Patriarchy does not exercise the hold it had on a previous generation: in *Northanger Abbey*, Catherine's parents are unperturbed by her solitary journey home when she is exiled from the Abbey by General Tilney. Pieties are receding: her departure from home for Bath is handled with 'moderation and composure' rather than with 'the refined sensibilities, the tender emotions which the first separation of a heroine from her family ought always to excite'.[62] Notwithstanding the need for women to lead lives of privacy and domesticity, Catherine, at the Upper Rooms in Bath, is unashamedly pleased with her share of 'public attention' (*NA* 11). Unlike the passive and physically weak heroine of earlier romances, Catherine, as a child, is 'fond of all boy's plays' (*NA* 1, 2). She was 'noisy and wild, hated confinement and cleanliness, and loved nothing so well in the world as rolling down the green slope at the back of the house' (*NA* 2). Against the pronouncement made by Richardson, in *Rambler* 97, that a young woman could not, in the interests of prudence and policy, fall in love with a man before he had declared his love for her, Austen hints that this was exactly what happened to Catherine after dancing with Henry Tilney. In what might be read as a quiet but overt acknowledgement of female sexuality, Catherine, with her friend Isabella, sets off in pursuit of two unknown men. The novel ends with Catherine's marriage to Henry, but the representation of this climactic event is nearly as flat and dismissive as Lennox's brief account of Arabella's submission to Mr. Glanville in *The Female Quixote*. The conservative position, as represented here, has absorbed much that was radical.

Where the radical and conservative also meet is in the conception that fiction itself could serve a serious purpose and that the novelist was a person of some importance and influence. M.O. Grenby argues that the use of fiction in the conservative cause in this period helped to legitimize the novel as a form·

---

62   Jane Austen, *Northanger Abbey*, ed. John Davie, with an introduction by Terry Castle (Oxford: Oxford University Press, 1990), 6.

the number of anti-Jacobin novels far outweighed that of Jacobin novels.[63] If *Caleb Williams* has been able to achieve anything, in Godwin's novel, it has been through his work of writing: 'With this engine, this little pen I defeat all his [Falkland's] machinations' (*CW* 315). *Northanger Abbey* makes a striking claim for the importance of fiction, and the capabilities of an author:

> while the abilities of the nine-hundredth abridger of the History of England, or of the man who collects and publishes in a volume some dozen lines of Milton, Pope, and Prior, with a paper from the Spectator, and a chapter from Sterne, are eulogized by a thousand pens,—there seems almost a general wish of decrying the capacity and undervaluing the labour of the novelist, and of slighting the performances which have only genius, wit and taste to recommend them. 'I am no novel reader—I seldom look into novels—Do not imagine that *I* often read novels—It is very well for a novel'.—Such is the common cant.—'And what are you reading, Miss—?' 'Oh! it is only a novel!' replies the young lady; while she lays down her book with affected indifference, or momentary shame.—'It is only Cecilia, or Camilla, or Belinda;' or, in short, only some work in which the greatest powers of the mind are displayed, in which the most thorough knowledge of human nature, the happiest delineation of its varieties, the liveliest effusions of wit and humour are conveyed to the world in the best chosen language. (*NA* 22)

For Austen, fiction is of vital importance. Ann Radcliffe's *The Mysteries of Udolpho* (1794) needs to be corrected because this is what women read, and, like Mary Wollstonecraft, Austen believes that women are, or can be, rational creatures. Austen's novel exploits the potential of Gothic fiction, as imagined by Radcliffe, to allow for female adventures and explorations, but it does so in a rational spirit. In *Northanger Abbey*, both Henry Tilney and his sister read fiction *and* history, demonstrating the fact that these genres may be of equal importance. The portrait of a man as an avid and unembarrassed consumer of novels further legitimizes the novel as a genre.

In the letters which form a kind of preface to *Humphry Clinker*, the Rev. Jonathan Dustwich proposes to discuss with bookseller Henry Davis the possible sale of a parcel of sermons, which were composed by a clergyman now deceased. 'You need not take the trouble to bring up your sermons on my account', replies Davis,' – No body reads sermons but Methodists and Dissenters' (*HC* 29). In reality, the idea that fiction had completely taken the place of sermons with the reading public hardly stands up to scrutiny. Sterne's *Sermons of Mr. Yorick* outsold *Tristram Shandy*. In 1773 and 1774 were published the nine volumes of *The English Preacher: or, sermons on the principal subjects of religion and morality, selected, revised, and abridged from various authors*. Richard Graves, author of *The Spiritual Quixote*, published a collection of his own sermons in 1799, presumably using his career as the author of four novels to promote his homiletic works. The relative status of novels and religious works might also be judged by the reading of one educated

---

[63]   M.O. Grenby, *The Anti-Jacobin Novel, British Conservatism and the French Revolution* (Cambridge: Cambridge University Press, 2001), 27.

and not necessarily typical female reader, over a 10-year period. Anna Larpent, daughter of a diplomat and wife of a successful civil servant, recorded reading 46 English novels and 22 works of French fiction. Her reading of fiction was almost matched by her reading in history, biography and social science: some 60 titles, including works by Gibbon, Hume, Adam Smith, Monboddo and Ferguson. She also read 46 sermons and other pious works.[64] Looking at the purchase of printed material by servants, as recorded by one provincial bookseller between 1746 and 1784, Jan Fergus found that conduct books and religious works were the most popular, though closely followed by plays, fiction and *belles lettres*.[65] Smollett's fictional dismissal of the sermon is polemical, rather than a matter of empirically verifiable fact.

Nevertheless, Smollett had a point. The market for fiction in the latter part of the eighteenth century made it possible for individuals who might otherwise have been outsiders to put forward ideas about the organisation of society, in a form which would reach a wide audience. In 'A View of the Commencement and Progress of Romance' (1797), John Moore, novelist, doctor of medicine and friend of Smollett, writes:

> It may be said, that … people had much better study books of science, or read moral essays or sermons. Unquestionably they had: but unfortunately they will not; for although some authors have shewn that it is possible to write sermons so that they shall be as much or more read than the best romance, yet this talent is extremely rare; and it is often lamented that sermons and moral essays, containing much good instruction, are less universally perused than many novels, more inelegantly written. What does this prove, but that there is something so peculiarly attractive in this species of writing, that performances, which would have been neglected in any other form, find readers in this?[66]

The novelist was now, potentially, in the position of cultural arbiter. This is not a transformation which came easily, even for those who would profit from it. The question posed by Holcroft in *Hugh Trevor*, about the social position of the 'man of principle, who is desirous to promote individual and general happiness', is in fact never satisfactorily answered. Paul Keen, writing about the 1790s, has spoken of a 'radical struggle by authors to re-imagine their social status by insisting on a set of values which identified the middle class rather than the aristocracy as society's moral centre, and the energetic transactions of print culture rather than the privileged leisure of a landed élite as the cornerstone of the public good'.[67] Holcroft does not mention the profession of author in his preface, but the

---

[64]   John Brewer, 'Reconstructing the reader: prescriptions, texts and strategies in Anna Larpent's reading', *The Practice and Representation of Reading in England*, eds James Raven, Helen Small and Naomi Tadmor (Cambridge: Cambridge University Press, 1996), 229.

[65]   Jan Fergus, 'Provincial servants' reading in the late eighteenth century', *The Practice and Representation of Reading*, ed. Raven, 202–3.

[66]   Williams, 441.

[67]   Keen, 77.

eponymous hero tries it, only to find himself dogged by disappointments and the same corruption that he discovers in the Church, medicine and the legal profession. The novel actually ends with the hero as an independent country gentleman, just as Hermsprong, the unconventional hero of Robert Bage's radical novel of 1796, proves to be a gentleman by birth and the true heir to the estate. The old conception that birth, and the ownership of estates, constituted an essential qualification for participation in the political process was hard to dispel.

Many eighteenth-century novels feature heroes or heroines of mysterious birth, who must wait to discover their true parentage and good fortune. These figures might be seen as analogues for the situation of fiction. At the beginning of the period considered in this study, prose fiction was itself an outsider and an outcast. Fiction was given some legitimacy when it began to do the work the Church of England was perceived as incapable of doing. The novel could picture a social order constructed in increasingly secular terms. With the expansion of the market, aristocratic influence dwindled, and a more democratic 'republic of letters' could be imagined as the source of public influence. By the end of the period one heroine, at least, does not need to wait to discover who her parents really are. We might leave the last word with Jane Austen and *Northanger Abbey*.

The novel begins, defiantly, with a girl who has none of the usual characteristics of the heroine. There is no mystery about who Catherine Morland's parents are: they are both alive, and her father is a respectable clergyman, neither neglected nor poor. Where the Morland family live, '[t]here was not one lord ... no – not even a baronet' (*NA* 4). Further:

> There was not one family among their aquaintance who had reared and supported a boy accidentally found at their door—not one young man whose origins was unknown. Her father had no ward, and the squire of the parish no children. (*NA* 4)

Here, the middle classes have truly taken centre stage. There is no need for the presence of a title to convey value or virtue – a tendency that is still apparent in *Emmeline*, *A Simple Story* and even the radical *Hermsprong*. There is no one, in any traditional sense, waiting to ascend into a position of worth from unpromising beginnings, despite Austen's own starting point: 'No one who had ever seen Catherine Morland in her infancy, would have supposed her to be born an heroine' (*NA* 1). Austen believes in the worthiness of her subject matter, the powers of the novelist and the validity of novelistic discourse. So far from embodying 'hurtful insignificance', then, the novel, by the end of the eighteenth century had come to occupy a position of moral value.

Works Cited

Primary Sources

Anonymous. *A Faithful Narrative of the Base and inhuman Arts That were lately practised upon the Brain of Habbakkuk Hilding, Justice, Dealer, and Chapman, Who now lies at his House in* Covent-garden, *in a deplorable State of Lunacy; a dreadful Monument of* false Friendship *and* Delusion. London: 1752.

Anonymous. *Observations upon the Conduct and Behaviour of a Certain Sect, Usually distinguished by the Name of Methodists.* n.p., n.d.

Astell, Mary. *Astell: Political Writings.* Edited by Patricia Springborg. Cambridge: Cambridge University Press, 1996.

Austen, Jane. *Northanger Abbey* (1818). Edited by John Davie, with an introduction by Terry Castle. Oxford: Oxford University Press, World's Classics, 1990.

Bage, Robert. *Hermsprong, or Man As He Is Not* (1796). Edited by Peter Faulkner. Oxford: Oxford University Press, 1988.

Barrow, Isaac. *The Works.* Edited by John Tillotson. 3 vols. London: 1716.

Baxter, Richard. *A Christian Directory: or, a Summ of Practical Theologie and Cases of Conscience.* London: 1673.

Bayle, Pierre. *Historical and Critical Dictionary. Selections.* Translated by Richard H. Popkin. Indianapolis: Bobbs-Merrill, 1965.

Beattie, James. *Dissertations Moral and Critical* (1783). New York: Garland, 1971.

Blackburne, Francis. *The Confessional, or a Full and Free Enquiry into the Right, Utility, Edification, and Success, of Establishing Systematical Confessions of Faith and Doctrine in Protestant Churches.* n.p.: 1767.

Bond, Donald F., ed. *The Spectator.* 5 vols. Oxford: Clarendon Press, 1965.

———. *The Tatler.* 3 vols. Oxford: Clarendon Press, 1987.

Boswell, James. *The Life of Samuel Johnson* (1791). Edited by R.W. Chapman, corrected by J.D. Fleeman. Oxford: Oxford University Press, 1970.

British Moralists 1650–1800. Edited by D.D. Raphael. 2 vols. Indianapolis: Hackett, 1991.

Burney, Frances. *Evelina* (1778). Edited by Kristina Straub. London: Macmillan, 1997.

Burton, Robert. *The Anatomy of Melancholy* (1621–1651). 6 vols. Edited by Thomas C. Faulkner, Nicolas K. Kiessling and Rhonda L. Blair, with an introduction by J.B. Bamborough. Oxford: Clarendon Press, 1989.

Cambridge Platonists, The (1969). Edited by C.A. Patrides. Cambridge: Cambridge University Press, 1980.

Chillingworth, William. *The Religion of Protestants, A Safe Way to Salvation.* n.p., 1638.

Collins, Anthony. *A Discourse of Free-Thinking* (1713) bound with *An Answer to Mr. Clark's Third Defence of his Letter to Mr. Dodwell* (1708). In *Atheism in Britain*, with an introduction by David Berman. Bristol: Thoemmes Press, 1996.

Confession of Faith, The. Glasgow: 1749.

English Sermon, The. 3 vols. Edited by C.H. Sisson. Cheadle: Carcanet, 1976.

Fielding, Henry. *The Adventures of Joseph Andrews, and his Friend Mr. Abraham Adams* (1742). Edited by Martin C. Battestin. Oxford: Clarendon Press, 1967.

———. *The History of Tom Jones, A Foundling* (1749). 2 vols. With an Introduction and Commentary by Martin Battestin, and edited by Fredson Bowers. Oxford: Clarendon Press, 1974.

———. *Amelia* (1751). Edited by Martin C. Battestin. Oxford: Clarendon Press, 1983.

———. *The Covent Garden Journal* and *A Plan of the Universal Register-office*. Edited by Bertrand A. Goldgar. Oxford: Clarendon Press, 1988.

———. *Contributions to* The Champion *and Related Writings*. Edited by W.B. Coley. The Wesleyan Edition of the Works of Henry Fielding. Oxford: Clarendon, 2003.

Fielding, Sarah. *The Lives of Cleopatra and Octavia* (1757). Edited by R. Brimley Johnson. n.p.: Scholartis Press, 1928.

———. *Remarks on Clarissa* (1749). Introduction by Peter Sabor. *Augustan Reprint Society* 231–2. Los Angeles: William Andrews Clark Memorial Library, 1985.

———. *The Adventures of David Simple* (1744) and *The Adventures of David Simple, Volume the Last* (1753). Edited by Peter Sabor. Lexington-Fayette, KY: The University Press of Kentucky, 1998.

Gentleman's Magazine.

Godwin, William. *Caleb Williams* (1794). Edited by David McCracken. Oxford: Oxford University Press,World's Classics, 1982.

Goldsmith, Oliver. *Collected Works of Oliver Goldsmith*. Edited by Arthur Friedman. 5 vols. Oxford: Clarendon Press, 1966.

Graves, Richard. *The Spiritual Quixote, or The Summer's Ramble of Mr. Geoffry Wildgoose. A Comic Romance* (1773). Edited by Clarence Tracy. London: Oxford University Press, 1967.

Hobbes, Thomas. *Leviathan* (1651). Edited by C.B. Macpherson. Harmondsworth: Penguin, 1985.

Holcroft, Thomas. *The Adventures of Hugh Trevor* (1794). Edited by Seamus Deane. Oxford: Oxford University Press, 1978.

Inchbald, Elizabeth. *A Simple Story* (1791). Edited by J.M.S. Tompkins with an Introduction by Jane Spencer. Oxford: Oxford University Press, Oxford World's Classics, 1988.

Knox, Vicesimus. *Elegant Extracts: or, useful and entertaining Passages in Prose, Selected for the Improvement of Young Persons* (1784). London: J. Johnson, 1808.

———. *Winter Evenings: or, Lucubrations on Life and Letters* (1788). 3 vols. New York: Garland, 1971.

————. *Essays, Moral and Literary* (1779). 2 vols. New York: Garland, 1972.

Law, William. *A Serious Call To a Devout and Holy Life* (1729). Edited by Halcyon and C. Backhouse. London: Hodder and Stoughton, 1987.

Lennox, Charlotte. *The Female Quixote* (1752). Edited by Margaret Dalziel. Oxford: Oxford University Press, World's Classics, 1989.

————. *The Life of Harriot Stuart, Written by Herself* (1750). Edited by Susan Kubica Howard. Madison: Fairleigh Dickinson University Press, 1995.

Locke, John. *Two Treatises of Government* (1690). Edited by Peter Laslett. 2nd. edition. Cambridge: Cambridge University Press, 1967.

————. *An Essay Concerning Human Understanding* (1690). Edited by Peter H. Nidditch. Oxford: Clarendon Press, 1975.

————. *The Reasonableness of Christianity: As Delivered in the Scriptures* (1695). Edited by John C. Higgins-Biddle. Oxford: Clarendon Press, 1999.

Mackenzie, Henry. *The Man of the World* (1773). In Vols I and II of *The Works of Henry Mackenzie*, (1808). With a new introduction by Susan Manning. 8 vols. London: Routledge/Thoemmes Press, 1996.

————. *Julia de Roubigné* (1779). Edited by Susan Manning. East Linton: Tuckwell Press, 1999.

————. *The Man of Feeling* (1771). Edited by Brian Vickers with an Introduction and Notes by Stephen Bending and Stephen Redgrave. Oxford: Oxford University Press, 2001.

Manley, Mary Delarivière. *The Secret History of Queen Zarah and the Zarazians* (1711). New York: Garland, 1972.

————. *The New Atalantis* (1709). Edited by Rosalind Ballaster. London: Penguin, 1991.

Montaigne, Michel de. *The Complete Works of Montaigne. Essays*, *Travel Journal*, *Letters*. Translated by Donald M. Frame. London: Hamish Hamilton, 1957.

Monthly Review.

Pamela Controversy, The. Criticisms and Adaptations of Samuel Richardson's Pamela. Edited by Thomas Keymer and Peter Sabor. 6 vols. London: Pickering and Chatto, 2001.

Perkins, William. *The Workes of That Famous and Worthy Minister of Christ, in the University of Cambridge, Mr. William Perkins*. 3 vols. London: 1613.

Pope, Alexander. *The Poems of Alexander Pope*. Edited by John Butt *et al.* 6 vols. London: Methuen and New Haven: Yale University Press, 1940–1961.

Popular Fiction by Women 1660–1730. An Anthology. Edited by Paula R. Backscheider and John J. Richetti. Oxford: Oxford University Press, 1996.

Reeve, Clara. *The Old English Baron. A Gothic Story*, (1778). Edited by James Trainer. London: Oxford University Press, 1967.

————. *The Progress of Romance* (1785). 2 vols. New York: Garland, 1970.

Richardson, Samuel. *Pamela, or Virtue Rewarded … and Afterwards in her Exalted Condition*. 4 vols. 1741–1742.

————. *The Correspondence of Samuel Richardson*. Edited by Anna Laetitia Barbauld. 6 vols. London: 1804.

———. *Familiar Letters on Important Occasions* (1741). Edited by J. Isaacs, with an Introduction by Brian Westerdale Downs. London: Routledge, 1928.

———. *Selected Letters of Samuel Richardson*. Edited by John Carroll. Oxford: Clarendon, 1964.

———. *The Apprentice's* Vade Mecum (1734). Introduction by A.D. McKillop. *The Augustan Reprint Society*, 169–70. Los Angeles: William Andrews Clark Memorial Library, 1975.

———. *Clarissa* (1747–1748). Edited by Angus Ross. London: Penguin, 1985.

———. *Samuel Richardson's Published Commentary on* Clarissa *1747–1765*. 3 vols. Edited by Thomas Keymer, with an Introduction by Jocelyn Harris. London: Pickering and Chatto, 1998

———. *Pamela, or Virtue Rewarded* (1740). Edited by Thomas Keymer and Alice Wakeley. Oxford: Oxford University Press, 2001.

Sheridan, Frances. *Memoirs of Miss Sidney Bidulph* (1761). Edited by Patricia Köster and Jean Coates Cleary. Oxford: Oxford University Press/World's Classics, 1995.

Smith, Charlotte. *The Old Manor House* (1793). Edited by Anne Henry Ehrenpreis. London: Oxford University Press, 1969.

———. *Emmeline. The Orphan of the Castle* (1788). Edited by Anne Henry Ehrenpreis. London: Oxford University Press, 1971.

Smollett, Tobias. *The Adventures of Peregrine Pickle* (1751). Edited by James L. Clifford. London: Oxford University Press, 1964.

———. *The Expedition of Humphry Clinker* (1771). Edited by Lewis M. Knapp. London: Oxford University Press, 1966.

———. *The Letters of Tobias Smollett*. Edited by Lewis M. Knapp. Oxford: Clarendon Press, 1970.

———. *The Adventures of Ferdinand Count Fathom* (1753). Edited by Damian Grant. London: Oxford University Press, 1971.

———. *The Life and Adventures of Sir Launcelot Greaves* (1760–1761). Edited by David Evans. London: Oxford University Press, 1973

———. *The Adventures of Roderick Random* (1748). Edited by Paul-Gabriel Boucé. Oxford: Oxford University Press, 1979.

———. *Travels Through France and Italy* (1766). Edited by Frank Felsenstein. Oxford: Oxford University Press, 1979.

———. *Poems, Plays and* The Briton. Edited by O.M. Brack, Jr., assisted by Leslie A. Chilton, with an introduction and notes by Byron Gassman. Athens: University of Georgia Press, 1993.

Steele, Richard. *The Christian Hero* (1701). Edited by Rae Blanchard. London: Oxford University Press, 1932.

Stephens, William, *An Account of the Growth of Deism in England* (1696). *The Augustan Reprint Society*, 261. Introduction by James E. Force. Los Angeles: William Andrews Clark Memorial Library, 1990.

Sterne, Laurence. *Letters of Laurence Sterne*. Edited by Lewis Perry Curtis. Oxford: Clarendon Press, 1935.

————. *A Sentimental Journey Through France and Italy by Mr. Yorick* (1771). Edited by Gardner D. Stout, Jr., Berkeley: University of California Press, 1967.

————. *The Life and Opinions of Tristram Shandy, Gentleman*, (1759–1567). Edited by Ian Campbell Ross. Oxford: Clarendon Press, 1983.

————. *The Sermons of Laurence Sterne*. Edited by Melvyn New. Vols IV and V of The Florida Edition of the Works of Laurence Sterne. 5 vols. Gainesville: University Press of Florida, 1996.

Swift, Jonathan, *Sermons*. Edited by Louis Landa. Bound with *Irish Tracts 1720–23*. Edited by Herbert Davis. Oxford: Basil Blackwell, 1968.

Taylor, Jeremy. *Ductor Dubitantium*. 3rd. ed. London: 1676.

————. *A Discourse of the Liberty of Prophesying*. London: 1702.

Tillotson, John. *The Rule of Faith: or an Answer to the Treatise of Mr. I.S. entituled* Sure Footing *etc*. London: 1676.

————. *Works*. Edited by R. Barker. 3 vols. London: 1728.

Tindal, Matthew. *The Rights of the Christian Church Asserted, Against the Romish, and all other Priests who claim an Independent Power over it*. London, 1706.

————. *Christianity as Old as the Creation* (1730). Edited by John Valdimir Price. London: Routledge, Thoemmes Press, 1995.

Trapp, Joseph. 'The Nature, Folly, Sin and Danger of being Righteous over-much; with a particular view to the Doctrines and Practices of Certain Modern Enthusiasts.' 3rd ed. London: 1739.

Trenchard, J., and Thomas Gordon. *The Independent Whig*, XLV, Wednesday, November 23, 1720.

————. *The Independent Whig*, LIV, Wednesday, January 18, 1721.

Walpole, Horace. *The Castle of Otranto* (1764). Edited by Michael Gamer. London: Penguin, 2001.

Whitefield, George. *Select Sermons*. London: Banner of Truth, 1958.

————. *George Whitefield's Journals*. Edinburgh: Banner of Truth Trust, 1960.

Wollstonecraft, Mary. *The Works of Mary Wollstonecraft*. Edited by Janet Todd and Mailyn Butler. 8 vols. London: William Pickering, 1989.

Secondary Sources

Addy, John. *Sin and Society in the Seventeenth Century*. London: Routledge, 1989.

Allison, C.F. *The Rise of Moralism: The Proclamation of the Gospel from Hooker to Baxter*. London: SPCK, 1966.

Armstrong, Nancy. *Desire and Domestic Fiction. A Political History of the Novel*. Oxford: Oxford University Press, 1987.

Bahlman, Dudley. *The Moral Revolution of 1688*. New Haven: Yale University Press, 1957.

Bakhtin, Mikhail. *The Dialogic Imagination*. Edited by Michael Holquist. Translated by Caryl Emerson and Michael Holquist. Austin: University of Texas Press, 1981.

————. *Rabelais and his World*. Translated by Helene Iswolsky. Bloomington: University of Indiana Press, 1984.

Ballaster, Ros. *Seductive Forms. Women's Amatory Fiction from 1684 to 1740*. Oxford: Clarendon, 1992.

Barchas, Janine. 'Sarah Fielding's Dashing Style and Eighteenth-Century Print Culture.' *ELH* 63 (1996): 633–56.

Barrell, John. *English Literature in History, 1730–1780. An Equal, Wide Survey*. London: Hutchinson, 1983.

Basker, James. *Tobias Smollett, Critic and Journalist*. Newark: University of Delaware Press, 1988.

Battestin, Martin C. *The Moral Basis of Fielding's Art: A Study of Joseph Andrews*. Middletown, CT: Wesleyan University Press, 1959.

————. 'Fielding's Revisions of Joseph Andrews.' *Studies in Bibliography* XVI (1963): 81–117.

————. *The Providence of Wit*. Oxford: Clarendon Press, 1974.

Battestin, Martin C., with Ruthe R. Battestin: *Henry Fielding: A Life*. London: Routledge, 1989.

Bennet, G.V. 'Conflict in the Church.' In *Britain after the Glorious Revolution 1689–1714*, edited by Geoffrey Holmes, 155–75. London: Macmillan, 1969.

————. *The Tory Crisis in Church and State 1688–1730. The Career of Francis Atterbury, Bishop of Rochester*. Oxford: Clarendon Press, 1975.

Berman, David. *A History of Atheism in Britain: From Hobbes to Russell*. London: Croom Helm, 1988.

Bloom, Edward A., and Lillian D. Bloom, eds. *Addison and Steele: The Critical Heritage*. London: Routledge and Kegan Paul, 1980.

Botting, Fred. 'In Gothic Darkly: Heterotopia, History, Culture.' In *A Companion to the Gothic*. Edited by David Punter, 3–14. Oxford: Blackwell, 2000.

Boucé, Paul-Gabriel. *The Novels of Tobias Smollett*. Translated by Antonia White. London: Longman, 1976.

Brack, O.M. Jr. 'Smollett and the Authorship of "The Memoirs of Lady of Quality."' In Tobias Smollett, *Scotland's First Novelist*. Edited by O.M. Brack, Jr., 35–73. Newark: University of Delaware Press, 2007.

Bree, Linda. *Introduction to David Simple, by Sarah Fielding*. London: Penguin, 2002.

Brewer, John, 'Reconstructing the reader: prescriptions, texts and strategies in Anna Larpent's reading.' In *The Practice and Representation of Reading in England*, edited by James Raven, Helen Small and Naomi Tadmor, 226–245. Cambridge: Cambridge University Press, 1996.

Bruce, Steve. *Religion and Modernization. Sociologists and Historians Debate the Secularization Thesis*. Oxford: Clarendon, 1992.

Buck, Howard. *A Study in Smollett*. New Haven, CT: Yale University Press, 1925.

————. 'Smollett and Dr. Akenside.' *JEGP* 31 (1932): 10–26.

Campbell, Jill. *Natural Masques: Gender and Identity in Fielding's Plays and Novels*. Palo Alto, CA: Stanford University Press, 1995.

Carlton, Peter J. 'The Mitigated Truth: Tom Jones's Double Heroism.' *Studies in the Novel* 19 (1987): 397–409.

Castle, Terry. *Clarissa's Ciphers: Meaning and Disruption* in *Richardson's Clarissa*. Ithaca, NY: Cornell University Press, 1982.

Clark, Anna. 'Whores and gossips: sexual reputation in London 1770–1825.' In *Current Issues in Women's History*. Edited by Ariana Angerman *et al.*, 231–48. London: Routledge, 1989.

Clark, J.C.D. *English Society 1688–1832: Ideology, Social Structure and the Ancien Regime*. Cambridge: Cambridge University Press, 1985.

Coffey, John. *Persecution and Toleration in Protestant England, 1558–1689*. Harlow, UK: Longman, 2000.

Cohen, Michèle. *Fashioning Masculinity: National Identity and Language in the Eighteenth Century*. London: Routledge, 1996.

Colley, Linda. *Britons. Forging the Nation 1707–1837*. New Haven, CT: Yale University Press, 1992.

Cragg, G.R. *From Puritanism to the Age of Reason. A Study of Changes in Religious Thought within the Church of England 1660 to 1700*. Cambridge: Cambridge University Press, 1966.

Curtis, T.C., and W.A. Speck. 'The Societies for the Reformation of Manners. A Case Study in the Theory and Practice of Moral Reform.' *Literature and History* 3 (1976): 45–64.

Davie, Grace. *Religion in Modern Europe: A Memory Mutates*. Oxford: Oxford University Press, 2000.

Donoghue, Frank. *The Fame Machine. Book Reviewing and Eighteenth-Century Literary Careers*. Palo Alto, CA: Stanford University Press, 1996.

Doody, Margaret Anne. 'Frances Sheridan. Morality and Annihilated Time.' In *Fetter'd or Free? British Women Novelists, 1670–1815*. Edited by Mary Anne Schofield and Cecilia Macheski, 324–58. Athens, OH: Ohio University Press, 1986.

———. *The True Story of the Novel*. New Brunswick, NJ: Rutgers University Press, 1996.

Douglas, Aileen. *Uneasy Sensations. Smollett and the Body*. Chicago: University of Chicago Press, 1995.

Dussinger, John A. '"Stealing in the great doctrines of Christianity": Samuel Richardson as Journalist.' *Eighteenth-Century Fiction* 15, No. 3–4 (2003): 451–506.

Eaves, T., C. Duncan, and Ben D. Kimpel. 'Richardson's Revisions of Pamela.' *Studies in Bibliography* 20 (1967): 61–88.

———. 'The Composition of *Clarissa* and its Revision before Publication.' *PMLA* 83 (1968): 416–28.

———. *Samuel Richardson. A Biography*. Oxford: Clarendon Press, 1971.

Fergus, Jan. 'Provincial servants' reading in the late eighteenth century.' In *The Practice and Representation of Reading in England*. Edited by James Raven, Helen Small and Naomi Tadmor, 202–25. Cambridge: Cambridge University Press, 1996.

Fitzer, Anna M. 'Mrs. Sheridan's Active Demon: *Memoirs of Miss Sidney Bidulph* and the Sly Rake in Petticoats.' *Eighteenth-Century Ireland* 18 (2003): 39–62.

Fitzpatrick, Martin. 'Latitudinarianism at the Parting of the Ways: A Suggestion.' In *The Church of England c.1689–c.1833. From Toleration to Tractarianism.* Edited by John Walsh, Colin Haydon and Stephen Taylor, 209–27. Cambridge: Cambridge University Press, 1993.

Fletcher, Anthony. *Gender, Sex and Subordination in England 1500–1800.* New Haven, CT: Yale University Press, 1995.

Gallagher, Catherine. *Nobody's Story. The Vanishing Acts of Women Writers in the Marketplace, 1670–1820.* Oxford: Clarendon Press, 1994.

Gallagher, Lowell. *Medusa's Gaze. Casuistry and Conscience in the Renaissance.* Palo Alto, CA: Stanford University Press, 1991.

Galloway, W.F. 'The Conservative Attitude Toward Fiction, 1770–1830.' *PMLA* 55 (1940): 1041–59.

Gascoigne, John. 'Anglican Latitudinarianism and Political Radicalism in the Late Eighteenth Century.' *History* 71 (1986): 22–38.

———. *Cambridge in the Age of the Enlightenment. Science, Religion and Politics from the Restoration to the French Revolution.* Cambridge, MA: Cambridge University Press, 1989.

Golden, Morris. 'Public Context and Imagining Self in Clarissa.' *Studies in English Literature 1500–1900* 25 (1985): 575–98.

Goldgar, Bertrand. *The Curse of Party. Swift's Relations with Addison and Steele.* Lincoln: University of Nebraska Press, 1961.

Gordon, Scott Paul. 'The Space of Romance in Lennox's The Female Quixote.' *Studies in English Literature 1500–1900* (1998): 499–516.

Goring, Paul. 'Thomas Weales's *The Christian Orator Delineated* (1778) and the Early Reception of Sterne's Sermons.' *The Shandean* 13 (2002): 87–97.

Green, I.M. *The Re-Establishment of the Church of England 1660–1663.* Oxford: Oxford University Press, 1978.

Green, Richard. *Anti-Methodist Publications Issued during the Eighteenth Century.* London: C.H. Kelly, 1902.

Grenby, M.O. *The Anti-Jacobin Novel, British Conservatism and the French Revolution.* Cambridge: Cambridge University Press, 2001.

Haakonssen, Knud. 'Enlightened Dissent: an introduction.' In *Enlightenment and Religion. Rational Dissent in eighteenth-century Britain.* Edited by Knud Haakonssen, 1–11. Cambridge: Cambridge University Press, 1996.

Hammond, Brean. *Professional Imaginative Writing in England, 1670–1740.* 'Hackney for Bread.' Oxford: Clarendon, 1997.

Hammond, Brean, and Shaun Regan. *Making the Novel: Fiction and Society in Britain, 1660–1789.* Houndmills, UK: Palgrave Macmillan, 2006.

Hammond, Lansing Van Der Heyden. *Laurence Sterne's Sermons of Mr. Yorick.* New Haven, CT: Yale University Press, 1948.

Hanley, Brian. 'Henry Fielding, Samuel Johnson, Samuel Richardson and the Reception of Charlotte Lennox's *The Female Quixote* in the Popular Press.' *ANQ* 13.3 (2000): 27–32.

Harris, Jocelyn. *Samuel Richardson*. Cambridge: Cambridge University Press, 1987.

Harrison, Bernard. *Henry Fielding's* Tom Jones. *The Novelist as Moral Philosopher*. London: Sussex University Press, 1975.

Hawley, Judith. 'Yorick in the Pulpit', review article, *Essays in Criticism* 48 (1998): 80–88.

Haydon, Colin. *Anti-Catholicism in Eighteenth-Century England, c.1714–1780. A political and social study*. Manchester, UK: Manchester University Press, 1993.

Hayton, David. 'Moral Reform and Country Politics in the Late Seventeenth Century House of Commons.' *Past and Present* 128 (1990): 48–91.

Hill, Christopher. *Society and Puritanism in Pre-Revolutionary England*. London: Secker and Warburg, 1964.

Hirst, Derek. 'The Failure of Godly Rule in England.' *Past and Present* 132 (1991): 33–66.

Holmes, Geoffrey. *The Making of a Great Power. Late Stuart and Early Georgian Britain 1660–1722*. London: Longman, 1993.

Howes, Alan B. Sterne. *The Critical Heritage*. London: Routledge and Kegan Paul, 1974.

H.R.P.C. 'A Mistake in Tristram Shandy.' *Notes and Queries*, 8th series, 7, January 12, 1895, 28–9.

Hudson, Nicholas. 'Fielding's Hierarchy of Dialogue: "Meta-Response" and the Reader of Tom Jones.' *Philological Quarterly* 68 (1969): 177–94.

Hunter, J. Paul. 'Clocks, Calendars and Names. The Troubles of Tristram and the Aesthetics of Uncertainty.' In *Rhetorics of Order/Ordering Rhetorics in English Neoclassical Literature*. Edited by J. Douglas Canfield and J. Paul Hunter, 173–98. Newark: University of Delaware Press, 1989.

Hunter, Michael. 'Casuistry in Action: Robert Boyle's Confessional Interviews with Gilbert Burnet and Edward Stillingfleet, 1691.' *Journal of Ecclesiastical History* 44 (1993): 80–98.

Ingram, Martin. *The Church Courts, Sex and Marriage in England, 1570–1660*. Cambridge: Cambridge University Press, 1987.

———. 'Reformation of Manners in Early Modern England.' In *The Experience of Authority in Early Modern England*. Edited by Paul Griffiths, Adam Fox and Steve Hindle, 47–88. Houndmills, UKI: Macmillan, 1996.

Innes, Joanna. 'Politics and Morals. The Reformation of Manners Movement in Later Eighteenth-Century England.' In *The Transformation of Political Culture in the Late Eighteenth Century*. Edited by Eckhart Hellmuth, 57–118. London: Oxford University Press, 1990.

Irvine, Robert. *Enlightenment and Romance. Gender and Agency in Smollett and Scott*. Oxford: Peter Lang, 2000.

Isaacs, Tina. 'The Anglican Hierarchy and the Reformation of Manners 1688–1738.' *Journal of Ecclesiastical History* 33 (1982): 391–411.

Isles, Duncan. 'The Lennox Collection.' *Harvard Library Bulletin* 18–19, 1970–1971.

Jones, Chris. *Radical Sensibility. Literature and Ideas in the 1790s*. London: Routledge, 1993.

Jones, M.G. *The Charity School Movement. A Study of Eighteenth Century Puritanism in Action*. Cambridge: Cambridge University Press, 1938.

Kay, Carol. *Political Constructions. Defoe, Richardson and Sterne in Relation to Hobbes, Hume and Burke*. Ithaca, NY: Cornell, 1988.

Keen, Paul. *The Crisis of Literature in the 1790s. Print Culture and the Public Sphere*. Cambridge: Cambridge University Press, 1999.

Kelly, Gary. *The English Jacobin Novel, 1780–1805*. Oxford: Clarendon Press, 1976.

Kelly, Lionel, ed. *Tobias Smollett. The Critical Heritage*. London: Routledge and Kegan Paul, 1987.

Kenyon, J.P. *Revolution Principles, The Politics of Party 1689–1720*. Cambridge: Cambridge University Press, 1977.

Keymer, Thomas. 'Richardson's *Meditations*: Clarissa's *Clarissa*.' In *Samuel Richardson. Tercentenary Essays*, edited by Margaret Anne Doody and Peter Sabor, 89–109. Cambridge: Cambridge University Press, 1989.

———. *Richardson's* Clarissa *and the Eighteenth-Century Reader*. Cambridge: Cambridge University Press, 1992.

Keymer, Thomas, and Peter Sabor, eds. *Pamela in the Marketplace. Literary Controversy and Print Culture in Eighteenth Century Britain and Ireland*. Cambridge: Cambridge University Press, 2005.

Klein, Lawrence. 'The Political Significance of "Politeness" in Early Eighteenth Century England.' In *Politics, Politeness and Patriotism*, edited by Gordon J. Schochet, Patricia E. Tatspaugh and Carol Brobeck, V, 73–108. Washington, DC: The Folger Shakespeare Library, 1993.

———. 'Gender and the Public/Private Distinction in the Eighteenth Century: Some Questions about Evidence and Analytic Procedure.' *ECS* 29.1 (Fall 1995): 97–109.

Knapp, Lewis. *Tobias Smollett. Doctor of Men and Manners*. Princeton, NJ: Princeton University Press, 1949.

Landa, Louis A. 'The Shandean Homunculus: The Background of Sterne's "Little Gentleman."' In *Restoration and Eighteenth-Century Literature: Essays in Honor of Alan Dugald McKillop*. Edited by Carroll Camden, 49–68. Chicago: University of Chicago Press, 1963.

Langbauer, Laurie. *Women and Romance. The Consolations of Gender in the English Novel*. Ithaca, NY: Cornell, 1990.

Langford, Paul. *A Polite and Commercial People. England 1727–1783*. Oxford: Clarendon Press, 1989.

Laqueur, Thomas. *Making Sex. Body and Gender from the Greeks to Freud*. Cambridge, MA: Harvard University Press, 1990.

Leeuwen, H. Van. *The Pursuit of Certainty in English Thought 1630–1690*. 2nd ed. The Hague: Martinus Nijhoff, 1970.

Lefanu, Alicia. *Memoirs of the Life and Writings of Mrs. Frances Sheridan*. London: 1824.

Leites, Edmund. 'Good Humor at Home, Good Humor Abroad: The Intimacies of Marriage and the Civilities of Social Life in the Ethic of Richard Steele.' In *Educating the Audience: Addison, Steele, and Eighteenth Century Culture*. Edited by Edward A. and Lillian D. Bloom and Edmund Leites, 51–89. University of California, Los Angeles: William Andrews Clark Memorial Library, 1984.

Leppert, Richard. *Music and Image. Domesticity, ideology and socio-cultural formation in eighteenth-century England*. Cambridge: Cambridge University Press, 1988.

Loftis, John. *The Politics of Drama in Augustan England*. Oxford: Clarendon Press, 1963.

Loveridge, Mark. *Laurence Sterne and the Argument about Design*. London: Macmilllan, 1982.

Lyles, Albert M. *Methodism Mocked. The Satiric Reaction to Methodism in the Eighteenth Century*. London: Epworth Press, 1960.

McKendrick, Neil, John Brewer and J.H. Plumb. *The Birth of a Consumer Society. The Commercialization of Eighteenth-Century England*. London: Europa, 1982.

McKeon, Michael. *Origins of the English Novel, 1600–1740*. Baltimore, MD: Johns Hopkins University Press, 1987.

McKeon, Michael. 'Historicizing Patriarchy: The Emergence of Gender Difference in England, 1660–1760.' *Eighteenth-Century Studies* 28.3 (1995): 295–322.

Martinich, A.P. *The Two Gods of Leviathan: Thomas Hobbes on Religion and Politics*. Cambridge: Cambridge University Press, 1992.

Martz, Louis. *The Later Career of Tobias Smollett*. New Haven, CT: Yale University Press, 1942.

Morse, David. *The Age of Virtue. British Culture from the Restoration to Romanticism*. London: Macmillan, 2000.

Mullan, John. *Sentiment and Sociability. The Language of Feeling in the Eighteenth Century*. Oxford: Clarendon Press, 1990.

Myers, Sylvia Harcstark. *The Bluestocking Circle. Women, Friendship, and the Life of the Mind in Eighteenth-Century England*. Oxford: Clarendon Press, 1990.

Nestor, Deborah J. 'Virtue Rarely Rewarded: Ideological Subversion and Narrative Form in Haywood's Later Fiction.' *Studies in English Literature 1500–1900* 34 (1994): 579–98.

New, Melvyn. *Laurence Sterne as Satirist. A Reading of Tristram Shandy*. Gainesville: University Press of Florida, 1969.

———. 'Sterne's Rabelaisian Fragment: A Text from the Holograph Manuscript.' *PMLA* 87 (1972): 1083–92.

New, Melvyn, ed. Notes *to Tristram Shandy*. Vol. III of The Florida Edition of the Works of Laurence Sterne. 5 vols. Gainesville: University Press of Florida, 1978–84.

Orr, Robert. *Reason and Authority. The Thought of William Chillingworth*. Oxford: Clarendon Press, 1967.

Outhwaite, R.B. *Clandestine Marriage in England 1500–1800*. London: Hambledon Press, 1995.

Pateman, Carole. *The Sexual Contract*. Cambridge: Polity, 1988.

Paulson, Ronald. 'Smollett and Hogarth: The Identity of Pallet.' *Studies in English Literature 1500–1900* 4 (1964): 351–59.

Pecora, Vincent P. *Secularization and Cultural Criticism: Religion, Nation and Modernity*. Chicago: University of Chicago Press, 2006.

Perkins, Pamela. Introduction, In *Hermsprong, or Man as He Is Not* (1796), by Robert Bage. Peterborough, Ontario: Broadview, 2002.

Perry, Ruth. *Women, Letters, and the Novel*. New York: AMS Press, 1980.

———. 'Colonizing the Breast: Sexuality and Maternity in Eighteenth-Century England.' In *Forbidden History: the State, Society and the Regulation of Sexuality in Modern Europe*. Edited by John C. Fout, 107–37. Chicago: University of Chicago Press, 1990.

Phillipson, Nicholas. 'Adam Smith as Civic Moralist.' In *Wealth and Virtue. The Shaping of Political Economy in the Scottish Enlightenment*. Edited by Istvan Hont and Michael Ignatieff, 179–202. Cambridge: Cambridge University Press, 1983.

Pocock, J.G.A. *The Machiavellian Moment, Florentine Political Thought and the Atlantic Republican Tradition*. Princeton: Princeton University Press, 1975.

———. 'Post-Puritan England and the Problem of the Enlightenment.' In *Culture and Politics from Puritanism to the Enlightenment*. Edited by Peter Zagorin, 91–111. Berkeley: University of California Press, 1980.

Poovey, Mary. *The Proper Lady and the Woman Writer, Ideology as Style in the Works of Mary Wollstonecraft, Mary Shelley and Jane Austen*. Chicago: University of Chicago Press, 1984.

Popkin, Richard. *The History of Scepticism from Savanarola to Bayle*. Revised edition. Oxford: Oxford University Press, 2003.

Price, John Valdimir. 'Smollett and the Reader in Sir Launcelot Greaves.' In *Smollett: Author of the First Distinction*, edited by Alan Bold, 193–208. London: Vision and Barnes and Noble, 1982.

Raphael, D.D. *Hobbes: Morals and Politics*. London: Allen and Unwin, 1977.

Raven, James. *Judging New Wealth, Popular Publishing and Responses to Commerce in England*, 1750–1800. Oxford: Clarendon, 1992.

Raven, James, and Antonia Forster, eds. *The English Novel 1770–1829: A Bibliographical Survey of Prose Fiction Published in the British Isles*. 3 vols. Vol I, 1770–1799, Oxford: Oxford University Press, 2000.

Richetti, John J. *Popular Fiction Before Richardson. Narrative Patterns 1700–1739*. Oxford: Clarendon Press, 1969.

Rivers, Isabel. 'Dissenting and Methodist Books of Practical Divinity.' In *Books and their Readers in Eighteenth-Century England*. Edited by Isabel Rivers, 127–64. Leicester, UK: Leicester University Press, 1982.

———. *Reason, Grace and Sentiment: A Study of the Language of Religion and Ethics in England, 1660–1780*. Vol. I, *Whichcote to Wesley*, Cambridge: Cambridge University Press, 1991. Vol. II, *Shaftesbury to Hume*, Cambridge: Cambridge University Press, 2000.

Rizzo, Betty. 'Renegotiating the Gothic.' In *Revising Women. Eighteenth-Century "Women's Fiction" and Social Engagement*. Edited by Paula R. Backscheider, 58–103. Baltimore, MD: The Johns Hopkins University Press, 2000.

Robertson, John. 'The Scottish Enlightenment at the limits of the civic tradition.' In *Wealth and Virtue. The Shaping of the Political Economy in the Scottish Enlightenment*, edited by Istvan Hont and Michael Ignatieff, 137–78. Cambridge: Cambridge University Press, 1983.

Rock, Henry. 'Religious Societies and the Origins of Methodism.' *Journal of Ecclesiastical History* 38 (1987): 582–95.

Rose, Elliot. *Cases of Conscience. Alternatives open to Recusants and Puritans under Elizabeth I and James I*. London: Cambridge University Press, 1975.

Ross, Angus, ed. *Selections from* The Tatler *and* The Spectator. London: Penguin, 1982.

Ross, Deborah. 'Mirror, Mirror: The Didactic Dilemma of The Female Quixote.' *SEL* 27 (1987): 455–73.

Ross, Ian Campbell. 'Tobias Smollett: Gentleman by Birth, Education and Profession.' *British Journal for Eighteenth-Century Studies* 5 (1982): 179–190.

———. '"With Dignity and Importance": Peregrine Pickle as Country Gentleman.' In *Smollett: Author of the First Distinction*. Edited by Alan Bold, 148–169. London: Vision and Barnes and Noble, 1982.

———. *Laurence Sterne: A Life*. Oxford: Oxford University Press, 2001.

Rousseau, G.S., ed. *Goldsmith: The Critical Heritage*. London: Routledge and Kegan Paul, 1974.

Rupp, Gordon. *Introductory Essay. A History of the Methodist Church in Great Britain*. Edited by Rupert Davies and Gordon Rupp, Vol. I, xiii–xl. London: Epworth Press, 1965.

———. *Religion in England 1688–1791*. Oxford: Clarendon, 1986.

Sampson, Margaret. 'Laxity and Liberty in Seventeenth-Century English Political Thought.' In: *Conscience and Casuistry in Early Modern Europe*. Edited by Edmund Leites, 72–118. Cambridge: Cambridge University Press, 1988.

Schellenberg, Betty A. *The Professionalization of Women Writers in Eighteenth-Century England*. Cambridge: Cambridge University Press, 2005.

Schochet, Gordon J. *Patriarchalism in Political Thought. The Authoritarian Family and Political Speculation and Attitudes Especially in Seventeenth Century England*. Oxford: Basil Blackwell, 1975.

Schonhorn, Manuel. 'Fielding's Ecphrastic Moment: Tom Jones and His Egyptian Majesty.' *Studies in Philology* 78 (1981): 305–23.

Sekora, John. *Luxury. The Concept in Western Thought from Eden to Smollett.* Baltimore, MD: The Johns Hopkins University Press, 1977.

Shevelow, Kathryn. *Women and Print Culture. The Construction of Femininity in the Early Periodical.* London: Routledge, 1989.

Shumaker, Wayne. *The Occult Sciences in the Renaissance. A Study in Intellectual Patterns.* Los Angeles: University of California Press, 1972.

Slights, Camille Wells. *The Casuistical Tradition in Shakespeare, Donne, Herbert and Milton.* Princeton, NJ: Princeton University Press, 1981.

Small, Miriam Rossiter. *Charlotte Ramsay Lennox. An Eighteenth Century Lady of Letters.* New Haven, CT: Yale University Press, 1935.

Smithers, Peter. *The Life of Joseph Addison.* Oxford: Clarendon Press, 1954.

Spacks, Patricia Meyer. *Desire and Truth. Functions of Plot in Eighteenth-Century English Novels.* Chicago: University of Chicago Press, 1994.

Speck, W.A. *Stability and Strife: England, 1714–60.* London: Edward Arnold, 1977.

Spencer, Jane. *The Rise of the Woman Novelist. From Aphra Behn to Jane Austen.* Oxford: Basil Blackwell, 1986.

Spurr, John. *The Restoration Church of England, 1646–1689.* New Haven: Yale University Press, 1991.

———. 'The Church, the Societies and the Moral Revolution of 1688.' In *The Church of England c.1689–c.1833. From Toleration to Tractarianism.* Edited by John Walsh, Colin Haydon and Stephen Taylor, 127–42. Cambridge: Cambridge University Press, 1993.

Stachniewski, John. *The Persecutory Imagination. English Puritanism and the Literature of Despair.* Oxford: Clarendon Press, 1991.

Starr, G.A. *Defoe and Casuistry.* Princeton, NJ: Princeton University Press, 1971.

Staves, Susan. *A Literary History of Women's Writing in Britain, 1660–1789.* Cambridge: Cambridge University Press, 2006.

Stevenson, John Allen. 'Black George and the Black Act.' *Eighteenth Century Fiction* 8.3 (April 1996): 355–82.

Stone, Lawrence. *The Family, Sex and Marriage in England 1500–1800.* London: Weidenfeld and Nicholson, 1977.

———. *The Road to Divorce, England 1530–1987.* Oxford: Oxford University Press, 1990.

Sykes, Norman. *From Sheldon to Secker, Aspects of Church History 1660–1768.* Cambridge: University Press, 1959.

———. *Church and State in England in the XVIIIth Century* (1934). Hamden, CT: Archon Books, 1962.

Taylor, John Tinnon. *Early Opposition to the English Novel.* New York: King's Crown Press, 1943.

Thomas, Keith. 'Cases of Conscience in Seventeenth Century England.' In *Public Duty and Private Conscience in Seventeenth Century England.* Edited by John Morrill, Paul Slack and Daniel Woolf, 29–56. Oxford: Clarendon Press, 1993.

Todd, Janet. *The Sign of Angellica. Women, Writing, and Fiction 1660–1800.* London: Virago, 1989.

Traugott, John. Tristram Shandy's *World: Sterne's Philosphical Rhetoric*. Berkeley: University of California Press, 1954.

Tyacke, Nicholas. *Anti-Calvinists: The Rise of English Arminianism c.1590–1640*. Oxford: Clarendon Press, 1987.

Vickery, Amanda. 'Golden Age to Separate Spheres? A Review of the Categories and Chronology of English Women's History.' *The Historical Journal* 36 (1993): 383–414.

———. *The Gentleman's Daughter, Women's Lives in Georgian England*. London: The Folio Society, 2006.

Walsh, John, and Stephen Taylor. 'Introduction: The Church and Anglicanism in the "Long" Eighteenth Century.' In *The Church of England c.1689–c.1833. From Toleration to Tractarianism*. Edited by John Walsh, Colin Haydon and Stephen Taylor, 1–64. Cambridge: Cambridge University Press, 1993.

Wardle, Ralph M. *Oliver Goldsmith*. Lawrence: University of Kansas Press, 1957.

Warner, William B. *Reading* Clarissa: *The Struggles of Interpretation*. New Haven, CT: Yale University Press, 1979.

———. *Licensing Entertainment: The Elevation of Novel Reading in Britain, 1684–1750*. Berkeley: University of California Press, 1998.

Warrender, Howard. *The Political Theory of Hobbes, His Theory of Obligation*. Oxford: Clarendon Press, 1957.

Watt, Ian. *The Rise of the Novel*. London: Chatto and Windus, 1957.

Watt, James. *Contesting the Gothic. Fiction, Genre and Cultural Conflict, 1764–1832*. Cambridge: Cambridge University Press, 1999.

Weil, Rachel. *Political Passions. Gender, the family and political argument in England 1680–1714*. Manchester, UK: Manchester University Press, 1999.

Wilks, John S. *The Idea of Conscience in Renaissance Tragedy*. London: Routledge, 1990.

Williams, Carolyn D. *Pope, Homer and Manliness: Some Aspects of Eighteenth-Century Classical Learning*. London: Routledge, 1993.

Williams, Ioan, ed. *Novel and Romance 1700–1800. A Documentary Record*. London: Routledge and Kegan Paul, 1970.

Wilson. B.R. *Religion in Secular Society*. London: C.A. Watts, 1966.

Index